The Nordic Council and Scandinavian Integration

Erik Solem

The Nordic Council and Scandinavian Integration

PRAEGER SPECIAL STUDIES IN INTERNATIONAL POLITICS AND GOVERNMENT

Praeger Publishers New York London

Library of Congress Cataloging in Publication Data

Solem, Erik, 1938-
The Nordic Council and Scandinavian integration.

(Praeger special studies in international politics and government)
Bibliography: p. 181
Includes index.
1. Nordiske rad. 2. Scandinavian cooperation.
3. Scandinavia—Economic integration. 4. Scandinavia—Politics and government. I. Title.
JN7042.S65 341.24'2 75-19824
ISBN 0-275-24100-9

PRAEGER PUBLISHERS
200 Park Avenue, New York, N.Y. 10017, U.S.A.

Published in the United States of America in 1977
by Praeger Publishers, Inc.

Printed in the United States of America

FOREWORD

Frantz Wendt

Erik Solem, a scholar from outside Scandinavia who has an intimate acquaintance with the Scandinavian peoples and languages, has taken it upon himself to describe and analyze the main aspects of Nordic cooperation. His study is welcome, the more because it combines an insight into the actual working of this cooperation with a solid grasp of the various theories on regional integration. Anyone who has had to explain to non-Scandinavians the character of the working-together of the Nordic peoples and states will appreciate this book. It is a fact, often confirmed by experience, that the manifold ties established among the Scandinavians cannot be satisfactorily placed within any of the current theoretical systems.

Mr. Solem's book examines the ways in which Nordic cooperation differs from other kinds of regional integration. As background for this comparison he calls attention to the forces stimulating or hampering Nordic efforts. In so doing he rightly points out that the outside world is apt to exaggerate the homogeneity of the Nordic nations and at the same time to underestimate the results their cooperation has obtained.

The peoples of Scandinavia are bound together to a high degree by their common origins, and by their similar linguistic, religious, legal, social, and political developments, all of which facilitate their mutual contacts. Nevertheless, historically motivated prejudices and present-day economic self-interest sometimes slow up the process of integration. Still more important, superior influences from the outside world have caused serious setbacks in the fields of common defense, foreign policy, and economic cooperation. On the other hand, during the more than 100 years in which the Nordic idea has been a force in the lives of the Scandinavian nations, considerable results have been reached in most other fields, in almost every case by a pragmatic, step-by-step method. Until about 25 years ago the number of common institutions was very small, and even now the idea of supranational Nordic institutions finds no response in the Scandinavian family of nations.

Dr. Solem rightly emphasizes the role of private groups as a driving force in Nordic endeavors. None of the other modern attempts

---

Frantz Wendt is a former secretary general of the Danish Delegation to the Nordic Council.

at regional integration has enjoyed as much widespread popular support.

The Nordic Council is the most important of the common institutions created since the second world war as well as the central driving force in present-day Nordic cooperation. With all justice Dr. Solem makes it the central object of his study. He describes its origin and organization and its functions in the various fields of activity. He also analyzes the roles of the parliamentarians and experts involved and points out what he regards as the weakness of the Nordic Council. He suggests methods of improving its working methods and thereby strengthening its influence. He does all of this within the framework of "a case study in the theory and methods of regional political integration."

This book will be read with great interest by all who take part in Nordic cooperation. It is also most gratifying that the Nordic Council is here presented so competently to an international public.

CONTENTS

LIST OF TABLES AND FIGURES

DEMOGRAPHIC DISTRIBUTION IN THE NORDIC COUNTRIES

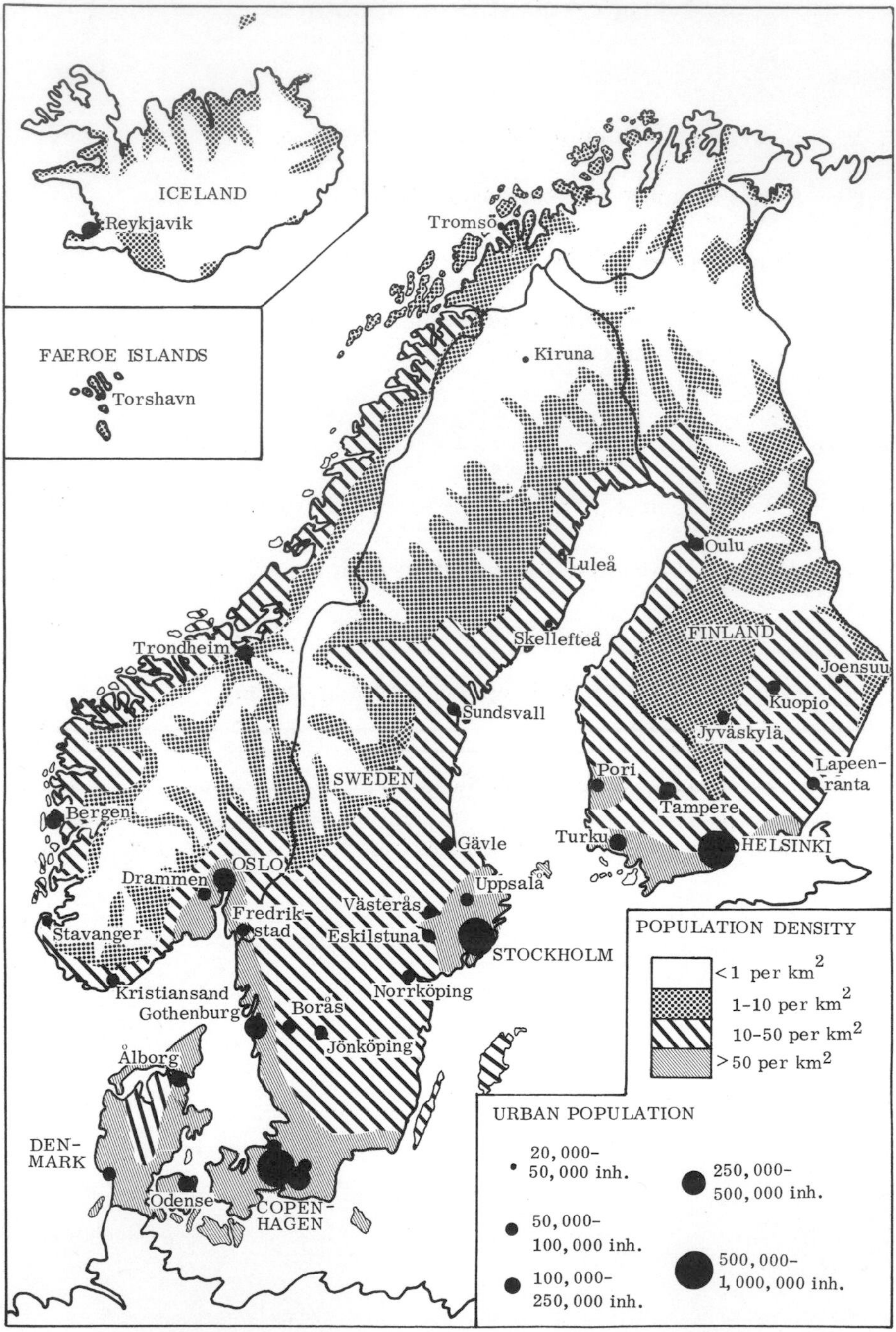

Source: Yearbook of Nordic Statistics (Stockholm: Nordic Council and Nordic Statistical Secretariat, 1976).

The Nordic Council and Scandinavian Integration

CHAPTER 1

INTRODUCTION

PRINCIPAL THEORIES OF REGIONAL POLITICAL INTEGRATION

The post-World War II period has brought major changes in the relationships among states. On the one hand there has been a proliferation of new nations, especially in the developing world, accompanied by a growing number of new member-countries in the United Nations. There has also been a tendency for parts of states—either geographical regions or cultural, linguistic, or religious groupings—to clamor for increased autonomy or independence. This is by no means a new phenomenon, but it is one that has been seen ever more frequently in the years since 1945.

On the other hand there has been an opposite, or complementary, tendency. Technological development has been so rapid and complex that it has become increasingly clear that national goals, be they economic, social, or political, are often best attained by cooperation and coordination among states. In fact, the problems facing the world demand not merely consultation and intergovernmental negotiations, but often organized cooperation that is binding on the participating states. This need is illustrated by the wide range of functioning international organizations which have been set up in recent years. More important, this development has led to some basic questioning of the assumed values that have been ascribed to the autonomous nation-states. To a much larger extent than before, the concept of national sovereignty has conflicted with other national and international goals.* The growth of so many new international organizations poses several

---

*I am here ignoring the immensely complex question of how, and under what conditions, a state is actually capable of acting independently of other states.

questions, one of which seems to be whether or not it makes sense to speak in terms of full national sovereignty or to behave as if this principle actually exists. If this question is answered in the negative, the next logical step is to try to establish what the legitimacy, usefulness, and purpose of a state are. Such questions are interesting and important, but the subject to which they address themselves is a vast and untidy one.

Has the nation-state always been, and will it continue to be, the basic unit in international politics? The assumption that it is, is still open to verification if we consider more than one or two dimensions of human activity. In grand politics, the signing of treaties and conducting of wars, it certainly seems to have been the case, although in other dimensions, such as trade and economics, this is not necessarily so. If we add such indicators as cultural exchange and communications, to the extent that impacts and transaction flows may be measured, it becomes even more doubtful whether the state "deserves" the powers and rights that it often claims. In the early 1960s political theorists looking at the international level of politics asked whether or not the nation-state was obsolete[1] and began to investigate the processes that seemed to be eroding the power and influence of the nation-states. At first the literature concerning the new sets of institutions, such as the European Coal and Steel Community (ECSC) and the European Economic Community (EEC) was primarily descriptive. The more detailed, careful analyses came a little later,[2] and the increased amount of speculation about the phenomenon is of fairly recent origin. Among the best-known theorists of integration are Karl W. Deutsch,[3] Ernst B. Haas,[4] Amitai Etzioni,[5] and Leon Lindberg.[6] Together they have made an important contribution to the understanding of the forces and processes that make up regional political integration.

There is no general and conclusive theory of regional integration, but scholars, especially American social scientists writing in the post-World War II period, have examined different aspects of this phenomenon.

The earliest group of theorists of unification and integration may be referred to as the classical institutionalists. This group assumed that with a minimum of cultural and political homogeneity among the peoples concerned, institutions could be made to bear the brunt of the political pressures. They argued that if supranational institutions were built "from the top," the rest would follow. Their concern about such matters as common loyalties was peripheral to their general idea of establishing sufficiently strong institutions. The advocates of Atlantic Union, "Pan-Europa," and World Federalism fall into this general category.[7]

A second group of theorists followed in the footsteps of Ernst Haas. Perhaps Haas's greatest contribution, as has been pointed out,[8] was to focus attention on the process of transforming loyalties to new institutions rather than on institution building by itself. The Uniting of Europe, the classic 1958 study by Haas of early unification in postwar Europe, carefully examined international community building, which he perceived as a process by which political actors are persuaded to shift their loyalties from the preexisting national states to new centers of authority. He analyzed the ECSC and its impact on the main political actors in the member states. Haas was much concerned about the creation of new political institutions capable of translating ideologies into law.[9] He is considered a main spokesman for functionalism in political integration.

To some extent such writers as Amitai Etzioni and Leon Lindberg shared the same basic concern as Haas. Lindberg, a pupil of Haas, looked for central institutions from which central policies must follow,[10] although he did not postulate so centralized an ideal-type as that of Haas. Lindberg's best-known contribution to integration theory was an attempt to apply the systems thinking of David Easton to the theory of political integration.[11]

Whereas Haas and Lindberg addressed themselves to the study of specific organizations, ECSC and EEC respectively, Amitai Etzioni attempted a comparative study of political unification, based on cases ranging from the United Arab Republic (1958-61) and the Federation of the West Indies (1958-62) to the EEC and Scandinavian integration. Etzioni's main contribution to integration theory was an attempt to create a paradigm for the study of political unification, on the basis of which the different cases in point could be tested and some generalizations formulated about the relative success or failure of each of them.[12] He followed Haas, being on the lookout for a "center of decision-making able to affect the allocation of resources and rewards throughout the community."[13]

The approach of Karl W. Deutsch, however, has been quite different. His major contribution to integration theory has been to focus attention away from institutions, and even away from loyalties to institutions, as ends in themselves. His main concern has been the avoidance of war under conditions of voluntary association and the creation of "security communities" for this purpose.[14] A need or lack of need for strong central institutions to accomplish this is not assumed, but becomes instead a subject for empirical investigation.[15]

DEFINITIONS AND CONCEPTS

Unification and Integration

According to Ernst B. Haas, integration is "the process whereby political actors in several distinct national settings are persuaded to shift their loyalties, expectations and political activities toward a new centre, whose institutions possess or demand jurisdiction over the pre-existing national states."[16] However, Haas is referring strictly to elites, having ruled out the importance of mass aspirations or attitudes in this process.[17] The emphasis on elites in the study of integration, he states, derives its justification from the bureaucratized nature of European organizations of long standing, in which "basic decisions are made by the leadership, sometimes over the opposition and usually over the indifference of the general membership."[18] His evidence for this claim is the public ignorance of, and lack of sustained interest in, matters of political integration and other aspects of foreign policy. This may well be the case with such an issue as the European Coal and Steel Community, the subject matter of his study, but it is doubtful whether the generalization would hold for other fields in which integration is pursued.

What is more important here is that the process of integration can only be fully understood and explained in terms of its goals. In this respect it becomes important to examine the type of political community that is to be derived from the process. In all fairness to Haas, it must be stated that he, particularly in his first book, attempts this to some extent, by examining both the doctrine of Europeanism and the expectations it raised, albeit among the elites only. As I have argued elsewhere, there is a need to consider these goals as early as possible.[19] Whereas an analysis of expectations is not exactly intrinsic to the analysis of a process of integration as such, it does greatly aid our understanding of what political integration as a whole is about. As for the process itself, we may benefit from examining it in a compartmentalized manner, that is, by analyzing the different fields in which integration occurs. In addition it would be useful to consider exactly what goes on in the lower, or "micro-," levels of integration within the functional level of analysis.

In Amitai Etzioni's conceptual framework, integration appears to be a state rather than a process.[20] This would seem to set him apart from Haas. A closer look, however, reveals that Etzioni's concept of unification closely resembles Haas's concept of integration. Although they use different terms, both authors are in fact looking at the same variables. Etzioni's process of unification reaches different "levels of integration," depending among other things upon the scope, that is, upon how many social functions are involved. This in turn depends upon the integrative power activated in the different stages of the unification process itself. The integrative power depends on effective distributions, effective compositions, and a dynamic perspective, which are all developed in his paradigm for political unification.[21] The question Etzioni is asking is, "Who is unifying, and by what kinds of power?" This question is similar to the questions asked by Haas in his earlier book.[22] Etzioni's propositions tend to be very general, and his analysis of integration theory has the added drawback, in three of his four cases, of considering a short period, from 1958 to 1964. Despite this, his contribution should not be undervalued, particularly his interesting analysis of the different kinds of power required to maintain the process of integration.[23] By this analysis he parts company with Haas, insofar as he is in part concerned about the importance of coercive power as a type of integration. At this point Etzioni is close to traditional power theory in his analysis, which varies somewhat from that of Haas. One might ask, however, whether Etzioni, in bringing in this element to his theorizing, is not widening his outlook to the extent that he has ceased theorizing about political integration alone and is instead concerned with the much more general question of relationships among states. This point has been raised by some writers,[24] but I do not subscribe to this view myself. Rather, I consider it an element of strength in Etzioni's theorizing that he also includes such elements as power politics when discussing the phenomenon of integration. In fact, his main contribution to integration theory, apart from the construction of a workable, although somewhat too general, paradigm for the study of political unification, is his realistic attitude.

Like Haas, however, Etzioni is very much concerned about institutions that are "capable of affecting the allocation of resources and rewards throughout the community,"[25] which makes his theorizing to a large extent an exercise in systems analysis.

Etzioni's particular interest here is that he is the only one of the above-mentioned theorists who uses a comparative framework and also the only one who has tried to incorporate the experience of the Scandinavian case.

Political Community

Of Deutsch, Haas, and Etzioni, the three main theorists of political integration, not one has, to my knowledge, put forward a consistent theory of cultural change, such as is found, more or less, in the writings of Pitirim Sorokin,[26] for example, or Arnold Toynbee.[27] This does not mean, however, that any of them has a limited conception of what the community will be—by "limited," I mean firm, definite, and not subject to change. Haas's earlier work,[28] for example, defines a political community as "a condition in which specific groups and individuals show more loyalty to their central political institutions than to any other political authority, in a specific period of time and in a definable geographic space."[29] As we can see, this definition, which he describes a "tight definition,"[30] although I cannot see that it really is, closely follows his definition of political integration. System and process are very close in his theorizing. At the same time, Haas takes some pains to bring in Max Weber's terminology and that writer's use of heuristic devices[31] in order to argue for the use of ideal types in theory. In his later writings Haas has shown himself keenly aware of the processes of political modernization, although his concept of the political community does not seem to have changed much.

Etzioni's "union" is, so it seems, an international system with a level of integration and a breadth of scope that are greater than those of an international organization and less than those of an established political community. "Union" refers to systems with an increasing, stable, or decreasing level of integration and breadth of scope; "unification" refers to the process of increasing; and "deunification" to decreasing. It is Etzioni's concept of a political community that provides the final clue to his frame of reference. According to Etzioni a political community possesses three kinds of integration: (1) effective control over the use of the means of violence (though it may delegate some of this to member units); (2) a center of decision making that can significantly affect the allocation of resources and rewards throughout the community; and (3) the dominance of the political identification of a large majority of politically aware citizens.[32] At the same time we see the similarity to and difference from the concepts of Haas.

To Etzioni, the political community is at the same time a state, an administrative-economic unit, and a focal point of identification. To his credit, Etzioni has brought into his definition both control over the means of violence and the ability to provide the dominant focus of identification for most citizens, rather than only the elite.

Karl Deutsch is even more specific about the latter point in his definition of a community. Integration, to him, is a means rather than an end. It is "the attainment within a territory of a 'sense of community' and of institutions and practices strong enough and widespread enough to assure for a long time, dependable expectations of 'peaceful change' among its population."[33] The sense of community referred to is equated with a belief on the part of the individuals in a group that they have come to agreement on at least the point that common social problems must and can be resolved by processes of peaceful change.

FIGURE 1

Security Communities and Integration

	Nonamalgamated		Amalgamated
Integrated	Pluralistic, security-community (Norway-Sweden today)	Threshold	Amalgamated, security-community (United States today)
	-----------------Integration	Threshold-----------------	
Nonintegrated	Not amalgamated, not security-community (United States-USSR today)	Amalgamation	Amalgamated, not security-community (Hapsburg Empire in 1914)

Source: Karl W. Deutsch, The Analysis of International Relations (Englewood Cliffs, N.J.: Prentice-Hall, 1968).

According to Deutsch, "peaceful change" means "the resolution of social problems, normally by institutionalized procedures, without resort to large scale physical force."[34] The purpose of this kind of integration is the establishment of what Deutsch calls a security community, of which he perceives two types, the amalgamated and the pluralistic. Amalgamation is a formal merger of two or more previously independent units into a single, larger unit with some form of common government. It may be unitary or, as in the case of the United States, federal. On the other hand, the pluralistic security community retains the legal independence of separate governments. For instance, the United States and Canada are integrated, as are Norway and Sweden (presumably also Norway and Denmark, and Denmark and Sweden). The schematic presentation shown in Figure 1 may help to clarify these distinctions.

Haas is critical of the Deutsch study, stating that "the study proceeds on the basis of ten historical cases, none of which satisfy the conditions held essential in my inquiry, because they were confined to pre-industrial and pre-mass mobilization settings,"[35] and that "one misses the appeals [to integration] heard most often in the contemporary setting: economic equality, industrial democracy, larger markets."[36] This criticism is somewhat unjust and also incorrect. Deutsch and his coauthors are entitled to pursue the study of the phenomenon of political integration based upon historical cases if they so wish, so long as they apply their own criteria consistently and try to do what they set out to do. The fact that such ideals as economic equality and, in particular, industrial democracy were not on the agenda of the day during the periods covered by the Deutsch study is not particularly relevant here.

Furthermore, Haas misses an important point. The emphasis in Deutsch's concept of a security community is on the avoidance of violence without coercion, and coercion may in fact include strong, central institutions. In fact, Haas misses two points, since the Deutsch study is very much concerned with person-to-person relationships as a necessary component. As a sociological study, Deutsch's book goes deeper than Haas seems willing to give it credit for. In his own study Deutsch's emphasis on this particular type of loyalty is, in fact, spelled out quite clearly as follows (my emphasis):

> The kind of sense of community that is relevant for integration, and therefore, for our study, turned out to be rather a matter of mutual sympathy and loyalties; of "we-feeling," trust and mutual consideration; of <u>mutually successful prediction of behaviour</u> and of co-operative action in accordance with it.[37]

Contrary to Haas, then, Karl Deutsch includes all the politically relevant strata of the population, as being important for the development of the required loyalties. Deutsch also found that the enlisting of popular participation was one of the most successful methods used to successfully promote a movement for amalgamation.[38] Furthermore, "mutually successful prediction of behaviour" is not a loose use of sociological terminology but rather a specific demand, drawing attention to important sectors outside the realm of institutions themselves. The emphasis is on methods and values rather than primarily on institutions. It is partly for this reason that Deutsch's theories are important for our study of the Scandinavian case. The development of community ties at the mass level is a slower process than the elite transfer of loyalties that interests Haas.

Supranationality

The concept of supranationality has been subject to some controversy among scholars of regional integration. Although a guarantee of supranationality was explicitly written into Article 9 of the ECSC treaty, there was no explicit mention made of it in the Treaty of Rome, which established the EEC some seven years later. Within the context of ECSC a supranational institution could be taken to mean one that possesses the following types of power: (1) direct relations with individuals within states; (2) authority to tax, borrow, and lend; (3) decisions by majority voting of the representatives of states. To this claim, critics have replied that some of these powers have long been held by other international organizations, particularly functionally specific ones. In briefly comparing the Treaty of Rome to that of the ECSC, one finds that the former deliberately restricts access by individuals to the Community Courts, gives no independent power of taxation to its commission, and has fewer cases of majority voting. Despite this the EEC Commission was not weaker than the ECSC High Authority; this would lead observers to revise their opinions of the importance of formal supranationality.

We may now try to broaden our definition of a supranational organization. "It is an organization which (a) bypasses the nation-state's authority and deals directly with the citizen: which (b) takes over some functions traditionally exercised by the nation-state; and (c) is in the position to originate decisions not only on behalf of the State but despite it."[39] This may seem to be a useful definition for our purposes, but it avoids certain important problems. What is meant by the authority of the nation-state? What, precisely, is involved in making decisions despite the state? It is easy to see that these problems may involve us in a detailed discussion of the nature, and possibly the legitimacy, of authority. In this context, for the sake of understanding, authority can only be seen in conjunction with the concept of sovereignty, which includes some tricky questions about the nature of power. It could be argued that from a legal, institutional point of view the notion of supranationality carries with it more problems than it actually solves.[40]

Supranationality, from a conceptual point of view, evokes problems similar to those evoked by federalism.[41] We may be able to meet these problems by conceiving of supranationality in a broader sense, as we would the concept of federalism. This would mean looking at it not so much as a political system, but as a technique for political action and a method of political analysis. Max Beloff, for example, argues the value of looking at federalism in this way, stating that this would more easily tell us important things about a particular society.[42] He points to the fact that modern societies are highly complex and that power is distributed not merely on a territorial basis but also among occupational and other groupings that may theoretically be amenable to some legal sovereign, but that these groupings can only be dealt with by the political authority with a "judicious combination per persuasion and co-ercion, with persuasion normally playing the leading role."[43]

The supranational element in an organization often rests on the view of key persons or leaders that the organization and the secretariat or leadership unit within the organization will succeed in carrying out certain important tasks. For example, as Beloff points out,[44] the supranational element of the United Nations rested with Dag Hammarskjöld's views about the possibilities of its secretariat. These views were based on the belief that it is possible to recruit individuals who are able and willing to exercise their powers in the interest of the community rather than for the benefit of their own countries. They also stem from a belief in the ability of the organization to perform certain tasks, given the rules of human organization.

It matters greatly what the persons serving an organization think of that organization, of its potential, and of its aims. The methods used for dealing with a problem and the beliefs held by the people who direct the efforts may matter as much as, and at times more than, the particular institutions with which they are working.

Nevertheless, we are still interested in the authority and power of the international organization, both in terms of the secretariat and in terms of intergovernmental conference aspects. To what extent are member states prepared to give up some of their power and to create, or rather to allow the creation of, strong central institutions? How much are central institutions really needed in order for a regional integration process to be initiated and maintained? Are there important differences between a regional organization and a universal one in this respect? If so, what are these differences? Since we are interested in the authoritativeness of an organization, it may be useful to apply a scheme for organizational procedures, as has been suggested by William D. Coplin.[45] Six types of tasks are important:

1. Gathering, analyzing, and distributing information;
2. Recommending national laws and actions;
3. Evaluating state activities in terms of the goals of the organization;
4. Creating and administering regulations;
5. Performing specific actions involving expenditure of funds with important impacts on the resources of some or all of the members; and
6. Formulating policies indirectly by expanding the scope of existing tasks.

Rather than examine the importance and influence of an organization in terms of sovereignty and supranationality, it may be more fruitful to proceed by attempting to penetrate or "cut into" its authoritativeness in the manner stated above. This may enable us to obtain answers to some important questions about the nature and function of the organization that could otherwise quite easily be lost in the labyrinthine aspects of supranationality.

THE NORDIC CASE: SOME HYPOTHESES

Amitai Etzioni saw a union as "an international system whose level of integration and scope are higher than that of an international organization and lower than that of an established political community."[46] He used the term to refer to systems with an increasing, stable, or decreasing level of integration and breadth of scope. In his frame of reference the Nordic countries constitute a stable union.

Now, to suggest that a political union exists among these countries is to take a risk. This union would certainly be denied by several observers who are incumbent to the region or living outside it. Further, the term "union" has a low political currency value among the Nordic countries, which may tend to complicate matters. The claim does, however, deserve to be examined carefully. Analytically speaking, the concept is useful, especially in conjunction with the type of political community Etzioni has in mind. His first type of integration, which is effective control over the use of the means of violence, would not seem to be met in the case of Scandinavia. In the remaining two types of integration, the center of decision making is able to affect significantly the allocation of resources and rewards throughout the community and is the dominant focus of the political identification of a large majority of politically aware citizens. These two types may be subject to verification. Etzioni's research on the Nordic associational web as a stable union according to the above criteria is useful insofar as it contributes to an understanding of the working of Scandinavian integration in general and possibly to some extent to an understanding of the position of the Nordic Council within it.

If integration in this sense is taken for the time being to mean levels or stages in a process that is called unification, it may enable us to attempt to measure the process in terms of stages (integration) and, admittedly to a lesser extent, to measure it on a time dimension. In principle I have nothing against such an exercise, which may even allow us to undertake empirical testing and to make predictions about both strength and direction. My scepticism centers on the somewhat lighthearted manner in which the central concept of "political community" is treated and the failure on the part of integration theorists to combine and connect it with the processes and structures of which they wish to speak. Although among the three main theorists of political integration mentioned above, Etzioni is the one who seems to be most perceptive with regard to the Nordic case, I differ from him on this point: his work suggests that the Nordic states are a stable union because they are very much a natural entity, which in turn is because of such factors as geographic proximity, cultural and religious semblances, and past joint experiences of a politico-administrative nature.

First, it seems to me that there is some type of methodological confusion here, between the conditions favoring integration and the results of it, on the one hand, and integration itself, on the other. Second, the dichotomy between homogeneity and heterogeneity is not taken into account. Just as it is possible for extreme heterogeneity to nullify community development, it may likewise be observed that extreme homogeneity also may cause a community to break down, along the lines of the old adage, "Familiarity breeds contempt." It may be suggested that heterogeneity is necessary for advancing development and the community process in the course of attempts to resolve differences and by the stimulation inherent in differences. However, the initial attempts to develop a sense of community seem to be dependent upon the perception of similarities of both purpose and function.

However, some of the important reasons for stability in the Nordic union have little to do with the belief that it constitutes a natural entity. In fact, in some cases the stability exists in spite of this. To a large extent it may even be decided by forces external to the union itself. We may also get closer to the truth by tracing and examining the methods of unification that are applied within the framework of the Nordic Council and of the rest of the Scandinavian machinery for cooperation and coordination. This may also show us how and where the process is weak and may offer some clues to why this is so or to what may come about as a result of it.

There has been a rapid development on the formal, organizational side of Nordic cooperation during the last few years. Its essence has been the formalization of governmental cooperation and the setting up of a Council of Ministers, a Committee of Permanent Representatives, a Secretariat (responsible to the Council of Ministers), a Cultural Secretariat, and various committees directly connected with the latter. In part this has been done to fill a gap that has existed for some time, that is, to satisfy a need for more formal institutions on the governmental side. This development has also come about because of events elsewhere, primarily in Western Europe; and to some extent it represents an effort to safeguard already existing types of cooperation. Hopefully the case study will show how, in part, the Nordic Council has been implicated in this development.

In a sense the Nordic Council is the most prominent organ for Scandinavian regionalism, serving as the focus of cooperation, coordination, and unification in the Nordic area. Theoretically speaking, it is an intergovernmental organization rather than a supranational one; in reality, however, it appears to be somewhere between these two archetypes. If this observation is correct, it leads to several important questions that may be difficult to answer but that should nevertheless be attempted. For example, how important is supranationality in the process of political integration and unification? How much, if any, and what type of integration may be achieved without the existence of supranational elements? At what point, if this is the case, or even if the reverse applies, are these supranational elements crucial for the continuance and durability of integration? How important are strong institutions, and what types of institutions are required? Do methods ever matter as much as, or more than, institutions? What are the sources of support and strain for the process and for the institutions of integration? Is it possible to determine the extent to which political integration takes place because of the role of institutions and/or the methods and conditions that contribute to it? What are other important factors?

As for the Nordic Council in particular, to what extent, if any, are supranational elements actually developing within its framework? To what extent, and by whom, is such a development desired? Who opposes it and for what reasons? Finally, what kinds of general observations about integration and unification can be made on the basis of specific examples? Which observations are particularly important in the Nordic case?

It may well be that Scandinavian integration is better understood if examined in a wider framework and that it may be more easily explained if seen against the background of existing theories about political integration. Conversely, integration theory, such as it is, may well prove to be inconclusive without the Scandinavian example and such lessons as may be drawn from it.

Theorists of political integration have produced propositions and hypotheses regarding this phenomenon, both as system and process. It seems to me that some of the hypotheses are doubtful, for reasons that I will explore, and that other hypotheses merit further investigation. Concerning the Scandinavian case, for example, the following statements have quite frequently been advanced by observers and are presumably thought to be correct:

1. Recommendations dealing with noncontroversial issues have little effect on political integration.

2. Because the measures taken by the Nordic Council are not binding, and because its procedures remain somewhat informal, the impact of the organization on political integration is minimal.

3. The Nordic Council does not play an active or important role in the integrative process of Scandinavia because the organization has no supranational powers.

To my mind these statements are at best misleading and at worst incorrect, for reasons that I will explore. In addition, there are several points of importance arising out of the Scandinavian case that seem to have been underplayed or even ignored. These are of central importance for the understanding of Scandinavian regionalism, but they may also be important for integration theory in general.

It is important to attempt to ascertain whether the Nordic associational web today is a stable union in the way Etzioni saw it. If the Scandinavian case is a story of success, is this because of structure, methods, or something else? It would also be interesting to see what the present sources of political support are and how these are likely to change in the future.

Naturally the Nordic union cannot be considered as somehow existing in a vacuum. We want to know what are the general effects on it of external systems and plural memberships. Finally, we want to find out how and in what sense the Nordic case may be of importance for integration theory and policy.

In order to try to get at some of the elements of importance, it should be useful to break up the notion and activities of integration into different sectors or fields of particular activity, such as the economic, legal, communicational, social, and cultural sectors or fields. Proceeding along these lines should provide us with an empirical framework within which several propositions can be advanced. It should also enable us to isolate specific instances from which useful understanding or insight may be gleaned.

Some activities, even entire fields or sectors of activities, are often considered to be of little or no political importance by theorists of international, or even transnational, politics. Traditionally, for example, both the cultural and social sectors of activity have tended to fall into this category. It seems to me that with respect to integration and community formation, since these concepts are closely connected, such an evaluation is inadequate to say the least. Social change and cultural change take place in accelerated form, and areas and types of human activity that may be considered of very slight political importance may well become important, both in theory and in fact, in the future and possibly even in the near future. Conversely, as other types of human or social activity become subject to increased technical and scientific planning and management or control, their political importance may well become deemphasized. Types of activity that are considered less political may, subject to such pressures as exist in the evolution of society, become politicized. Large-scale economic, and to some extent technical, social planning may well shift the political content to areas having more to do with private life, with cultural manifestations, or with life styles. I foresee a depoliticization of the economic dimension or sector of activity and also an obverse effect taking place in the social, the cultural, and possibly the communicational sectors.

It is important to stress at the outset that the Nordic states are members of several multinational systems, although not necessarily the same ones. Finland, for example, is not a member of the Organization for Economic Cooperation and Development (OECD) or of the

North Atlantic Treaty Organization (NATO) and only an associate member of the European Free Trade Association (EFTA), an organization that until 1960-61 did not include Iceland. As we know, Sweden is not a member of NATO either, because of her neutrality, which incidentally prevents her from entering into a full membership in the European Economic Community (EEC), an organization of which Denmark is a full member. Participation by Sweden in various military and economic arrangements has been prevented or delayed by her own decision, whereas participation by Finland in such schemes is prevented by the influence of an outside power.

Since such organizations as EFTA and NATO are essentially monofunctional, whereas the Nordic Council is designedly multifunctional, it may be possible to make some comparisons that will aid in understanding both types. Does membership in the one type of organization create barriers to active or useful membership in another? Are memberships in some cases irreconcilable, and if so, what are these cases and why is this so? We should like to know something about the roles of units of these organizations. If, let us say, an organization has several units that perform different functions, is this advantageous for political integration in short-term and/or in long-term cases? If the organization is supported by several social groups (and if the representation is of a certain size), as opposed to being supported by one or two social groups, is the likelihood of unification increased?

We may now suggest some hypotheses concerning the Nordic case:

1. Recommendations dealing with noncontroversial issues have little effect on political integration.

2. Micro-, or low-level, integration is a major and perhaps necessary factor favoring unification.

3. Issues that are considered noncontroversial may not necessarily remain so in the future or in some different context, with the result that recommendations dealing with them may in fact become useful for political integration.

4. Since the methods of the Nordic Council are informal and its measures are not binding, the impact of the organization on political integration is minimal.

5. For some dimensions of integration, the less such formalized institutions as binding guidelines and timetables, rules of conduct, and penalty clauses are applied, the greater is the chance of successful long-term unification.

6. However, economics is probably not one of these dimensions.

7. The Nordic Council does not play an active or important role in the integration process of Scandinavia because the organization has no supranational powers.

8. The approach used by the Nordic Council, since it involves several levels of action other than that of economics, is conducive to a welcome long-term unification.

9. In the Scandinavian case unification remains a poorly articulated and somewhat ambiguous goal that may therefore be difficult to achieve.

10. This ambiguity is maintained, deliberately or not, for national, local, or party reasons, although it may otherwise serve useful purposes.

11. Integrative dysfunctionality may be intrinsic to the political structures and processes of the Scandinavian states.

A hypothesis does not require proof unless or until it becomes part of a theory. It will be seen that the main hypotheses are Hypotheses 1, 4, and 7, with 2, 3, 5, 6, and 8 serving as alternative or supportive hypotheses. Finally, Hypotheses 9, 10, and 11 are part hypotheses and part "hunches."

Powerful short-run devices in key dimensions, such as economics, do not necessarily generate general support. Tight schemes superimposed upon political reality in different national settings may only last to the crucial point at which national self-interest is affected or the spirit of cooperation ceases. Concerning the usage of the concept of national self-interest in Scandinavian politics, this may turn out to be nothing more than the collective self-interest of politicians, individual national public servants, and administrators.

As for the Nordic group of states, it may be necessary, possibly even crucial, to attempt to achieve some sort of large-scale economy or some other measure of increased economic or political efficiency. If so, the states may decide to amend, add to, make changes in the structure and/or the methods of the organization, or even bypass it altogether. The last change is unlikely so far as the Nordic Council is concerned, for reasons that will be shown; but nevertheless if any of the first three changes were to be made, they would merely shed more light on the particular phenomenon we are examining without necessarily invalidating our propositions.

The unification process, then, is one in which control of the means of violence, the capacity to allocate resources and rewards, and the locus of identification are transferred from the member units to the system in which they are members. I will argue that the degree to which the units are initially integrated internally is likely to affect their potential resistance to unification and therefore the success of any specific unification effort and that there are some peculiar consequences flowing from this. The Nordic Council is a good example for this kind of study since (1) the units are internally well-integrated to start with; (2) the organization is clearly so multifunctional that specifications of integrative efforts on different dimensions may be made and contrasted with each other; and (3) the organization has been operative for a comparatively long time.

Two other factors of considerable importance for this and other studies of unification and integration are communication and responsiveness. As Karl Deutsch has shown, the communicational capacity of a unit is a major determining element in the unification process. The effectiveness of the communication network of a unit or system affects the degree to which assets are converted into policy. This may be significant as far as the Nordic Council is concerned, as I will argue, to to extent that the lines of communication are deliberately kept open in this sense.

Many of the integrative measures in the Nordic case are taken by nongovernmental agencies, including such semiprivate groups as the Norden Associations, as cultural and social interest groups, as private firms, and as businessmen and private individuals in the different countries. Therefore, we may in fact be able to answer some additional important questions. For example, what is the exact role of governments and of individual parliamentarians and civil servants in the process of integration in general and in the Nordic case in particular, as opposed to the role of private groups and individuals? Is it not possible that the former, institutionalized groups, which are said to be in favor of unification and which are also given credit for this when it occurs, may in fact be opposed to at least aspects of the process, and/or stages of it? In fact, the roles and functions of the institutionalized groups may be dysfunctional to integration in the Nordic area. On the other hand, not nearly enough is known about the various activities of the semiprivate and private sectors in this process. For example, it could be that there is a fair amount of identitive power in the Nordic union that is so far unfocused. Furthermore, the utilitarian power of these groups may not be quite so low as the state administrators and government members often proclaim it to be. In this region, as well as elsewhere, both national administrators and politicians of different backgrounds have special interests of their own to look after. These interests may or may not necessarily coincide with those of private groups or individuals within the same union. They may even go against majority interests.

I shall try to isolate the areas within the above-mentioned fields of integration in which the interests do not seem to coincide and, if possible, explore the reasons for this. This exercise is one to which the Nordic Council lends itself, and it may clarify the roles of governments, of individual parliamentarians and bureaucrats, and of the semiprivate and private sectors in the process of unification in Scandinavia, giving credit where it is due, whether for positive or negative action. Finally, this exercise may be of some use as a contribution to the understanding of Scandinavian policy in general and to the possible lessons that may be drawn from it, for theory as well as for practice.

NOTES

1. Some of the earlier writings on European integration pose this question.

2. For example, see U. W. Kitzinger, The Challenge of the Common Market (Oxford: Basil Blackwell, 1962).

3. See Karl W. Deutsch, Nationalism and Social Communication (Cambridge, Mass.: M.I.T. Press, 1953); Karl W. Deutsch, Sidney A. Burrell, Robert A. Kann, Maurice Lee, Jr., Martin Lichterman, Raymond E. Undgren, and Richard W. Van Wagenen, Political Community and the North Atlantic Area: International Organization in the Light of Historical Experience (Princeton, N.J.: Princeton University Press, 1957); and Deutsch, The Analysis of International Relations (Englewood Cliffs, N.J.: Prentice-Hall, 1968).

4. See Ernst Haas, The Uniting of Europe: Political, Economic and Social Forces (Stanford, Calif.: Stanford University Press, 1958); Haas, Beyond the Nation-State: Functionalism and International Organization (Stanford, Calif.: Stanford University Press, 1964); and Haas, "Technocracy, Pluralism and the New Europe," in A New Europe?, edited by Stephen Graubard (Boston: Houghton-Mifflin Co., 1964).

5. See Amitai Etzioni, A Hard Way to Peace (New York: Collier Books, 1962) and Etzioni, Political Unification: A Comparative Study of Leaders and Forces (New York: Holt, Rinehart and Winston, 1965).

6. See Leon Lindberg, The Political Dynamics of European Economic Integration (Stanford, Calif.: Stanford University Press, 1963); and Lindberg, "Integration as a Source of Stress on the European Community System," International Organization 20, no. 2 (Spring 1966).

7. See for example, Count Coudenhove, An Idea Conquers the World (London: Hutchinson, 1953); and Crusade for Pan-Europe (New York: G. P. Putnam's Sons, 1943); Edouard Herriot, The United States of Europe (New York: Viking, 1930).

8. By Bruce Russett in "Transactions, Community, and International Political Integration" (mimeographed, 1970).

9. See Haas, The Uniting of Europe, op. cit., pp. 5-7.

10. See Lindberg, The Political Dynamics of European Economic Integration, op. cit.

11. See Leon N. Lindberg, "The European Community as a Political System," Journal of Common Market Studies 5, no. 4 (June

1967): 344-87; and Lindberg, Europe's Would-Be Policy (Englewood Cliffs, N.J.: Prentice-Hall, 1970).

12. See Etzioni, Political Unification, op. cit., Chapters 1-4.

13. Etzioni, "A Paradigm for the Study of Political Unification," World Politics 15, no. 1 (1963/64): 45.

14. See Deutsch et al., Political Community and the North Atlantic Area, op. cit.

15. Deutsch, Nationalism and Social Communication, op. cit., especially Chapter 3.

16. Haas, The Uniting of Europe, op. cit., p. 16.

17. Ibid., p. 17.

18. Ibid.

19. See Eric Solem, "Nordic Integration: Problems and Possibilities," European Studies 9 (1969).

20. See Etzioni, Political Unification, op. cit.

21. Ibid., Part 1.

22. See Haas, The Uniting of Europe, op. cit.

23. Etzioni, Political Unification, op. cit.

24. See Martin Saeter, "Hva er integrasjon?" Internasjonal politikk, no. 4 (1965).

25. Etzioni, "A Paradigm for the Study of Political Integration," op. cit., p. 45; Pitirim Sorokin, Social and Cultural Dynamics (New York: American Book Co., 1937).

26. See Pitirim Sorokin, The Crisis of Our Age (New York: E. P. Dutton, 1941).

27. See Arnold Toynbee, A Study of History (London: Oxford University Press, 1934); Toynbee, The World & The West (London: Oxford University Press, 1953); Toynbee, The Present Day Experience in Western Civilization (London: Oxford University Press, 1962); and Toynbee, with Philip Toynbee, Comparing Notes: A Dialogue across a Generation (London: Weinfeld & Nicholson, 1963).

28. See Haas, The Uniting of Europe, op. cit.

29. Ibid., p. 5.

30. Ibid., p. 11.

31. Ibid., p. 10.

32. Etzioni, Political Unification, op. cit., p. 4.

33. See Deutsch et al., Political Community and the North Atlantic Area, op. cit., p. 36.

34. Ibid.

35. See Haas, The Uniting of Europe, op. cit., p. xv.

36. Ibid.

37. Deutsch et al., Political Community and the North Atlantic Area, op. cit., p. 36.

38. Ibid., p. 93.

39. See Nina Heathcote, "The Crisis of European Supranationality," Journal of Common Market Studies 5, no. 2 (1966): 141.

40. See Francis Rosenstiel, "Reflections on the Notion of Supranationality," Journal of Common Market Studies 2, no. 2 (November 1963).

41. Ibid.

42. See Max Beloff, "International Integration and the Modern State," Journal of Common Market Studies 2, no. 1.

43. Ibid., p. 54.

44. Ibid., p. 56.

45. See William D. Coplin, The Functions of International Law: An Introduction to the Role of International Law in the Contemporary World (Chicago: Rand McNally & Co., 1966), p. 152.

46. See Etzioni, Political Unification, op. cit.

CHAPTER

2

SCANDINAVIAN ADMINISTRATIVE COOPERATION

THE ROOTS OF SCANDINAVIAN COOPERATION

Viewed historically, Scandinavian cooperation is a relatively new phenomenon. Scandinavianism, on the other hand, goes back further in time. The first major attempt at unification, in part by coercion, was the Kalmar Union (1397-1520), which was initiated under Queen Margareta. The union extended from Greenland in the west to Finland in the east, and it included Norway, Sweden, Denmark, and a small part of northern Germany. However, this union, based on the power of the throne, did not last.

A period of consolidation in the Nordic region followed, and two large power blocs emerged. The western bloc consisted of Denmark, Norway, Iceland, the Faeroe Islands, and Greenland, while the eastern bloc was made up of Sweden and Finland. The strong partners in these blocs were Denmark and Sweden respectively. The western bloc dominated at first, only to be overtaken by the eastern bloc later on. Despite several attempts to change the situation, the latest of which was the Nordic Seven Years War (1563-1570), the eastern bloc remained dominant. This state of affairs lasted for nearly 300 years.

Following the Treaty of Kiel in January 1814, Norway was ceded to Sweden, and she remained under Swedish government for nearly a century, until independence was achieved in 1905. Finland had been incorporated into the Russian czardom during the Napoleonic Wars, although she retained her own administrative and legal institutions as well as her own Diet. Nevertheless, the centuries-old and deeply integrated relations between Sweden and Finland were severed. This was the situation when the first waves of the romantic nationalist movement on the European continent reached the Nordic region.

The Scandinavianism of 1840–70 appears to have been primarily romantic, with an element of liberalism in it. As with the national-liberal movements of Germany and Italy, its adherents tended to come from academic circles and from the upper middle classes. This was the time of Student Scandinavianism, with the drinking of punch and the toasting of the Nordic Idea.

However, some practical work was also initiated at this time. As early as 1839, for example, a joint meeting of Scandinavian natural scientists took place. Other professional groups were drawn into this type of cooperation, which progressed without interruption. Beginning in the middle of the century, several fraternal societies and professional groups became increasingly involved in efforts to intensify the social and cultural interplay in the region. There was interest in the development of a common literature, for example, as well as in establishing a common basis, and common concepts, of law. Unity in patent legislation had been on the program of the pan-Scandinavians, and as early as 1861 an agreement was made through which Denmark and Sweden entered into an exchange of verdicts and legal decisions. The first meeting of lawyers was held in 1872, and it included professors of law, judges, and experts from the administrations. The legal meetings have been carried out regularly ever since that time, and they have been of considerable importance, as we shall see. Economic cooperation also grew out of these early practical experiences of Scandinavianism, as did cooperation in the social and cultural fields.

However, strong political forces were also at work. For example, Denmark wanted a defense alliance with Sweden-Norway in order to try to stop German expansion in Schleswig. The more radical spokesmen for this type of Scandinavianism were prepared to offer the Crown of Denmark to the King of Sweden and Norway in return for an alliance. A united parliament and common institutions were some of the goals of the pan-Scandinavians. Forces were pulling in the opposite direction as well. Nationalism, for example, had already raised up its head in Iceland, Finland, and Norway.

Iceland was still a Danish dependency, and Finland remained politically tied to Russia. In Norway a determined campaign was staged, the purpose of which was to reinstate the old language of the country as spoken by the farmers and rural people at the expense of the Danish-influenced language of the city dwellers. This battle of languages, as it soon became, developed into something much wider, a cultural conflict that is still not resolved as far as Norway is concerned. Norway was becoming antagonistic not only toward her union with Sweden, but also toward foreign influence and, as she saw it, "dominance" in general. This struggle between centripetal and centrifugal forces was detrimental to unification in the Scandinavian region.

The first meeting of Scandinavian economists had been held in 1862. At two following conferences, one in Stockholm in 1866 and the other in Copenhagen in 1872, the economists directed their attention toward the possibility of creating a monetary union. A recommendation was passed, calling on the governments to set up a joint commission to study this question. One month after it had been appointed, the joint commission produced its report and the first steps toward a monetary union were taken. Norway, Denmark, and Sweden were urged to adopt the gold standard; bring conformity to their currencies; and make Norwegian, Swedish, and Danish coins legal tender in all three countries. This proposal was accepted by Sweden and Denmark, and the Monetary Union came into being early in 1873. Norway, having at first objected to the plan, joined this union in 1875.

By 1885 the three central banks had agreed to issue drafts on each other without interest or commission. The rate of exchange was now constantly at par. In 1894 Sweden and Norway decided that their bills could be used interchangeably. This agreement was widened to incorporate Denmark, which became a partner to it in 1901. The Scandinavian monetary union lasted until 1924.

A system of free trade had been in existence between Sweden and Norway since 1874; this system had resulted in a considerable increase in trade flow between the two states. However, since such a system could only work well as long as the states followed similar trade policies of a liberal nature, it was brought to an end in 1874, when Sweden opted for a more restrictive and protective system.

One of the main reasons why the Scandinavianism of the nineteenth century did not result in political unity may have been the lack of popular support. At the same time, no one state was quite strong enough to impose its will on the other states, and the days of unification by coercion seemed to be over. Nevertheless, the support base had been broadened. In 1866, for example, the first Scandinavian labor congress met, and the labor movement soon became one of the strongest forces behind Scandinavian solidarity. Also, the many "folk high schools" of the 1860s were actively advocating Scandinavian solidarity, mostly among the rural populations. Interestingly enough, more than a century later in 1970-71, the only group within Scandinavia that was wholeheartedly in favor of setting up a Nordic customs union was the Scandinavian Labor Union Congresses.

In a sense World War I brought the three Scandinavian states closer together. They issued identical notes of neutrality to indicate a joint position on foreign policy. The so-called three kings' meeting took place on December 18, 1914, when Christian X of Denmark, Gustav V of Sweden, and Haakon VII of Norway all met in Malmo, Sweden. The idea was to create a symbol of unity in foreign policy, which was temporarily achieved, although it later turned out to be basically unsound.

Because of the unrestricted submarine warfare by Germany and the retaliatory tightening of the blockade, a crisis situation arose with regard to supplies of vital commodities to Scandinavia. The practical results of this showed up quickly in the intra-Scandinavian system of exchange of commodities, which was based on national needs as well as on reciprocity. Because of this barter system, intra-Scandinavian trade showed an increase from 12 or 13 percent before the war to 30 percent by 1918.[1]

The experience of the war situation brought home to the Scandinavians the value of cooperation in general. Several new contacts were created, and organizations that were intended to further cooperation were set up. One of the most important of these was the Norden Association, which was established in order to promote, maintain, and strengthen cultural ties among the Nordic peoples. This organization, founded by private persons, still has many branches throughout the region and is active in all the Nordic countries. It was set up in Denmark, Sweden, and Norway in 1919; in Iceland in 1922; and in Finland in 1924. Iceland became a sovereign state in 1917, followed by Finland one year later. Both states became republics and were from then on able to make their own valuable contribution to Nordic cooperation.* The Faeroe Islands were granted home rule, and their own flag, within the Danish kingdom in 1948, whereas Greenland, which had remained a Danish colony, was incorporated into the kingdom of Denmark in 1953. It is represented in the Danish parliament on an equal footing with the other parts of the country.

In spite of these changes, World War I had also been a setback to Scandinavian unity. Dissimilar economic conditions and monetary policies in the war years had led to the suspension of the currency union, although it was never formally dissolved. Although there had been no attempt to create the necessary formal machinery of coordination, the Scandinavians had come fairly close to this with the Interparliamentary Union, which had been set up privately by members of the Scandinavian parliaments in 1907, two years after the dissolution of the Swedish-Norwegian Union. Owing to the lack of a sufficiently effective coordinating machinery, among other things, economic cooperation was allowed to decline after the war years.

Nevertheless, new fields of cooperation were opened up. The Nordic states became increasingly involved in the work of the League of Nations, and they put their trust in this new international body for securing peace and world order. In a sense it was a two-way traffic, since the Nordic countries were assigned one seat on the council of

---

*Norway, Sweden, and Denmark are still monarchies. Denmark is the world's oldest existing kingdom, dating back to Gorm the Old, 900-50.

the League of Nations. From then on, partly because of the expectations of that organization and partly from the experience of neutralism in the war, the image of the natural entity of the Nordic states was born.

There was little internal progress within Scandinavia as far as unification was concerned, however. Official contact among the governments was also less frequent than during the war. Much work was put into some of the activities of the League of Nations, however, and coordination of policies by the Nordic states took place on this level of activity.

Although during the 1920s no major progress was achieved as far as economic cooperation was concerned, cooperation among the states in the administration of justice and in social policy increased. However, no major upward turn in cooperation occurred until the 1930s, when the Scandinavian states created the so-called Oslo Bloc.

The world depression, the rise of Nazism in Germany, and the growing danger of war in Europe again led the Scandinavian states to try to increase their cooperation in various fields. Meetings were held by the foreign ministers on a regular basis, beginning in January 1932. Regular meetings of the ministers of Commerce, Social Welfare, and Justice were by now a regular practice. Of added importance was the fact that Finland was drawn into this network. Nevertheless, the Scandinavians had put too much trust in the League of Nations and had also drawn false conclusions from their World War I experience about the viability of neutralism. For this reason, as we know, there was a marked failure to make a common show of force against Nazi Germany. Instead, the Scandinavian states became splintered and forced into isolation from one another.

Denmark and Norway were occupied by German troops, although they were officially "protected" by Hitler. Sweden, the only country that was strong enough to defend itself, became neutral during World War II, after having profited handsomely from German armament. It also gave the German troops access to Norway on its own territory, no doubt because it was under heavy pressure. Understandably, this fact was not easily forgotten in Norway. It provided a strong basis for postwar suspicion and a psychological blockage among the Norwegians as far as perception of Swedish foreign policy motives was concerned. Viable arguments were put forward to the effect that Sweden really had very little choice and that in retrospect she might have taken the right decision; but at the same time it is easy to see that what happened had extremely important consequences for inter-Scandinavian relations in years to come and that it precipitated a decline in mutual trust and amplified already existing suspicions.

As it turned out, Denmark fared relatively well during the German occupation, although some atrocities were committed by

Germany, especially the attempt to round up all Danish Jews. Norway and Finland were severely damaged. Because of her relationship with the Soviet Union, Finland found herself siding with Germany, suffering both attacks by Soviet troops and dominance by Germany. Needless to say, the years 1940-45 meant a virtual standstill in Nordic cooperation.

POSTWAR DEVELOPMENTS

Following the peace in 1945, some plans were laid for the establishment of a defense alliance among the Scandinavian states. Sweden was eager to maintain her own successful policy of neutrality, which meant that she did not want to join the newly created North Atlantic Treaty Organization in 1949. For this reason Sweden suggested a Scandinavian pact based on mutual defense and neutrality. For several reasons this was not acceptable to other Scandinavians, in particular to the Norwegians. When the U.S. administration, for understandable reasons, insisted upon membership in NATO as a prerequisite for the supply of U.S. arms to the Nordic countries, the proposed defense union collapsed.

The question of a defense union had been brought up shortly after the Communist takeover of Czechoslovakia in February 1948. For obvious reasons, Finland was not able to take part in the discussions of the pact by a preliminary study group set up by Sweden, Denmark, and Norway. Rather, Finland felt compelled to conclude a treaty of friendship and mutual assistance with the Soviet Union in that year.

It should be stated that the military problems and security issues were not identical for Denmark, Sweden, and Norway. For that reason alone, a solution would have been difficult to find. The two main political actors were Sweden and Norway. Whereas Norway was to some extent attracted by the emerging Atlantic security project, Sweden was not. From a strategic point of view the situation appeared less than attractive to her. A constellation inside the Nordic area that would put Sweden between rival blocs was obviously an undesirable development seen from the Swedish point of view. Furthermore such a development, which would pull Norway into a tighter Atlantic security arrangement while Finland became more closely drawn into the Soviet sphere of influence, would contribute toward a further disintegration in Scandinavia. Participation in an Atlantic security system was out of the question for Sweden because of her policy of neutrality, but isolated neutrality would put a severe strain on Sweden if her neighboring Nordic countries to the west and south became firmly committed. On the other hand, if a Scandinavian defense alliance could be set up, according to which Sweden, Denmark, and Norway would carry out a Swedish-type policy of neutrality, Scandinavia could be turned into a credible neutral zone. This type of thinking led the Swedes to suggest a defense alliance to their Danish and Norwegian neighbors.

The proposed treaty would have three main principles. First, there should be a joint pledge from all three states that an attack on one of them should be considered an attack on them all. Second, a declaration of neutrality should be made. This would of course mean that none of the states could conclude any military treaty with a third power and that all would endeavor to keep out of any military conflict. Third, the joint Scandinavian neutrality should be an armed neutrality, with plans for joint defense and joint control of armaments to be worked out, within a reasonable period of time. The joint military effort would be brought up to such a level as would be deemed necessary, but with due regard to economic capabilities.

This plan presented several difficulties, in particular to the Norwegians, who insisted that the plan be supplemented with arrangements in advance for outside help if it should be required; this demand was unacceptable to Sweden. The question of costs presented another difficulty. It must be remembered that Norway, which was practically defenseless at this stage, was faced with a need for considerable reconstruction, especially in its northern regions. The United States was an obvious source of cheap weapons, but these were reserved for future NATO members, as previously stated, as well as for states with which the United States had special arrangements.

Needless to say there were other forces at work of more regional or of domestic origin. There was the bitterness felt by the Norwegians toward Sweden, dating back to the Union and more recently to World War II, when the compromised neutrality of Sweden had allowed Germany to cross through Swedish territory when advancing upon Norway. There was also the traditional orientation toward the West by Norway because of trade patterns and other factors. Finally there was the general scepticism toward neutrality as a viable policy, particularly with regard to the reasonable chances of small states being able to carry it out and stay out of war. Some of the pessimism on the last point was probably related to the larger issue of the unsuccessful and possibly devastating defense policy that had been conducted by Norway prior to the outbreak of World War II.

Throughout this period Denmark had played a rather passive role, while trying to moderate between the Norwegian and Swedish views. After Norway decided not to accept the Swedish proposal, Denmark investigated the possibility of some kind of bilateral arrangement between the two remaining countries. From the Swedish point of view this was considered an inadequate substitute, and not a viable solution strategically or politically. The net result was that Denmark followed the Norwegian example of accepting membership in NATO.

In retrospect it seems that some of the fears that prompted Sweden to make the initial defense alliance proposal have so far not materialized. On the other hand, the different security policies of the Scandinavian states seem to represent fundamental and possibly even unbridgeable political separation. As NATO members, Denmark and Norway have both succeeded in acquiring protection with very specific conditions. For example, they have refused to receive permanently stationed Allied forces on their territories and have turned down the idea of nuclear arms installments. Until the Czechoslovakian crisis of 1968, and possibly even since that event, there has been a certain diversity of feeling about the NATO affiliation and about the nature of the threat from the east. Both countries have unambiguously confirmed their intention of retaining their membership in the alliance, however.

Finland has faced different problems. Although it falls within the Soviet security orbit, Finland is not a member of the Warsaw Pact and has to a considerable extent succeeded in moving toward, if not actually achieving, the status of a basically neutral state. This neutrality is of course qualified by its 1948 treaty of friendship and mutual assistance with the Soviet Union. The Finnish situation seems to have remained almost unalterable as seen from the Finnish point of view. There is little that Finland can do, especially in the light of her own preferred policy toward her eastern neighbor, the so-called Paasikivi-Kekkonen line. The other Scandinavian states have understood the Finnish position or have at least accepted it with some sympathy.

Sweden has refrained from applying her technological capability to the development of nuclear weapons and has carried out her policy of neutrality. The doctrine of nonalignment and neutrality is now firmly entrenched, to the extent that it would cause political discomfort to consider a relationship with the EEC that would go much beyond that of an associational arrangement.

Although they produced no direct positive results with regard to defense, the initial talks about a defense alliance among the Nordic states were nevertheless useful. For example, the matter was considered so important that it became clear that a special type of international forum was required in which the parliamentarian members of Scandinavian legislatures would be able to meet and express themselves. Although this did not imply a distrust on the part of the governments or in the relationship among these governments as such, it meant a widening of the circle of political participation in Nordic affairs. The seeds had now been planted for what was later to become the Nordic Council.

PRESENT FORMS OF COOPERATION

If by integration we mean, as some writers seem to mean, chiefly or even only the merger of national economies, we may quite easily speak of the Scandinavian countries as not very well integrated. On the other hand, there is really nothing to prevent us from including in our definition of that term such areas as the social, legal, communicational, and cultural fields of human activity. In fact, our understanding of what integration is all about would probably benefit from this way of looking at reality. It is possible that the Scandinavian group of countries would then appear to be highly integrated in several of these fields.

Take social legislation, for example. The social services in the Scandinavian region are now coordinated to a point at which there is nearly complete equality in treatment, irrespective of nationality. Workers, for example, may take their social benefits with them when crossing the boundaries within Scandinavia, including their pension rights, should they so desire. Through their own national health insurance, the citizens of Scandinavia have free access to hospital services and medical treatment throughout the region.

Since 1954 Sweden, Denmark, Norway, and Finland have had a common labor market. One of the basic principles of this labor market has been the maintenance of full employment, and a joint Nordic Labor Committee has been set up to coordinate the efforts of the governments and to implement this policy.

There are other fields in which the national boundaries in Scandinavia are being broken down. For example, there are no passport boundaries for the inhabitants of the region. As a rule foreigners entering Scandinavia need only show their passports once, after which they move about very much as if they were inside one country. Integration is also taking place in such fields as public and private law, road traffic and safety, regional planning, communications, education, research, cultural affairs, and a host of other fields of human activity. As a result there has been a broadening in national allegiances to incorporate allegiance to the region as well as to the individual countries.

The different levels at which intergovernmental cooperation and coordination are carried out in Scandinavia fall into three categories. First, direct contact is maintained at the level of ministers. This contact includes the Nordic Council of Ministers. The foreign ministers, for example, meet at least twice a year. The ministries of justice cooperate even more extensively, holding three or more meetings per year and attempting to coordinate legislation throughout Scandinavia. In addition, meetings of the ministers of social affairs, of health and hygiene, of education, of communications, and of

TABLE 1

Newly Established Joint Nordic Organs, 1945-74

Time Period	Number of New Organs	Percentage of New Organs
1945-49	7	6.7
1950-54	4	3.8
1955-59	9	8.7
1960-64	19	18.3
1965-69	33	31.7
1970-74	32	30.8
1945-74	104	100.0

Source: Nordic Council, Nordiska Samarbetsorgan (Stockholm: the Council, 1974); Nordic Council, Nordisk Statutsamling, 1970-73 (Stockholm: the Council, 1971-74).

commerce have been enlarged and increased in frequency, partly because of the operations of the Nordic Council.

Prior to 1940 there was no systematic machinery for collaboration among the governments of Scandinavia. Certain ministers, such as the ministers of social affairs and the foreign ministers, had adopted a system of more or less regular meetings. Also there was fairly close contact among the civil servants of some ministries, primarily those of the social affairs ministries. However, the change since the end of World War II has been considerable.

The development of cooperation in traffic matters and communications, which has also resulted in the setting up of the Scandinavian Airlines System (SAS), has necessitated closer collaboration among the traffic ministers than used to be the case. Also the operation of Scandinavian troops under UN auspices in the Gaza Strip, which meant that the participating countries shared interests, has led to an increase in the number of meetings and discussions among the ministers of defense in Scandinavia.

Since 1954 the ministers of trade, in particular, have held several joint meetings intended to further Nordic economic collaboration.

In addition to the increasingly regular meetings among the ministers, which are necessitated by the continuing problems of joint concern, there are some extraordinary meetings at which specific tasks that require quick decisions are taken up. It should also be mentioned that in addition to the regular meetings with their Nordic counterparts, several of the ministers meet during the annual sessions of the Nordic Council, where they often jointly take part in the work. This is of considerable practical importance in several ways. The trend toward developing new joint Nordic organs is illustrated in Table 1.

As of June 1975 there were fourteen permanent committees of national civil servants operating under the auspices of the Nordic Council of Ministers. This can be compared with the eight committees and working groups in the parliamentary sphere under the Nordic Council. From these simple figures it is obvious that the Nordic regional institutional structure cannot be identified solely in terms of the Nordic Council itself. In reality its structure is even more complex than this, since it is only a small proportion of the total number of joint organs that are incorporated into the Nordic Council and Nordic Council of Ministers. It may even be fair to say that no one knows exactly how many joint institutions exist in the region today. The most recent and reliable listing includes no less than 83 permanent governmental organs of Nordic cooperation, in addition to the committees already mentioned. Hence what we have is a complex set of small, decentralized institutions, each functioning within its particular field of operations.

FUTURE IMPLICATIONS

In addition to the permanent bodies of cooperation, which regularly report on their activities to the Nordic Council, there are regular meetings of the heads of certain departments of public services. Among these may be mentioned the postal services, the state railways, the departments of health, the customs authorities, and the trade departments of the foreign offices of the Scandinavian states.

As more areas have become subjects for systematic Nordic cooperation, it has been necessary to set up special committees for the purpose of carrying out this work. Examples of some of these are the Nordic Labor Market Committee, the Committee for Transport Research, the Contact Committee for Nuclear Energy Questions, the Select Committee on Immigrants and Foreigners, the Nordic Committee for Coordination of Wage Statistics, and the Nordic Committee for Social Statistics.[2] There are an estimated 100 or more ad hoc committees working on specific aspects of Nordic cooperation.

Interparliamentarian Cooperation

Finally there is a tradition of constant contact among several public offices and departments on a day-to-day basis, wherever this is required. This contact is often direct rather than restricted to the traditional channels of the foreign offices or the embassies.

Several factors have been important in stimulating Scandinavian cooperation, and they have been decisive in shaping this particular type of collaboration. There are often joint Nordic associations, or meetings as they are called, the purpose of which has been to further unity in specific fields of human activity. Particular traditions of cooperation frequently pull in the same direction. For example, several joint Nordic projects in the legal field may be traced back to informal discussions held in Nordic legal meetings. Often the participants in such discussions have later been appointed to select committees or commissions set up to implement proposals arising out of the earlier discussions. In the case of Marine Law, collections of Nordic legal judgments were published as early as 1900; and in other areas of law collections of judgments have been published since 1958, following initiatives taken by the Nordic Council.

There is little doubt that the tradition of internationalism in the labor movements of Scandinavia has been fundamental to the growth of collaboration in the field of social policy. The first Scandinavian labor conference was held as early as 1886. In 1913 a Committee for Cooperation of the Scandinavian Labor Movements was set up. This in turn led to increased cooperation among Scandinavian employers. Congresses for particular labor unions were also set up, resulting, among other things, in promises of mutual financial support in the case of conflict. Cooperation among the Scandinavian unemployment funds was initiated at an early stage; for example, mention is made of it in Danish statutes of law as early as 1914.

There is a striking presence of and role played by the different Norden Associations in cultural affairs. See Chapter 10. The importance to cultural affairs of these organizations must have been recognized quite early, since they were soon drawn into the activities of the Nordic Cultural Commission. In addition to the above-mentioned Scandinavian organizations for cultural collaboration, there are several bodies and committees that deal with this area within the sector of education and research.

We also find evidence of early collaboration in such fields as trade and economics. For example, the first Nordic meeting for economists was held as early as 1863. The participants were prominent business leaders, professors, and civil servants. These meetings resembled those of the legal profession, insofar as resolutions were passed on to the governments of Scandinavia asking for specific action on certain matters. However, these meetings were not as successful as those of the legal practitioners. The currency union of 1872-75 may have been influenced by the early meetings of the economists. The breakup of the Swedish-Norwegian Union in 1905 was a setback to economic collaboration in Scandinavia. The Nordic Association for Economic Cooperation, which had been set up shortly before the breakup, had only one meeting, although it was instrumental in initiating ad hoc cooperation among the statistical offices of Scandinavia, resulting in a statistical report on inter-Scandinavian trade for the period 1900-06.

The above sets forth the framework within which this interparliamentary organization operates, and without which it cannot be fully comprehended. I will proceed with a discussion of certain important forms of cooperation that I have refrained from describing before this point.

Intergovernmental Cooperation

Whereas Nordic interparliamentarian cooperation and coordination could justly be described as quite well organized in terms of institutional levels, the same cannot be said about governmental cooperation. There have been, of course, frequent consultations, both on ministerial and high civil service levels, as well as close contacts among different ministries in and out of the Nordic Council; but until recently Nordic governmental cooperation showed a lack of organizational form, a situation that has been somewhat alleviated by recent developments.

The Nordic Council of Ministers was established in 1971 in accordance with the agreement revising the Helsinki Treaty, giving intergovernmental cooperation in the Nordic countries a firmer basis. By this agreement the Nordic governments cooperate in the Nordic Council of Ministers, and in addition the informal Nordic ministerial meetings continue.

The Council of Ministers makes decisions to the extent provided for in the Helsinki Treaty and in other agreements that have been made among the Nordic countries. The Council of Ministers also concerns itself with cooperation among the Nordic governments as well as with cooperation between the governments and the Nordic Council itself.

In accordance with the treaty, each government nominates a Cooperation Minister, who coordinates the work of the Council of Ministers and Nordic governmental cooperation in general, as well as contacts by his or her government with the Nordic Council.

The Council of Ministers is not supranational; hence it cannot impose obligations on a country against its will. The chairmanship circulates annually from one country to another.

The present results of the recent institutional proliferation in Scandinavia is quite impressive. Figure 2 illustrates this graphically.

FIGURE 2

Nordic Cooperation

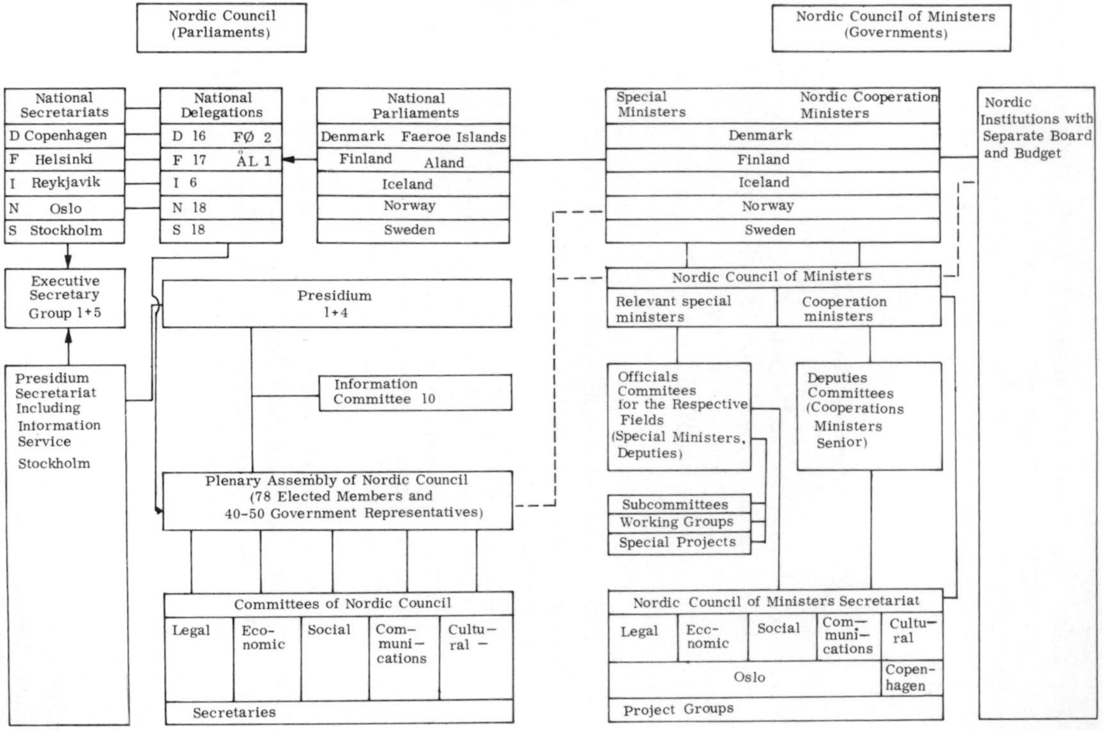

Source: Compiled by the author.

Hopefully, these new organs will succeed in achieving their original aims: an improvement and simplification of Nordic integrative measures. However, as I shall attempt to demonstrate, for this to come about true weight and importance must be given to the Nordic Council.

NOTES

1. See Frantz Wendt, The Nordic Council and Co-operation in Scandinavia (Copenhagen: Munksgaard, 1959), p. 28.

2. See Frantz Wendt, "Nogle Resultator af Nordisk Samarkejde Gennem 15 ar: 1945-1960," mimeographed (Copenhagen: Nordic Council, 1960).

CHAPTER

3

ORIGIN AND DEVELOPMENT OF THE NORDIC COUNCIL

GEOGRAPHIC AND INSTITUTIONAL FRAMEWORK

The Nordic Council is a purely consultative organization consisting of parliamentarians and members of the governments of the Nordic states, which are Denmark, Norway, Sweden, Finland, and Iceland. The Aland and Faeroe Islands are represented in the Finnish and the Danish delegations respectively. The council has no authority to make decisions that are binding on its individual members. Its statutes, which are written in all five different languages, were accepted by national decision rather than by an international convention. In other words, each member state may leave the Nordic Council at will, but none have yet done so.

Article I of the statutes defines the Nordic Council as "an organ for consultation between the Danish Rigsdag, the Icelandic Althing, the Norwegian Storting, the Swedish Riksdag, and the Finnish Riksdag together with the governments of these countries with reference to questions concerning co-operation between the countries, or between some of them." This means that for a matter to be raised in the Nordic Council, it is sufficient for it to be of interest to two of the countries involved. There is no limitation on the kinds of questions that may be discussed and dealt with. The statutes were deliberately formulated in indefinite terms. On the other hand, there is no obligation for parliamentarians or governments to submit any specific matters to the council.

Although the competence of the Nordic Council is unlimited in principle, its concern is primarily with matters of common interest to two or more countries, on which it is thought that joint action may be taken. According to Article 10 of the statutes, the main duty of the council is to discuss questions of common interest to the countries and to make recommendations to the governments concerning these matters, suggesting actions to be taken. If a question is of concern to only some of the states, only the delegates of those states participate in the decision on the matter. Members of the governments of the states concerned may take part in the discussion, but they have no vote.

The Nordic Council makes its own decisions about its organization and work as well as about the organization and work of its secretariats. Until 1972 there was no central secretariat, but there were five national ones. In the opinion of some of its founding fathers, the Nordic Council seems to have been conceived primarily as an inter-Nordic forum for debate and an instigator of joint action by means of exchanges of ideas, rather than as a producer of recommendations to the governments, which is what it may be turning itself into.

Questions are raised and matters introduced in the Nordic Council by the governments and, more often, by the parliamentarian members. Outsiders may also submit proposals, but only through the council members. Nonmembers and interest groups who wish to introduce a matter in the council are encouraged to do so. However, they must act through some members of the national delegations to the council or through a government.

Although the explanatory statement to the statutes holds that the Nordic Council should function in terms of those matters and problems that are considered suitable for immediate and specific action, there has as yet been no attempt to adhere very strictly to this ideal. If anything, the criticism in the press and media in general has been that the council has taken upon itself too vast a number of questions.* The counterargument is that the Nordic Council should diversify its attention to a host of matters that for one reason or another are considered important. Experience has also shown that the members have not hesitated to introduce questions and problems in a variety of fields concerning which the governments have not considered that time was ripe for action. It would be interesting to try to ascertain to what extent the governments have taken action that in the absence of the council would have been delayed, postponed, or not taken at all; part of this influence may be seen, but only in an indirect fashion.

Detailed discussions about foreign policy or about defense have so far not taken place in the Nordic Council. Because of differences

---

*My own findings partly substantiate this view. See the results of interviews with ministers, parliamentarians, and top civil servants in the following sections.

among the Nordic states, such discussions are difficult to foresee in the near future. The examples that spring to mind are the Swedish policy of neutrality and the relations of Finland with the USSR. During the first few years of the existence of the Nordic Council, Finland was under pressure by Moscow not to join the council, and in fact she did not do so until October 1955. Finland still seems very sensitive about dealing with or discussing foreign policy or defense issues in the Council, more so than the other Nordic states. Nevertheless, it has been the Finnish communist members of the Nordic Council who have repeatedly put forward the proposal of a nuclear-free zone in the Nordic area, an issue of some considerable foreign policy importance to the member states.

Because of their geographic proximity, their similarity in size, and certain analogous cultural and social features, the Nordic states are often taken as a whole or mentioned simultaneously in international relations. For example, it is a fairly common belief that Denmark, Norway, Sweden, and to some extent Iceland and Finland, comprise some sort of a natural entity. It follows from this idea that cooperation and coordination among these states must work naturally, almost automatically, since they have so much in common. It may seem as if these countries have some inborn common denominator. Their geographical proximity, coupled with their social, cultural, and linguistic similarities, would seem to back up this view.

How does this notion of natural affinity fit political reality? Undeniably, several important similarities do exist among the Nordic states; but there are also some substantial differences. Geographically, for example, there are almost as many differences among the Nordic countries as there are similarities. It is true that they are all situated in northern Europe and that Sweden and Norway are approximately similar in shape and size. However, Sweden has twice as many inhabitants, or about 9 million, as Norway, with about 4 million. Denmark, Norway, and Finland are similar in population size, whereas Iceland is very much smaller. The Icelandic population is 205,000, while the population of Sweden is about 40 times as large.

The geographical positions of the Nordic countries also show some differences. Denmark is linked to the European continent, for instance, while Iceland is in an isolated position and surrounded by water.

It is true that most educated persons in Norway, Sweden, and Denmark can understand the languages of all three countries, although they do not speak them all. Only 10 percent of the Finns use Swedish, however, and they have great difficulty understanding Norwegian or Danish. The remaining 90 percent of the Finns speak Finnish, which is related to the language of the Hungarians and incomprehensible to the rest of the Scandinavians.

The Icelandic language is similar to Old Norse, which was used by the Vikings a thousand years ago. This means that in general the language is not understood outside Iceland. Old Norse is taught as a foreign language in a special branch of the secondary schools in Norway and enables the students who have taken the course to understand Icelandic.

Norway has two official languages, Riksmal and New Norwegian. The former is derived from Danish, whereas the latter is based upon rural dialects. This makes it easier for the Norwegians to understand either Danish or Swedish, according to which official language they use.

As far as the Nordic Council is concerned, the language problem has so far been dealt with by using Norwegian, Swedish, and Danish as the three official working languages of the organization. It is up to the Finns to make themselves understood by using Swedish and to Icelandics by using Danish.

My aim in stating these differences among the Nordic states is simply to try to strike a balance between what is common between them and what have been the chief barriers to closer unity. Let us take Norway for a historical example. As we have seen, from 1397 to 1520 Norway was part of the Kalmar Union, in which she was a minor partner. Following the collapse of the union, she became part of the western state of Scandinavia, in which Denmark played a dominant role for the next 300 years. This period was followed by one of Swedish dominance, from 1814 to 1905.

No doubt all this has been very important for Norway in her relations with the other Scandinavian states. It has, for example, been a source of similarities in administrative methods. These similarities, together with religious, social, and cultural proximity have probably aided the tendency toward unity. They are what may be referred to as favorable background conditions in the preunification stage.

On the other hand, it is also quite possible that experiences from a common past may have a detrimental effect on unity and integration. Union often meant dominance of the stronger over the weaker partners, with a Danish aristocracy residing in Norway and a Swedish one in Finland. Consequently it should come as no surprise that some segments of the Norwegian, Finnish, and Icelandic populations regarded their affiliations with the Danes and Swedes as inhibiting their own national development. Not only had local economic or political interests been neglected, this argument went, but language had suffered as well. The Finns resented the dominance of the Swedish language in Finland, and similar sentiments were voiced in Norway about the influence of Danish.

Since then there has been a section of the Norwegian population that has not and does not consider the experience with the other Nordic nations in such unions or international communities as beneficial to Norway. The seeds of the later Norwegian resistance to the idea of union in general, if perceived as a political merger, and to such techniques as supranational community building, may be found by an examination of these experiences.

This point was made publicly in Copenhagen at the formation of the Nordic Council in 1953, when C. J. Hambro, the then-prominent Norwegian parliamentarian, strongly warned against anything that smacked of union, no doubt with the Kalmar Union in mind.

This point may seem small, but it is an important one. First, it has a sobering effect on the belief that Scandinavian unification is to be expected almost automatically and achieved with relative ease.

More theoretically, it could perhaps be shown that geographic, religious, and cultural proximity, taken in conjunction with joint experiences in the preintegration stage, may at times be dysfunctional to integration. This is the reverse of views put forward by several writers and theorists in the field, including Karl Deutsch.

I will try to substantiate this point at a later stage; in the meantime, it may be stated that the Nordic countries have many important factors in common and that certain types of similarities exist that have traditionally been thought to be highly useful for the furtherance of unification. However, to deduce from this that the states themselves constitute some form of almost natural entity seems fallacious. What sort of entity is it, for instance, when one state is neutral (Sweden); one is under constant Soviet influence (Finland); and the remaining three are members of NATO, although one of them (Iceland) is grudgingly so.

THE CREATION OF THE NORDIC COUNCIL

Although the proposed defense union did not come about, it had an important impact on intra-Scandinavian relations. Two large meetings had been called, one in Copenhagen and one in Oslo, both in January 1949, in which members of the Scandinavian parliaments took part. There was a growing awareness of the importance of setting up some intergovernmental coordinative council. For example, the Norden Association started to pay attention to such a scheme, and the Danish Norden Association proposed in November 1949 that a Nordic common assembly be made the most important immediate objective of further Nordic cooperation.

This development is not too difficult to understand. Since 1945 the former intra-Nordic institutions and agencies had resumed their activities. Norway, Sweden, and Denmark had joined the Organization for Economic Cooperation and Development (OECD) when this organization was set up in 1948, and all the Scandinavian states except Finland became members of the Council of Europe, which was established the following year.

It was clear from the beginning, however, that the Scandinavians were not interested in setting up a political union as envisaged by the early federalist members of the Council of Europe. Instead, the Scandinavian countries wanted cooperation of a more traditional intergovernmental type, as did the United Kingdom. No doubt there is a strain of nationalism in the demand for political independence and integrity that has been a guideline of the Scandinavian position on political unity since the early postwar period.

Their rejection of a political union as envisaged by the federalists did not prevent the Nordic countries from moving closer to one another in several important areas. The need to facilitate the exchange of information and the desire to provide a wider forum for debate than that of intergovernmental cooperation were among the reasons why the Nordic Council was initiated. However, there were other reasons as well, some of them going back to the prewar period. In 1938, for example, Peter Munch, then Danish foreign minister, had put forward a proposal for permanent parliamentary cooperation in Scandinavia. Some discussion had been carried out during the war years, and several persons, among them the Swedish statesman Per Albin Hansson, were in favor of institutionalized parliamentarian cooperation. This interest lingered on and was expressed by important opposition members of the Danish parliament such as Bertel Dahlgaard and Ole Björn Kraft. In October 1950 the Norwegian Prime Minister, Einar Gerhardsen, went on record as stating that it would be useful if members of different political parties could be able to take part in Nordic meetings more often.

This idea gathered momentum, partly as a reaction to the Norwegian and Danish entry into NATO and partly as a response to the failure of the Nordic defense union talks. A private group of Scandinavian members of parliament, called the Nordic Interparliamentarian Union, met as usual in Stockholm in August 1951. At this meeting, to the general surprise of many members there, Hans Hedtoft, the leader of the Danish Delegation, put forward a proposal to set up a permanent Nordic council of parliamentarians. The legislators should meet, he suggested, on a regular basis for consultation among themselves and with the Nordic governments concerning questions relating to Scandinavian cooperation. Several persons from different national and party backgrounds backed this proposal, which was unanimously endorsed. The resolution called on the Interparliamentary Union to investigate ways in which this proposal could be realized.

A committee of five, with three Social Democrats and two Conservatives, was set up and charged with the task of studying the possibilities and plans for the proposed organization. Apart from Hans Hedtoft himself, the committee consisted of Oscar Torp (Norway, Social Democrat), Karl-August Fagerholm (Finland, Social Democrat), Sigurdur Bjarnason (Iceland, Conservative), and Nils Herlitz (Sweden, Conservative). Because of the difficulties traditionally facing Finland with regard to foreign policy, Fagerholm's position became one of passive approval and wait-and-see. The biggest part of the work at the early stages seems to have fallen on Herlitz of Sweden and Hedtoft of Denmark.

The committee met once, on October 24, 1951, in Copenhagen. The participants were Herlitz, Hedtoft, Fagerholm, and Bjarnason. Bjarnason stated that no definite decision regarding the matter had been taken by Iceland. Torp, who had been urged by Hedtoft to attend, was unable to take part. He had sent a message to the effect that his own position was positive, but for a number of reasons, to which I will return, the situation was somewhat uncertain in Norway.

Herlitz was under the impression that a Danish proposal for the council's statutes would be forthcoming. However, this was not the case, and his own proposal, which had been written in one morning, became the basis for the discussions.[1] Although forced by the foreign policy guidelines of his own country to play a passive role, Fagerholm of Finland made an important contribution. He suggested that according to the council's statutes the governments be asked to report matters back to the council, and that special mention be made of this. As we shall see, this particular feature of the operation of the council has proven to be important.

Having completed its task, the committee submitted its proposal to the Nordic Interparliamentary Union on November 8. So far there had been no important opposition. Finland was definitely unable to be a partner in the proposed Nordic Council, as expected, but the other Scandinavian states were all in favor of setting up this organization. Although the matter had aroused some debate in Norwegian newspapers, the delegates from Norway who took part in the Nordic Interparliamentary Union meeting in Stockholm on December 3, 1951, were positively inclined toward the proposed council. However, there was some opposition within the Norwegian Conservative Party, and a second meeting of the Nordic Interparliamentary Union was called for on February 9, 1952. One of the most important questions discussed was the idea of giving the government members, or some of them, the right to vote in the proposed council.

The Nordic foreign ministers met in Copenhagen on March 15 and 16, but the question was still not answered. It was no secret, however, that the Norwegians were opposed to this arrangement.

Subsequently an agreement was reached giving some government members the right of membership but not the right to vote. Apart from this, general agreement was reached, and the draft proposals were submitted to the Nordic governments shortly afterward. They were passed by the legislative assemblies of Denmark, Sweden, and Norway in June 1952.

INITIAL POLITICAL PROBLEMS AND THEIR SOLUTION

In retrospect it seems that the greatest amount of enthusiasm about the Nordic Council was generated from Denmark and Sweden. The Danes were quite optimistic about the council. According to Hans Hedtoft, although the militaristic pan-Scandinavianism of the nineteenth century was dead, its social and spiritual aspects had survived.[2] Mr. Hedtoft urged, against predictable Norwegian opposition, that there be closer economic cooperation among the Nordic states. Largely because of the role played by Norway, it was decided that the emphasis should be put on cooperation rather than on integration. There was general agreement concerning the need for an organization such as the Nordic Council, although the hopes and expectations of the parliamentarians seem to have differed somewhat. Notes of caution were struck by both Halvard Lange, the Norwegian foreign minister, a statesman of considerable international reputation, and by his fellow countryman, Finn Moe. Lange issued a warning against too close economic cooperation, and Moe expressed his opposition to the idea of a general customs union, declaring that it would be detrimental to trade relations with Finland and other countries.[3]

The only organized political opposition to the Nordic Council came, as expected, from the Scandinavian communists. Moscow had already declared that the Nordic Council was "a creature of NATO aggression," and as such an instrument serving the function of drawing Sweden further into the U.S. sphere of dominance. For obvious reasons it was impossible for Finland to become a member of the council.

Gradually the Soviet attitude softened somewhat, with the result that Finland was able to join the Nordic Council by 1956. The conditions under which Finland joined gave certain lines of direction. If the Nordic Council were ever to consider questions of military or strategic content, Finland could not participate in these discussions. Interestingly enough, several times it has been the Finnish, albeit communist, delegates to the Nordic Council who have suggested matters of clearly strategic importance, such as the setting up of a nuclear-free zone in Scandinavia. The communists have also been requesting stronger ties with Eastern Europe.

Apart from its geographic proximity to Finland, there are several distinct reasons why the USSR has a hold on its western neighbor's freedom with regard to international affairs in general and participation in international organizations in particular. The Paris Peace Treaty of 1947 set out the conditions for Finnish reparations to the Soviet Union and also limited the size and nature of the armed forces of Finland. Just as important, if not more so, to Soviet-Finnish relations is the so-called Treaty of Friendship, Cooperation, and Mutual Assistance of 1948. The essence of this treaty is that Finland undertakes to defend her soil against any attack by Germany or by a German ally and to consult with the Soviet Union if such an attack should threaten.

Both treaties state that neither the USSR nor Finland must conclude any alliance or join any coalition directed against the other party. This means that the Kremlin has a pretty effective veto over entry by Finland into any international organization, should this in any way seem to be against Soviet interests as interpreted by the Soviet Union. Finland, with her interest in further developing her ties with the rest of Scandinavia, let alone in maintaining these ties, is understandably in a delicate position, of which the other Nordic countries are aware. The Paasikivi Line sets out the need for Finland to avoid any appearance of evil as far as Soviet suspicions are concerned.

Although the doctrine is adhered to by all the Finnish political parties, it is of primary concern to Finland to maintain and strengthen her ties with the rest of Scandinavia. These may or may not bolster Finnish security, but they do provide contact with the Western European markets. Despite the partial economic dependence of Finland on the Eastern bloc and the pressures applied by domestic communists and supporters, Finland is at least economically turned to the West.

The other Nordic states are aware of the problems facing the Finns. It is quite clear that Finland has had little leeway with regard to the Nordic Council or any other international organization in which she has been interested. When Norway, Sweden, and Denmark joined the Organization for European Economic Cooperation (OEEC), which was the predecessor of OECD, in 1949 and the European Free Trade Association (EFTA) in 1960, for example, Finland was also inhibited from participating in either scheme. She was allowed to join EFTA in 1960-61 on an associate basis and has remained so since. The problems of Finland are perhaps intensified by her sizeable communist party, which has played a decisive coalition role in her government.

Since communism has not been strongly represented in any of the other Scandinavian states, no strong party opposition to the Nordic Council was found in them except in Norway. The situation of Norway differed somewhat from that of Denmark, Sweden, and Iceland. The nonsocialist parties of Norway were considerably less enthusiastic about this new organization. There was no open hostility, but the general climate was one of lukewarm approval. Some of the nonsocialist politicians saw little or no use for yet another international organization of the type the Nordic Council was meant to be. As they saw it, there were already enough organizations, albeit under private auspices, that had the purpose of increasing Nordic unity or looking after joint interests.

Aftenposten (Conservative), the largest daily newspaper in Norway, supported the Nordic Council, but Dagbladet (Left-Liberal), another large Oslo paper, was less in favor, emphasizing the difficulties the Nordic Council would create for Norway with regard to the Atlantic pact. This concern has proven to be totally unfounded, of course. Arbeiderbladet, the government paper, naturally was in favor of the Nordic Council.

The parliamentarians were somewhat split in their opinion of the importance and value of this new organization. The most outspoken individual critic of the whole idea of the council and what went with it was C. J. Hambro of the Conservative Party. He was sceptical of the expectations of parliamentarians in Norway and elsewhere in Scandinavia, and of the ways in which this new organization had been initiated. With considerable eloquence this outstanding figure in Norwegian politics acted as the chief critic of what he considered the faulty expectations of his fellow countrymen. A mass meeting was held at the Farmers' House (Farmer's Association Building) in Oslo on February 2, at which Hambro voiced his firm criticism.

There was also scepticism in other quarters. For example, Finn Moe, the foreign expert of the Norwegian Labor party, went on record as stating that the Nordic Council should not be a parliament, but merely a negotiating organ. No decisions that might be unacceptable to the governments should be taken; nor should any such proposals be made, as had been the case with the United Nations and the Council of Europe. In this way there seems to have been a split within the government party, since Gerhardsen, the former Prime Minister, had stated the very day before that the Nordic Council should not avoid taking up matters that might be controversial.

Despite the fact that opinion was divided both among the parties and within them, a much smaller group than had been expected voted against the Nordic Council in the Norwegian parliament. The Labor Party, with the majority government, voted in favor; the Liberals split; and the Christian Peoples' Party and the Agrarians both opposed the council. The compromise whereby it was decided not to give the right of vote to the government members of the council reduced the opposition drastically.

Nevertheless, whereas the Danish and Swedish legislatures had both unanimously accepted the draft proposals for the Nordic

Council, the Norwegian Storting accepted them by a vote of 74 to 39. It is quite clear, in other words, that Norway was by far the most hesitant of the three initiating countries.

NOTES

1. See Nils Herlitz, "Nordiska radets tillkomst: Minnen fran 1951-1953," supplement to Nordisk Kontakt (1962).
2. Nordic Council, Minutes of meetings, 1st Session.
3. New York Herald Tribune, March 10, 1953.

CHAPTER

4

OPERATIONAL FEATURES OF THE NORDIC COUNCIL

AREAS OF COMPETENCE

Thus far the Nordic Council has been working on problems falling within the following main categories: economic matters, legal questions, communications, social issues, and cultural affairs. Although it is a Nordic organization, the council's existence does not prevent the member countries from promoting wider unity. Hans Hedtoft, the late Danish prime minister and one of the founding fathers of the Nordic Council, stated that by working for close cooperation among the Northern European countries the council would allow its member countries to serve the larger unity better. He saw the development of regional units such as the northern group of countries as a natural stage toward larger international endeavors.

Questions relating to any of the above-mentioned fields concerning which it is believed that joint action may be undertaken can be introduced to the Nordic Council in several ways. Matters may be submitted by the governments in the form of government motions. They may also be introduced as individual motions, by individual parliamentarian members who have been elected to the council, or as joint motions by several members acting together.

RESPONSIBILITIES AND POWERS

As we have seen, the main duty of the Nordic Council is to discuss questions in the above-mentioned fields of activity, to the extent that such questions are of importance to relations between two or more Nordic countries, and to try to solve problems on a Nordic level. However, this interparliamentary debate on economic, legal, communicational, social, and cultural matters is followed by recommendations that, if accepted, are passed on to the governments. According to Article 11 of the statutes, the governments must report back to the Nordic Council at each session, indicating what action has been taken regarding the recommendations passed in the previous session. We may refer to this arrangement as the call-back, or control, clause of the statutes. It enables the Nordic Council to check on the progress that has been made, if any, on each recommendation it has passed to see how much remains to be done in any specific case. It is up to the council to decide, if it so wishes, whether a recommendation is considered as having been implemented. The council may also decide that a full or final report regarding a particular recommendation is not required until a later session. It may also decide that a particular matter is no longer relevant or that sufficient action on it is already being taken elsewhere.

The importance of this rule is twofold. First, attention is kept on individual recommendations all along, and the progress or lack of progress is constantly checked in each case. The recommendation may be called back several times if the Nordic Council so desires, until the council has decided that the matter is concluded, that nothing more can be done, or that circumstances have rendered the particular recommendation obsolete.

Second, this rule constitutes an indirect pressure on the governments to do something about the recommendations they have received. Although the council has no legislative powers, it can nevertheless act as a sort of pressure group. The governments are exposed to both parliamentary and interparliamentary criticism, as well as to news publicity on an inter-Nordic level.

Apart from this, the Nordic Council also serves as a tribunal for the discussion of general Nordic or at times international problems of policy coordination, even when no direct question is posed. At times such discussion arises from some of the many reports that are submitted to the council at each sessional meeting by the different Nordic agencies and organizations. At other times the problems may be raised during the general debate of the council. The general debate, which takes place during the first two days of each plenary session, tends to focus attention on the past sessions as well as on some of the larger underlying problems of interest and importance to the member countries.

How can a consultative intergovernmental organization contribute in any important way toward the implementation of decisions it has arrived at? As we have seen, the Nordic Council has no formal powers of decision making in respect to the governments. There seem to be several reasons. The different political parties of the Scandinavian states have chosen to select their most influential members as delegates to the council. Although without the right of vote, all the important ministers, headed by the prime ministers, attend the sessions. Recommendations that have been adopted by a large majority of the council, as very many of them have been, would therefore carry substantial weight. Attention is given to the Nordic Council by the news media, in Scandinavia as well as abroad.

The council is perceived by some as a promoter and in a way as a guardian of the Nordic Idea, which in itself is powerful politically. No political group in Scandinavia would come out against the Nordic Idea, although it no doubt has different meanings in different circles.

Underlying the influence of the council, however, is the well-developed spirit of cooperation and good will that prevails in the organization. How far these motives could carry Nordic integration if national policies or the interests of parliamentarians or administrators were at stake remains to be seen. It could well be that the positive spirit with which the Nordic Council generally operates is partly caused by the fact that the organization is not equipped with what would seem to be the needed supranational authority, although too much should probably not be made of this point. As we shall see, this lack of authority quite clearly also works against the effectiveness of the organization. On the other hand, it may be possible that the present careful, step-by-step functional method of cooperation and coordination has added to its positive spirit.

STRUCTURE AND METHODS

The Nordic Council is composed of 78 members elected by the parliaments of the member countries and of governmental representatives who are appointed for each session. The Danish parliament elects 16 members to the council; the Finnish parliament, 17 members; the Icelandic parliament, 6 members; and the Norwegian and Swedish parliaments, 18 members each. The Danish delegation also includes 2 members elected by the legislature of the Faeroe Islands, and the Finnish delegation includes 1 member elected by the legislature of the Aland Islands. The governmental representatives (ministers) and the representatives of the provincial governments of the Faeroe Islands and the Aland Islands take part in the work of the Nordic Council but do not have any voting rights.

The council meets annually for a session in one of the Nordic capitals. The standing committees prepare the business of the session and meet 4 to 6 times a year. Each national delegation has a secretariat of its own attached to the national parliament. Since 1971 the presidium of the council has had a secretariat in Stockholm. The

Nordic Council of Ministers has a secretariat for Nordic cultural cooperation in Copenhagen and a secretariat for other fields of cooperation in Oslo.

The parliamentarian delegates are nominated by their own parties, and their term of service is one year. In practice, however, they are often renominated with little difficulty if they wish, as they apparently often do. These members constitute their country's delegations, each of which appoints a working committee. The chairman and vice-chairman of the committee are elected, and the chairmen of the five delegations constitute the presidium of the Nordic Council for the session. The chairman of the delegation of the host country becomes the president until the next plenary session.

The presidium meets several times during the year, at some of these times with the prime ministers of the five countries, to plan the next plenary session. It also obtains the expert information that may be required to coordinate and carry out the work of the council in accordance with the decisions that have been made at previous sessions. Furthermore, the presidium follows up the work done by the respective governments to implement the recommendations that have been passed by the council. Joint meetings of the presidium and government representatives may take place several times a year.

Plenary meetings consist of all the members of the council. Until 1973 plenary sessions were held once a year, but it was decided to split the 21st session (1973) in two, and the fall session was held in Stockholm October 25-27. The same procedure was followed in 1974. Extraordinary sessions may be held when the plenary council or the presidium so desires, or when at least two governments or at least 25 elected members request them. As yet there have been no extraordinary meetings. The regular meetings are held in the different Nordic capitals. Extraordinary meetings may be held anywhere that is decided upon. The sessions last from 7 to 10 days each starting at a week-end, and the tendency has been to shorten them.

Although the main purpose of the council is to further Nordic unity, this does not mean that its agenda has been limited to Scandinavian matters. The external policies of member states, such as foreign aid and development, have often been discussed; in fact, some of these policies have been initiated in the Nordic Council. Likewise, planned joint action and conduct in international organizations, such as in the United Nations and under the General Agreement on Tariffs and Trade (GATT), are often discussed in the Nordic Council.

Proposals to the Nordic Council, whether from the governments, from the Nordic Council of Ministers, or from elected members, must be sent in written form to the secretariat as soon as possible, for circulation. Reports must be sent at least a month before the opening of the session. Proposals to be dealt with during the session must be circulated to the governments, the Council of Ministers, and the members and alternates no less than two weeks before the opening of the plenary meeting.

Following formal approval, a motion goes through the following stages: first reading, committee, and second reading. As a rule, the first reading is brief. So far most motions have been referred by the presidium to the committee stage without comment. Those of the members who are unable to participate in the committee stage for one reason or another and who wish to make their views known have the opportunity to do so at the first reading.

In the committee stage the ministers may be invited to participate. The proposals are discussed in considerable detail. At this stage close cooperation between parliamentarians and ministers is generally developed and makes itself strongly felt. Although the ministers do not have the right to vote, they normally attend the committee stage, participating in those meetings at which matters pertaining to their own departments are discussed. By cooperating directly with the ministers in this manner, the parliamentarians are able to obtain a realistic impression of the attitudes of the governments toward the questions on the agenda. This is conducive to both understanding and cooperation with regard to particular matters. On the other hand, it may well be that the method is conducive to "timidity," a charge that has been leveled at the Nordic Council from time to time. We shall later examine this claim in greater detail, and in doing so try to ascertain to what extent such timidity, if it is the case, has to do with structure and methods and to what extent the reasons for it may be found elsewhere.

After investigation and discussion, the committees report back to the council for the second reading. The proposals that have been arrived at may be amended either at the committee stage or during the plenary debate. The committees submit written statements to the council indicating whether the recommendations have been concluded, rejected, or postponed until the next plenary session. Supplementary proposals may be made at either of these stages.

As a rule, the plenary sessions are open to the general public, unless the council decides otherwise (Article 6). The documents of each session are published annually in complete volumes and are offered for sale through certain bookstores. The committee meetings are held in camera, although invited persons holding the status of observers are permitted to attend. As Stanley Anderson points out, the clear policy against open committee meetings of the Nordic Council developed in response to the attempts of the young people's auxiliaries of political parties to secure admission to committee hearings.[1]

A large number of matters are debated, and several members express themselves during the debate. There have been fewer contributions by the ministerial members than by the parliamentarians. Following the discussion, votes are taken. A recommendation is accepted when more than 50 percent of the members who are present vote in favor of it, provided this 50 percent constitutes more than 30 votes. Voting is by yes, no, or abstention. Provision is made for cloture if the president or five elected members so propose. A two-thirds vote by the council closes debate, and there is no debate on a motion of cloture.

The recommendations passed by the council are addressed to the governments or the Nordic Council of Ministers. A joint meeting between the presidium and the council of ministers is held following the plenary session, often by means of delegation of authority on high civil servants. Each government assumes the responsibility of supervising a certain number of recommendations, and the outcome of each recommendation is reported back to the council at the following session. This system of coordinating and directing the recommendations is meant to facilitate the work and prevent duplication of efforts.

During the sessions as well as between them, the Nordic Council is divided into the following kinds of committees: economic, legal, communicational, social, and cultural. Individual membership on the committees, as well as on the council, varies from one session to the next. Each delegate is a member of one committee, which elects its own chairman and vice-chairman according to national and party considerations. The presidium may appoint special committees. As a rule each country is given the chairmanship of one committee and the vice-chairmanship of another. When required, one or several countries appoint experts to the committees for hearings. A government official is also made available to each committee as a secretary. The committees used to serve only during the annual sessions, but they now meet regularly between the sessions. New committee members are elected by each session. Frequent meetings are held, both by the standing committees and by other bodies and groups that are involved in the work of the council.

Until 1972 the Nordic Council had no joint secretariat, but rather five small national secretariats. Since then the council is supported in its work by a secretariat consisting of one secretary who is appointed by the presidium and five secretaries appointed by the five national delegations. The secretaries and other personnel of the committees are appointed by the presidium. Each delegation hires such personnel as it deems necessary. The national delegations are staffed as follows: Finland has a secretary-general, a secretary, an information secretary, and office personnel; Iceland has a secretary-general; Denmark has a secretary-general, a bureau chief, and office personnel; and Norway has a secretary-general, a consultant, and office personnel.

There is considerable collaboration among the various staffs throughout the year, and the Norwegian, Swedish, Danish, and Finnish secretaries-general are in almost constant contact with each other. By 1972 the presidium had its secretariat, located in Stockholm. In the following year the Secretariat of the Nordic Council of Ministers had been established in Oslo. This increase in formal institutionalization without necessarily an increase or change in actual power will be discussed in some detail later on.

Most of the planning and implementation of the session also falls on the secretariat of the host country. This applies to administrative matters and information, but it does not cover research, for which the secretariats are not responsible.

The secretaries-general of the national delegations are prominent persons with considerable interest in and dedication to Nordic affairs. This is the case for all the secretaries-general, and in particular for the Danish delegation. Frantz Wendt of the Danish secretariat, for example, was the only full-time national secretary-general in Scandinavia during the formative years of the Nordic Council. Wendt was also instrumental in Nordic cooperation prior to the Nordic Council. The former Swedish secretary-general, Gustaf Petren, was an equally prominent person. For many years he was one of the most active and dynamic men involved in Nordic work. He was responsible not only to the Swedish delegation to the Nordic Council, but also to the Swedish parliament as a whole, as the head of the Nordic Council chancellery.

Apart from administrative work between and during the plenary sessions, the secretariats are involved in the information and public relations sectors. They produce pamphlets, distribute press releases, call meetings, and brief various educational personnel on the activities of the council.

Until recently there was an attempt at labor saving, insofar as the Danish secretariat looked after most of the information service of the council, whereas the Swedish secretariat took prime responsibility for legal questions. All along, the Finnish secretariat has to some extent been tied up with the problem of bridging the language gulf, since many of the Finnish delegates to the Nordic Council do not speak Swedish, Danish, or Norwegian, which are the three working languages of the council.

Although the secretariats have had equal status, some observers have argued that their importance seems to have varied from country to country. I found no clear evidence of this. Executive work on current matters of interest is entrusted to the presidium of the council.

NOTE

1. Stanley Anderson, The Nordic Council: A Study of Scandinavian Regionalism (Stockholm: Svenska Bokforlaget Norstedts, 1967), p. 80.

CHAPTER

5

GOVERNMENTS, PARTIES, AND THE NORDIC COUNCIL

MINISTERS AND PARLIAMENTARIANS

As we have seen, both government members and parliamentarians take part in the work of the Nordic Council. The size of the parliamentary group is fixed, but the governmental group varies in size from session to session. The ministers, depending upon the urgency or importance of the matter at hand, come and go throughout the session. They remain in close contact with the Nordic Council between annual sessions, especially with its presidium, as well as participating through the Nordic Council of Ministers.

The governments may send as many ministers to the Nordic Council sessions as they deem necessary. The range varied from 1 (Iceland) to 10 (Denmark, Finland, Sweden, and Norway) within the first five years. Generally about 45 to 50 ministers take part in the meetings.

Although the ministers do not vote, they express themselves freely. The prime ministers of Norway; Sweden; Denmark; and, since 1956, Finland have attended nearly all the meetings, and the ministers of justice and foreign affairs are also regular participants in the sessions. The holders of other portfolios, and also ministers without them, attend more sporadically. Iceland had no ministerial members present in the session meetings of 1955, 1957, 1958, and 1959 but had seven government members in the 1960 session (when she was host country) and has had ministerial representation ever since.

The ministers, as well as the parliamentarians, are seated alphabetically in the same chamber, which, it has been argued,[1] has been beneficial for the Nordic Council as a whole, insofar as it has probably made for more realistic recommendations than might otherwise have been the case.

Of greater importance, perhaps, is the possible interpenetration of civil services and bureaucracies that can take place, which will be examined more closely later in the book. Among the experts and the large group of government officials who attend the sessions, important collaboration has developed. This development, as we shall see, has not been without problems.

During the annual plenary sessions of the Nordic Council, the speeches given by the ministers are looked forward to with considerable interest, both by the parliamentarian members of the council and by the news media. Although it is true that the government members have not introduced a large number of matters to the Nordic Council, they have been the originators of some fairly large and important matters, such as the Nordic Economic (NORDEK) plan.

The parliamentarian members of the Nordic Council are practically all ranking members of their parliaments. In some cases they are committed "Nordists," but this is by no means a prerequisite for council membership or an exclusive characteristic of those who take part.

Since 1965, when the standing committees of the Nordic Council assumed interim functions, the appropriate cabinet members have attended the committee meetings during the sessions. Contact between the ministers and the parliamentarians is, naturally, kept within the different assemblies on a national basis.

PARTIES

According to Article 2 of the statutes of the Nordic Council, the council shall consist of 78 elected members as well as of ministerial representatives. The article states further, "Among the elected members of each country different political opinions must be represented."

The members elected to the council are chosen largely according to the method of proportional representation. A mathematical formula is applied that allocates the seats among the political parties of the member states. After the allocation has been made, it is up to each party to decide which members shall be chosen. To some extent it may be correct to say that the Nordic Council is a microcosm of the parent national bodies, except that in the multiparty systems of the Nordic states, tiny parties, of which there may be several, do not achieve representation in the council. Nevertheless, there is a feeling both among the members of the general public and among parliamentarians, government members, and civil servants that the different political parties are sufficiently represented in the Nordic Council.

The social democratic parties generally have roughly half of the elected members' seats or a little less, with the liberal, conservative, and centrist-agrarian parties represented by about the same number of seats each.

This method of representation has been significant in the development of Nordic cooperation, insofar as it allows full participation by the opposition parties in work that has hitherto been exclusively reserved for the governments.

Since the different political parties of the Nordic parliaments nominate their own delegates to the Nordic Council, subject of course to sufficient national strength, it is possible to argue that the Nordic Council is based on a more democratic principle than, say, the Council of Europe or until fairly recently the Parliament of the European Communities. In the latter, for example, no communists or fascists were allowed to participate, despite the fact that the communist parties of both France and Italy commanded fairly large followings and were at times considerably well represented in the national assemblies.

Preceding each annual session the parliamentarian members of the Nordic Council are elected for one year terms. Deputy delegates are usually elected at the same time and in a number equal to that of the delegates. Since the parties tend to send their most prominent members, both in the eyes of the parties and according to general opinion, it is hardly surprising that the council membership shows considerable continuity. On the whole the prominence of the members does not seem to fluctuate very much once they have established themselves. Nevertheless there has been some fluctuation, both by country (Finland in particular) and by party. In the case of Finland it could be argued that the council has been used somewhat more for general orientation than for the development of specialized competence.[2] On the other hand, this slight deviance in the case of Finland could be caused by its external relations. On the whole there has been little change in individual membership. With the presence of both prominent politicians and many of the cabinet ministers, the Nordic Council has an important potential for future political action that has so far hardly been exploited.

As expected, the strength of the representation of different political views differs from one plenary session to the next, according to the national strength of the parties represented. Discussing the political parties of the Nordic parliaments is difficult because it is hard to label them for comparative purposes. Some of the countries have parties that are more or less uniquely national in character and therefore difficult to fit into a comparative scheme, since they have no direct opposite numbers in other Nordic countries. Some of these are the Swedish Party of Finland, the Christian People's Party of Norway, and the Justice Party of Denmark. The last has suffered the fate of many other small parties in the multiparty system and is no longer represented nationally. Finland and Denmark each have a score of smaller parties. The Danish parliament also includes individual politicians representing Greenland and the Faeroe Islands. The Faeroe Islands are, as we have seen, represented in their own right in the Nordic Council.

The proliferation of parties that consider themselves leftist, again particularly in Denmark, where that term takes in a large spectrum of political opinion, blurs the picture. The left in Denmark consists of no less than seven parties, one of which has no representation in the Danish parliament. These parties are, in order of size if not importance, the Social Democrats, the Left (Venstre), the Radical Left (Radikale Venstre), the Socialist People's Party (Socialistisk Folkeparti), the Left Socialists (Venstresocialistene), the Socialist Working Group (Lösgängere), and finally the communists (DKP). Two of the parties on the left, the Left and the Radical Left, may to some extent be considered middle of the road parties. At times they are are mistakenly referred to as bourgeois parties, an inaccurate label. The party members would consider themselves as leftists or liberals in the case of the radical left or as centrists or liberals in the case of the left. These complications make it difficult to compare the strengths of organized political interests in the council.

Some observers have pointed out that it may be justifiable to talk about a special Nordic party system, presumably because the states have similar forms of government and somewhat parallel party systems, and most importantly because the democratic parties are united on basic philosophical points. The Social Democrats have abandoned doctrinaire socialism, and among the parties there is general unity of opinion concerning welfare issues and full employment policies.

What is more important is the extent, if any, to which the political parties have taken issues to the Nordic Council with the purpose of accomplishing what they have failed to do for some reason or other nationally. It is also important to find out to what extent crossnational parties have come into being.

Have the creation and existence of the Nordic Council brought about any changes in the relationships among the political parties of Scandinavia? Have they aligned themselves on issues connected with the council or its work? Is there any evidence that crossnational party alignments are being made? If so, will they increase?

To start with, the non-Socialist parties of Norway were initially somewhat negatively disposed to the idea of the Nordic Council. That view was held most strongly by conservative and agrarian politicians at the time, but parts of the liberal parties shared it. For example, Dagbladet, the mouthpiece of the city liberals of Oslo, was initially sceptical about the Nordic Council. That part of the Norwegian Liberal Party has turned around almost completely and is now actively propagating Nordic unity, especially in the field of economics. Opposition to the council from the other Norwegian nonsocialist parties has softened, but they are still suspicious of inroads by the council into areas of Norwegian sovereignty. Examples of bloc voting on this matter exists in the records of the council.

National bloc voting rarely occurs. An example of this is the occasion in 1969 when the whole Danish delegation, with the exception of the delegate Axel Larson of the Socialist People's Party, voted against the proposed recommendation regarding the prohibition of professional boxing (No. 6.1969).

Voting in party blocs, that is, across national borders, has occurred in several cases. In 1967 the council adopted a recommendation regarding unified marriage law (No. 2.1967) against the votes of several conservative members, including all the representatives of the Norwegian Christian People's Party, on the one hand and the most radical members on the other. Each of these groups had favored a different proposal for a recommendation.

At the same session in Helsinki in 1967, the voting on a proposal for a recommendation regarding the legal right to correction of information given on radio and television largely followed party lines. In 1970 there was a lively debate about a proposal regarding abortion legislation (A. 109.j). The motion was defeated: only representatives of communist parties, plus two social democrats, voted for it. In 1954 the members of the Norwegian nonsocialist parties abstained from voting for a recommendation (No. 22.1954) regarding economic cooperation.

The communist parties, as may perhaps be expected, have tended to show more crossnational party cohesion than any other group of Scandinavian parties. The communists of Finland, the Finnish Democratic People's League, exemplify the only ideological voting in the Nordic Council. This party has repeatedly tried to introduce recommendations into the council that would seem to fall outside the council's realm of competence. The Finnish communists have been consistently opposed to economic integration, both in Europe as a whole and in the Nordic area, as well as persistently bent on making that same area into a nuclear-free zone. This last was attempted in 1961 (proposed as Item A 27.1961), when the Finnish communists wanted Scandinavia to be publicly declared a region free from atomic weapons, and in this they received support from their Icelandic and

Danish comrades, a case of crossnational party cohesion. It was attempted again in 1963 by the same groups, in connection with the proposal by President Kekkonen of Finland to prohibit the introduction of atomic weapons; the communists were again unsuccessful, this time with faltering support.

At times proposals to the Nordic Council have been made by members of different political parties; in fact this happens quite often. This would seem to be neither an indication of crossnational party cohesion nor a prediction of the coming of crossnational parties, since on the whole the matters raised have tended to be noncontroversial in character. As long as this remains so, a measure of high positive correlation between coauthorship of proposals and similarity or dissimilarity of party background would not mean very much.

There are, however, two points worth noting in this connection. First, as we shall see, a phenomenon is developing that I shall call the cooperation ideology, which may bring about some changes. Second, the amount of controversy raised by an issue depends very much upon which states participate in the particular piece of negotiation or passing of a recommendation. It is therefore possible that matters that are not controversial to Scandinavians could prove rather controversial to, say, other European states with which the Scandinavians are entering into closer cooperation.

THE HELSINKI TREATY

Leading up to the Helsinki Treaty were Danish and Norwegian overtures toward the EEC during the summer and fall of 1961. In August of that year, Denmark formally decided to enter into negotiations with the EEC for full membership, on the understanding that this would be the course taken by Great Britain. Norway was also interested in joining as a full member under such circumstances, but Sweden wanted to consider associate membership because of its policy of neutrality. On account of her relations with the Soviet Union, Finland would in all likelihood have had no opportunity of applying for membership, should she have decided to do so, and the situation regarding Iceland in this respect was not at all clear.

In order to prevent a breakup of the Nordic community of interests and a weakening of ongoing cooperation, several of the members of the Nordic Council were to draw up a convention of cooperation among the Nordic states. As we have seen, much of that cooperation was informal in character and not based upon written agreements. Even the Nordic Council itself was based upon five national documents rather than on an international convention. Several members of the Nordic Council, among others, considered it important at this stage to confirm the areas, results, and importance of the cooperation pursued so far, in writing. Three of its most prominent members, who were the former Finnish prime minister, K. A. Fagerholm; the former Norwegian ambassador, Finn Moe; and the former vice-chairman of the Swedish delegation to the Nordic Council, Bertil Ohlin, submitted a proposal that the Nordic Council ask the governments to enter into such an agreement. This proposal was accepted by the council.

A joint meeting of the presidium of the Nordic Council and the prime ministers was held at Hangø, Finland on November 11, 1961, at which a provisional draft was produced and accepted in principle by the prime ministers. The final draft was introduced to the Nordic Council at Session 10 in Helsinki in March 1962. The agreement was signed by the five governments on March 23, to be fully implemented by July 1, 1962.

The document called the Helsinki Treaty is largely a declaration of intent, setting up certain general principles of cooperation and listing in 34 of its 65 articles the results of collaboration already achieved. One innovation was that the Nordic Council was given the right to be consulted on important questions. The treaty as such includes no binding obligations. It reflects the perceived need for a document recognizing the various types of previously noncodified cooperation among the Scandinavian states. Its importance could be said to be as a means of increasing Nordic identification and awareness. As such the treaty may carry weight psychologically and possibly morally.

Articles 2 through 7 of the treaty deal with law; 8 through 13 with culture; 14 through 17 with social cooperation; 18 through 25 with economics; 26 through 29 with communications; and 30 through 34 with other forms of Nordic cooperation. These other forms include joint efforts regarding external affairs where possible, especially consular help to Nordic citizens; aid to developing countries; and information services abroad. Article 1 of the treaty states that the contracting partners shall attempt to maintain and further cooperation among the states in the above-mentioned fields of activity.

A closer look at some of the articles indicates the general tone of the treaty. Article 14, dealing with social cooperation, reads as follows:

> The Contracting Parties shall strive to maintain and further develop the common Nordic labor market along the lines established in earlier agreements. The employment and vocational guidance services shall be coordinated. The exchange of student trainees shall be free.

> Uniformity shall be aimed at between the national provisions concerning industrial safety and similar matters.

The Helsinki Treaty was amended on February 13, 1971, to incorporate some direct mention of Nordic cooperation (Articles 35 and 36); of the Nordic Council (Articles 39 through 54), the role of which remains almost exactly the same as it was; and the newly formed Nordic Council of Ministers (Articles 55 through 62), the duties and powers of which were listed.

As to the general arrangements for Nordic Cooperation (Articles 35 through 38), there is nothing really new in the treaty other than the expressed aim of continued Nordic cooperation, to be carried out within the different organizations set up for this purpose. Referring specifically to the Nordic Council (Articles 39 through 54), the Helsinki Treaty states that the council may adopt recommendations and make other representations or statements to one or more of the Nordic countries' governments or to the Nordic Council of Ministers. The Nordic Council is to be assisted in its work by a secretariat consisting of one secretary appointed by the presidium and one secretary appointed by each of the five delegations. The presidium shall appoint the committee secretaries and other staff required for carrying out the joint secretarial duties of the council, and each delegation shall appoint its own secretariat staff (Article 49). The next article gives the Nordic Council of Ministers the right to submit proposals to the plenary assembly of the council.

There is a slight increase in the importance of the presidium of the Nordic Council according to Article 51 of the treaty. If it is not suitable to await consideration of a matter by the plenary assembly or if there are any other reasons for so doing, the presidium may make other forms of representations in lieu of recommendations. The presidium is to report to the plenary assembly on the measures taken by virtue of this arrangement. There are, in other words, no major or even minor changes in the powers of the Nordic Council according to the Helsinki Treaty.

The Nordic Council of Ministers was meant to be the main body of cooperation among the Nordic governments, each of which sends one member, assisted by an official. The council of ministers makes decisions to the extent provided for in the Helsinki Treaty as well as in other agreements among the Nordic countries. It is also responsible for cooperation in other matters among the governments of the Nordic countries and between the governments and the Nordic Council (Article 55).

The decisions of the council of ministers must be unanimous. Each country has one vote, and no decision regarding all the countries may be taken unless all the countries are represented in the council. With regard to questions that exclusively concern certain countries, only those countries need be represented (Article 57). On questions of procedure, decisions may be made by simple majority vote. An abstention constitutes no obstacle to a decision.

Decisions made by the Nordic council of ministers are binding on the individual countries. On matters that under the constitution of a country require parliamentary approval, the decisions are not binding until approved by parliament. Until parliamentary approval is given by all countries, no other country is bound by the decision.

The Nordic Council of Ministers submits a report to the Nordic Council prior to each ordinary session, in which it accounts for the cooperative efforts of the past year and sets forth plans for future cooperation. The council of ministers also submits statements to the Nordic Council on the measures taken in response to the council's recommendations and other representations (Article 60). The council of ministers adopts its own rules of procedure.

The Helsinki Treaty can be terminated in writing at six months' notice by any country signatory to it.

IMPLICATIONS FOR THE FUTURE

The Helsinki Treaty, both in its original and its amended form, is very much a statement of intent, an expression of solidarity with agreed-upon aims, as well as a general treaty of cooperation. Among other things, the signatories call on the Nordic Council to play a coordinating role. According to Article 41 of the amended treaty, the Nordic Council should be given the opportunity of stating its views on the more important questions of Nordic cooperation when this is not impracticable on account of shortage of time. Prior to amendment, this same idea was expressed as follows in the then Article 36:

> The Nordic Council ought to be given the opportunity to express its views on questions of Nordic cooperation which are of importance in principle, whenever this is not impossible due to lack of time.

The "ought" in the first line of the article was substituted for the "shall" that appeared in a draft version; with the added modification at the end of the article, this amounts to a very cautious formulation. This is probably because the countries involved were afraid of the impact of external systems upon their own Nordic cooperation. The fact that the binding provisions have been almost completely deleted or watered down by governmental experts may be yet another example of the deep-seated fear of supranationalism that appears wherever it is seen to rear its ugly head.

In 1962, although agreeing that the treaty could be said to have been watered down, the Finnish president of the Nordic Council nevertheless thought that there were reasons to be fairly content with the agreement,[3] especially since it had been concluded in such a short period of time. Six years later Gustaf Petren, another prominent Nordic Council spokesman, stated that Article 36 of the treaty had on the whole never been applied.[4] In general his criticism at this point was not so much aimed at the Helsinki Treaty itself as at certain practices of Nordic cooperation that had evolved by that time.

References have been made to the Treaty in connection with proposals raised in the Nordic Council. In the recommendation concerning a Nordic Institute for Elementary Particle (High Energy) Physics, a reference was made to Article 12 of the treaty, which deals with cooperation in research. Likewise, in a Danish proposal for a common agricultural market, Articles 18 and 21, concerning production and trade cooperation, were referred to. In addition, a number of Nordic Council recommendations may be said to be directly related to or based upon some clause in the Helsinki Treaty. As examples may be mentioned recommendations concerning the social rights of Nordic seamen (No. 2.1962) and regulations for Nordic drivers' licenses (No. 8.1965), which were both directly related to Article 2 of the Helsinki Treaty, dealing with legal equality. One might also mention the recommendations on common rules for the prescription of medicines (No. 13.1965) and Nordic patent legislation (No. 36.1965), which are based upon and partly result from Article 4 of the Helsinki Treaty, which deals with legal coordination.

Two additional implications of the Helsinki Agreement should be mentioned. First, from its moment of inauguration the treaty was seized upon by the Norden Association, an important grass-roots organization that is working for Nordic unity. The organization had previously been very active in increasing popular support for the treaty, trying to make its work known to as many individuals as possible. This is important for identification of support in the population as a whole, which matters a great deal if successful integrative steps are to be taken and integration maintained. The semiprivate Norden Association has of course no right of legislative action; as a result its role has been, and continues to be, that of a pressure group. The important fact to remember is the breadth of the basis of interests and professions of the organization, which I shall deal with in the section on the Norden Association.

NOTES

1. See Einar Löchen, "A Comparative Study of Certain European Parliamentary Assemblies," in The European Yearbook IV, 1958, p. 156.

2. See Stanley Anderson, The Nordic Council, A Study of Scandinavian Regionalism (Stockholm: Svenska Bokforlaget Norstedts, 1967).

3. K. A. Fagorholm in Nordisk Kontact (Stockholm: the Nordic Council, 1962), p. 302.

4. Gustaf Petren, in report on the conference at Storlien, September 2-4, 1968, Nordisk Udredningsserie 9 (1969): 43.

CHAPTER

6

INTEGRATION AND ECONOMICS

EARLY WORK

Economic cooperation among the Scandinavian states dates back at least to the end of the last century. As early as 1872 a monetary union was set up between Sweden and Denmark. Norway joined this union in 1875. Sweden and Norway were joined in a free trade area from 1871 to 1897, but political pressures and trade diversion terminated this arrangement. Despite several attempts by Denmark throughout the 1880s to create a larger Scandinavian market, no action was taken by the governments.[1]

One of the most ardent advocates of a Scandinavian customs union was the Danish financier C. F. Tietgen. His main argument, like that of Viggo Rothe, was the need for Scandinavia to create a large common market that would enable her to hold her own against the big industrial countries. Tietgen was active in the 1880s.

The disintegration of the Swedish-Norwegian union in 1905 was a serious setback to economic cooperation among the Scandinavian states. The suspension of the monetary union in 1914 was a further blow. Although ideas about economic and political cooperation persisted after this date, very little actually happened.*

Some economic cooperation was carried on during the 1930s, but the direct and practical results were few and of limited importance.

---

*The main reason for the breakup was the war. Finland and Iceland had remained outside the monetary union, although Iceland did in fact join the still-existing Scandinavian Monetary Convention in 1924.

THE CUSTOMS UNION PROPOSALS

Economic cooperation picked up momentum following the end of World War II. In July 1947, at a meeting of the foreign ministers of Denmark, Iceland, Norway, and Sweden, the Norwegian minister suggested that a special committee be established to investigate the means for further economic cooperation in Scandinavia. The following February the Joint Nordic Committee for Economic Cooperation was set up. Its purpose was to investigate the possibilities of establishing a common Nordic tariff as a preliminary step toward a customs union; reducing inter-Scandinavian tariffs and quantitative restrictions; increasing division of labor and specialization in Scandinavia, in cooperation with private organizations; and expanding previous Nordic commercial cooperation. Finland did not participate in this committee, primarily for political reasons.

The committee submitted its preliminary report to the governments of Denmark, Iceland, Norway, and Sweden in January 1950. The report itself was unanimous. The general belief of the committee members was that a customs union would be beneficial for the Scandinavian states for reasons of specialization, large-scale production, and rationalization. It would also, as the committee stated, make the countries more competitive internationally. The idea of a ten-year transitional period to cushion anticipated difficulties was discussed. However, the committee noted that a customs union would mean some problems for Norway, the economy of which had suffered during World War II. The spotty industrialization of Norway would have to be improved and filled out before a customs union would be profitable for her. The strong reservations that were voiced by Norway, and the status of Iceland as an observer, led the 1948 committee to conclude that it was not possible at that time to set up a customs union among the four countries.

Norway was not prepared to enter into any economic agreement that might prove detrimental to her own development, as it was perceived. She had concentrated on the rebuilding of her merchant marine following the war, since this had always been of primary concern to her overall economy. This meant, of course, that home industries had been given second priority to shipping in order to enable Norway to earn currency abroad, which was badly needed. For this reason, it was felt, she was not really in a position to cope with the increasing competition from the other Scandinavian states that would follow upon the introduction of a customs union. Although the other states argued that they had also suffered from the war and that some arrangements could be worked out, the Norwegians were not convinced of the strength of this argument. Some agreement was reached, however, and on Norwegian initiative it was decided to charge the committee with the task of investigating the possibilities of abolishing tariffs on some categories of goods, which were to be defined by joint consultation.[2]

Denmark, Sweden, Norway, and the United Kingdom had developed a tradition of thinking alike and acting together during the early postwar years. Following the split in the Council of Europe between the federalists and the functionalists, the above-mentioned countries found themselves together in the latter group. In 1949 UNISCAN (United Kingdom and Scandinavia) was set up, at the time when France, Italy, and the Benelux states were involved in discussions concerning a plan for linking up the Benelux customs union with the proposed Franco-Italian customs union. The latter plan, referred to as FINEBEL (France, Italy, the Netherlands, Belgium, Luxemberg) proved abortive, but UNISCAN, which was largely a riposte, was put into action.[3] UNISCAN was an Anglo-Scandinavian economic agreement that freed certain types of financial transactions and provided for consultation on certain types of economic questions. Throughout the negotiations of the Maudling Committee, there was frequent contact among the Scandinavian states and between them and Switzerland and Austria.

In its first session in Copenhagen in 1953, the Nordic Council did not discuss the report of its economic committee in any great detail, since the tariff question was still being studied by the experts. Instead the council asked the committee to have the final report ready by the following session in August 1954. The report was completed by the spring of 1954 and submitted to the Nordic Council at its second annual session, as had been requested. According to its frame of reference, the committee had concentrated its efforts on the study of 20 to 30 branches of industry to ascertain whether or not a common market could be established for some of them and what the possible implications of this would be.

Agricultural products were not included in the report, as had already been agreed upon during the negotiations that had led to the provisional report of 1950. The reasons for excluding agriculture at this stage were as follows. The climatic and soil conditions under which Norwegian and Swedish agriculture operate vary too much from those of Denmark. In fact, Denmark is so superior for farming that neither Norway nor Sweden would have much of a chance competing for the market within Scandinavia. Since Norway and Sweden carry out a system of heavy subsidization that keeps the domestic prices considerably above the level of world prices, free import of Danish food and fodder products would seriously upset Swedish and Norwegian farming. As a rule, practically all products from those two countries are sold on the home market, and competition for farming would be ruinous, should Denmark be allowed free access to the markets. The Danish farm leaders were well aware of these considerations and did not press for inclusion of agriculture in a customs union at that time, although they have since done so, as in connection with the abortive NORDEK talks of 1969-70.

Most of the Swedish and Danish industries that had been investigated by the Nordic Council economic committee had been in favor of setting up a customs union. The committee concluded that a customs union was both feasible and in the long run desirable. However, the Norwegians took the opposite view, as they had in 1950. Norwegian industry was opposed to the idea, stressing the same problems that had been emphasized four years earlier. Nevertheless, the Norwegian national trade unions were favorably disposed toward the customs union, and to a large extent the split in the Norwegian camp followed the dividing lines between the socialist and the nonsocialist parties. A joint Swedish-Danish statement approving the plan was produced.

The short-term drawbacks, which had been referred to in the 1950 report and claimed to be transitional, were no longer of the same significance. With a common market there would be a better division of labor among the countries, which in turn would improve their competitive abilities and enable them to take up new kinds of production for which the present home markets had proved too small. This would, according to the argument, pave the way for a higher standard of living in Scandinavia as a whole.

The Danish and Swedish committee members then urged the Scandinavian governments to open negotiations for the establishment of a common market for eight industries. These negotiations would be a preliminary step toward further integration of markets for 21 industries, and later for even more industries. The initial eight were furniture, heavy chemicals, dyes and lacquers, porcelain, leather and footwear, textiles, agricultural machinery and machine tools, and radio sets and accessories.

The Norwegian members of the committee pointed out that Norway would derive little benefit from a common market. Her most important commodities, they argued, could already be imported duty-free into the other Scandinavian states. Also, the competition from their industries would be too much for Norway, the industries of which were more highly protected by tariffs. Norway would also face competition from non-Scandinavian firms by way of the other Scandinavian countries.

Another argument used was that whereas Norway had no marketing organizations and was catering primarily to the home market, both Sweden and Denmark were accustomed to working in export markets. Many of the Swedish and Danish industries had in fact already established marketing organizations in Norway. Further, Norway was handicapped by the higher cost of raw materials because of its higher tariff levels. Since Norwegian plants were often situated at great distances from markets, in localities the economies of which were based on the presence of these plants, serious economic and social consequences could follow. All in all, Norway was in a much weaker position industrially than either Sweden or Denmark, so much so that the Norwegian committee members rejected the idea of a common market for Scandinavia.

The Norwegian Labor Government, however, issued a statement that was much more favorable than the views expressed by the committee members of the Norwegian group. It endorsed the general idea of a common market but suggested a different approach. Rather than starting with industries for which difficulties existed or would arise, the Norwegian government suggested that new industries for which there was no economic basis in a small home market be established. It also put forward the idea of a large-scale Scandinavian plan for cooperation in the production of hydroelectric power by means of Norwegian natural resources and Danish and Swedish manpower and capital. Finally, the Norwegian government suggested cooperation in industrial research in order to improve the competitive ability of Scandinavia as a whole.[4] In other words, an entirely new form of cooperation was being proposed by Norway.

The two main proposals were tabled at the 1954 session of the Nordic Council, the Danish-Swedish idea of a common market for certain industries and the new Norwegian proposal for cooperation and coordination in entirely new, large-scale industries. Agreement was finally reached on a compromise between the two proposals, although unanimity was not attained. The entire Swedish and Danish delegations, plus three of the five members from Iceland, voted for the compromise proposal. The Norwegian group, on the other hand, split on the issue. Half of the delegation, that is, the Labor Party members, were in favor, and all the non-Labor Party members were opposed.

The latter group wanted the proposal to be referred to the next annual session of the council, which would be held six months later in Stockholm, and this group tabled a motion to that effect. The council rejected this motion by a vote of 8 to 43, with two members absent. The majority proposal for a recommendation was then put forward and voted upon. The council passed Recommendation No. 22.1954 with 43 votes in favor, none opposed, 1 member absent, and 9 abstaining.

The recommendation urged the Scandinavian governments to pave the way for a common market that would cover as large an area of the economy as possible. The Nordic Council requested that endeavors be made to establish common tariffs on goods from non-Scandinavian countries and that steps be taken to remove existing inter-Scandinavian tariffs and trade barriers to such a degree and in such a way as would be acceptable to each country. The council urged the governments to start negotiations in the specific areas that could raise the standard of living and level of productivity in Scandinavia, especially in the production and transmission of electricity but also in the technological, agricultural, and research areas. Furthermore, the Nordic Council asked the governments to work on setting up organs charged with the task of developing and supervising this effort.

It should be mentioned that certain large-scale plans for cooperation in the production and distribution of hydroelectric power had already been discussed by Denmark, Norway, and Sweden during 1948-1951, and specific proposals had been put forward in this connection. There had also been negotiations between Stockholm and the city of Trondheim in Norway for the development of waterfalls in the Nea River, near Trondheim, by means of Swedish loans. The Norwegian Storting approved the plan, which was put into operation beginning in 1955.

Largely as a result of the 1954 recommendation of the Nordic Council, a conference was held in November 1954 at Harpsund, the official summer residence of the Swedish prime minister. The participants consisted of the prime ministers, the foreign ministers, the finance ministers, and the commerce ministers of Sweden, Denmark, and Norway. The main purpose of this conference was to establish a framework for the preparation of a Scandinavian common market.

The conference decided to appoint one cabinet minister from each country to a ministerial committee, the duty of which was to plan and organize economic cooperation. A Scandinavian cooperation committee was also set up, consisting of three to four government officials from each country. This committee was to undertake the necessary investigations. The members of the cooperation committee were to form national committees for coordinating internal administrative work and maintaining close contacts with industry, business, and labor organizations.

A survey of intra-Scandinavian trade patterns was to be carried out initially, to identify those fields in which customs duties and quantitative restrictions either did not exist or were of little importance. The Harpsund Conference wanted to know which sectors would lend themselves most easily to the introduction of a common market with mutual advantages for all three countries.

Among other duties the ministerial committee was charged with defining the conditions to be fulfilled if the Nordic market was to be compatible with trade with non-Scandinavian countries and with the GATT regulations.*

---

*In August 1956 Finland appointed a government member to participate in the cooperative work in this field.

Although the various committees and working groups that had been set up by the Harpsund Conference went to work right away, there were not results ready for the third annual session of the Nordic Council in Stockholm at the end of January 1955. By the following January, however, a comprehensive provisional report was submitted to the council. Although the committee had only managed to complete half of its work, the council put the common market on its agenda in order to arouse public interest. It may be assumed, therefore, that the council did not at this time intend to reach any final conclusion on the facts of the report. Rather, the council recommended unanimously that the committee carry out its work and present a complete report by the summer of 1957.

During the discussions of the 1956 session it again became clear that opposition to the whole scheme was still limited but strong, and that this opposition was to be found in the same groups as during the Oslo session in 1954. The nonsocialist members of the Norwegian delegation, who accounted for half of that group, were prepared to reject the plan outright. As they saw it, a common Scandinavian market would involve more drawbacks than advantages to Norway, both politically and economically. Politically the opponents of the proposal were afraid of supranational elements that could mean full political integration. This would mean encroachment upon the national autonomy of the individual countries, which would lose their sovereignty. Taking into account early Norwegian history and the past Norwegian experiences of dealing with Denmark and Sweden, it is possible to understand the Norwegian opposition from a political point of view. One broad area of Norway's reservations was undoubtedly the fact that she was running a planned economy, whereas the other two states, despite similar social-democratic governments, were much less interventionist.

From an economic point of view it was argued that no less than 80 percent of Norwegian exports could already be imported into Denmark and Sweden free of duty, whereas only 50 percent of the exports of the other two countries to Norway entered duty-free.[5] The problem with this argument is that it fails to take into account the question of potential reciprocity, in GATT negotiation terms, insofar as the issue is the relative height of the outstanding tariffs. However, it was argued that Norway had less to gain than the other two countries by the abolition of her customs barriers and that her industries were in no position to compete with those of Denmark and Sweden. Also, by participating in a venture such as that which was planned, Norway might risk additional drawbacks. For example, those involved in the export industries of Norway thought that they would be exposed to countermeasures, especially from the United Kingdom.

The counterarguments to this position were also familiar. First, as a unit of 20 million people Scandinavia would carry more weight in trade negotiations. All the countries involved would benefit from such an arrangement, Norway not least. Rather than seeing a decline in trade with the United Kingdom, the promarket spokesmen envisaged an increase, since Britain would have the incentive of export to one of the largest and best markets in Europe. By creating a bigger market, the Scandinavians would benefit with regard to both production and specialization. The Scandinavian states, the argument went, would be in a better position to offset any upheavals in the international economy.[6] Since all three countries had weak balances of trade and of payments, especially with Germany, it was necessary to create more competitive industrial exports, which in turn demanded a larger home market. If this could be carried out successfully, it would strengthen the currency reserves and raise the standard of living.

The committee presented its main report in July 1957. It had put forward a series of proposals concerning economic cooperation, the most important of which were the proposal for a Nordic common market for industrial products and the proposal to extend cooperation to the fields of commercial policy, production, energy, and investment, as well as finance and currency. The committee presented its report to the Nordic Council at its sixth session in Oslo in the fall of 1958.

Considering the investigatory and preparatory stages of the work to be covered, the Nordic Council now recommended that the Nordic governments take over and initiate the final negotiations for the setting up of a common market as envisaged by the report. The recommendation (No. 26.1958) led to a governmental meeting in Oslo in January 1959. This meeting suggested that certain changes be made, and the economic committee adopted these in its report to the Nordic Council at its seventh annual session in Stockholm in November 1959.

At this point it will be helpful to examine a bit closer the reasons for the abandonment of the customs union proposals of 1947-58. I shall note the underlying political reasons for this development and examine this series of episodes to see if it reveals an element of weakness or a peculiarity in the process of integration in Scandinavia.

Denmark made the initial proposals for a Scandinavian customs union in the postwar period. There was almost unanimous support for the idea throughout the Danish economic community. The close proximity of Denmark to the large European powers, particularly Germany, had traditionally led Denmark to attempt a balance between the powerful economic and cultural influence on her southern border and the Scandinavian pressures of orientation to the north. Neither Danish industry nor Danish agriculture had much to fear from a Scandinavian customs union. Even the fact that the other Scandinavian states were reluctant to include agriculture in the proposed union did not at first discourage the Danes. The rise of agricultural protectionism throughout Europe, the development of the EEC agricultural policy, and particularly the strong advantage to Dutch exports following from this brought about a change in the Danish position. Also, misgivings were voiced from time to time by certain sectors of Danish industry about the effect on industrial costs of raising the low Danish tariff on imported materials to the levels of the proposed customs union.

Norway, on the other hand, had since the end of the war been the least enthusiastic of the Nordic states about the idea of a customs union. In particular, there was fear in the Norwegian business community that the competition from Sweden would be too strong. Also, as we have seen, considerable opposition to the scheme was expressed by the nonsocialist delegates to the Nordic Council throughout its debates during 1956-57.

Sweden had a generally positive attitude toward the proposal all along, with less active support at the beginning than in the case of Denmark. Sweden was the most industrialized of the Nordic countries, with diversified production and high exports, low tariffs, and no war damage to her industry. Therefore she would have little to lose and possibly a great deal to gain from the proposed customs union.

Finland had a strong interest in a Nordic customs union and in strong economic ties with the Scandinavian countries in general, since she was dependent upon her exports to Western Europe. However, it would be very difficult or even impossible for Finland to reconcile an approach to the EEC with a preferred foreign policy line with regard to the Soviet Union and with the maintenance of friendly relations with that state.

The importance for Finland of the Scandinavian market could be found in commodity groups outside the wood sector. Although quantitatively speaking these commodity groups were of minor importance, they were nevertheless strategic for Finland, since they constituted new exports. Finnish exports had been very much concentrated in one sector, which meant that short-run erratic development of the relationship between world demand and world capacity would exert too strong an influence on the economy of the country. A related argument had to do with the need for industrial employment following the release of labor from the somewhat oversized and in a certain sense inefficient Finnish agricultural sector, which the increasingly capital-intensive wood-using industries would be unable to provide. Finally, it was thought that the proposed Nordic customs union might also provide an opportunity for Finland to obtain better treatment in her trade with the EEC without having to accept obligations that might be misinterpreted by her eastern neighbor. These are some reasons why the Finnish interest in the Nordic customs union issue lingered on and why Finland later came to play an important role in the NORDEK talks.

As I have noted, the most noticeable and possibly the chief stumbling block to a customs union had been the fears of Norway about her weak and highly protected industries. Her economic arguments may not always have stood up to close scrutiny, but by and large they were accepted politically by the other states.

The preliminary report of 1950 was not politically acceptable, although this was not admitted at the time. Expert bureaucrats had been involved to work out reports, referring reports back for more information and so on. Per Häkkerup, the former Danish foreign minister, summed up the drawback to this procedure as follows:

> Our approach was to ask experts to determine and describe the difficulties that had to be overcome before [such a] customs union could be formed. No stone was left unturned, no question unanswered. The outcome of concentrated work in the Nordic Council was thirteen thousand pages of documents for and against a customs union. But while we were discussing and elaborating these problems from every conceivable angle, developments in Europe passed us by.[7]

This painfully slow and detailed procedure must take most of the blame. This was allowed to happen partly because of the state of the democratic process itself in Scandinavia, that is, the need for opinions and suggestions by a large number of groups and the corresponding great increase in the amount of communication necessary among all these social and economic groups. Partly it may also have been caused by some of the built-in factors of dysfunctionality in Scandinavian integration. By way of contrast, as several writers have pointed out,[8] the political decision to form the Benelux customs union preceded any detailed technical elaboration. The experts were charged with the implementation of the decision, once taken, rather than with evaluations of its feasibility.

The difference between these two methods, and the shortcomings of the former, were summed up by the former chairman of the Norwegian group in the Nordic Economic Cooperational Committee, when he stated that the Nordic states

> ought . . . to . . . prevent their foreign economic policy from becoming a one-sided accommodation to situations which are created for them by other countries. They

> ought to be willing to make political decisions in this area without always demanding comprehensive and detailed study beforehand. The Six made the political decisions first, and then asked the experts for help in carrying them out.[9]

THE NORDIC COUNCIL AND THE EUROPEAN FREE TRADE ASSOCIATION (EFTA)

By now many important events had taken place outside Scandinavia, overshadowing what went on inside the region. As usual, these major world events proved to be decisive for the internal developments of Scandinavia as well. At a meeting of the governments in Kungälv in July 1959, it was decided that Denmark, Norway, and Sweden should take part in the creation of a free trade area, one main purpose of which would be to facilitate the entry of certain European countries into the European Economic Community (EEC), which at this stage had been successfully launched. The name of the new organization was the European Free Trade Association (EFTA). Although a Nordic customs union inside EFTA was theoretically feasible, it would nevertheless be awkward from a practical point of view. It was left for the Nordic Council at its Stockholm session in 1959 to declare that the plans for a Nordic customs union were no longer realistic.

The Norwegian opposition to the whole scheme had varied, but it had been maintained throughout. Both business and industry felt, as they still do, to some extent, that the major marketing opportunities for Norway could be found outside Scandinavia, particularly in the United Kingdom, in Western Europe, and in the United States. Thus in the opinion of the critics a Nordic market was too limited in importance to justify the costs and difficulties of introducing it, to say nothing of the drawbacks that might easily follow.

With EFTA as a going concern and the idea of a Nordic customs union temporarily abandoned, the Nordic Council had to limit its activities within the economic field. Since it is often easier for governments to recognize economic realities than to translate them quickly into terms of national policies, there were still several tasks open to the Nordic Council. For example it could, as it did, deal with problems of cooperation in commercial policy and in the fields of production, distribution, and energy.*

---

*The idea of a Nordic customs union, albeit in a limited form, was again put forward as the stillborn Nordic Economic (NORDEK) project of 1969-70.

It could be argued that it was a mistake for the Nordic countries not to pursue the plan for a customs union, EFTA or no EFTA. There were political reasons both for and against. It is even possible that a customs union will come about, although the NORDEK talks of 1969-70, which were shelved following the withdrawal of Finland from the talks, highlighted some of the difficulties with which Nordic economic integration seems to be permanently beset.

What was important in 1959, however, was the creation of a common industrial market within EFTA, which also meant free trade among four of the five countries.

At the 1959 session, the Nordic Council debated and passed a motion, No. 12.1959, in which it recommended that the governments encourage economic cooperation and build up an efficient machinery for that purpose. In reporting back to the Nordic Council, the governments stated that most of the economic cooperation among the Nordic countries was now taking place within the framework of EFTA, GATT, and the OEEC.

Trade among the four Scandinavian countries since 1959 has grown considerably faster than the total trade among all EFTA members. Exports within Scandinavia accounted for approximately one-third of total EFTA exports and rose by 164 percent from 1959 to 1966. At the same time the increase in Scandinavian exports to the rest of EFTA was only 77 percent, and the increase in Scandinavian exports to EEC was 75 percent in the same period. Not only has there been a strong growth in intra-Scandinavian trade from 1959 to 1966 following the setting up of EFTA, but this same growth has been one of the most dynamic elements of EFTA cooperation.

This makes it seem as if intra-Scandinavian trade as promoted by EFTA has overshadowed any remaining desire for a Nordic customs union. However, a closer look, such as that which was undertaken by the EFTA secretariat itself in 1969, questions this proposition.[10] This study shows that the estimated effects on trade by the Nordic countries, measured as percentages of the rise in foreign trade with member countries from 1959 to 1965, do not show any considerable difference from the effects on other countries. Because trade among the Nordic countries is more concentrated than the trade among the other member countries on the EFTA markets, its effect on total trade has been more significant.[11] Following the distinction between trade diversion and trade creation that is made in customs union theory, in imports the share of trade creation in the total import effect for the Nordic countries is on the whole above average. As the EFTA study shows, the Nordic countries made full use of the opportunities offered through increased specialization. As I will point out later, subcontracting increased considerably among the Nordic states. As for pulp and paper, Finland, Norway, and Sweden all benefitted from the increased exports. The major effect on imports for all the Nordic states was in textiles and clothing, as well as in metals and engineering products.[12]

Although they had been impressive in terms of dollars, during the period investigated (1959 to 1965), the effects of EFTA on intra-Nordic trade had been less significant in terms of an increase in trade among the Nordic countries. For example, intra-Nordic trade as a percentage of the actual growth in intra-Nordic trade was below the corresponding percentage for EFTA as a whole. One possible conclusion from this might be that the creation of EFTA has promoted trade among distant member countries to a greater extent than it has promoted trade among neighboring countries.[13]

Although the more important economic questions concerning four of the five Nordic states were dealt with within the framework of EFTA, this did not prevent the Nordic Council from taking an interest in the working of that organization. The importance of EFTA to the Nordic states was repeatedly emphasized by several representatives during the general debates of the Nordic Council.* Conversely, the council members were also fully aware of some of the shortcomings of the EFTA agreement. For example, the decision by the British government to impose an import surcharge triggered off a debate in the Nordic Council, the outcome of which was a recommendation (No. 25.1965), adopted by a vote of 58 to 0, in which the council requested that the Scandinavian governments press for a rapid elimination of the surcharge, which was seen to be in contradiction to EFTA principles. At the same time the Nordic Council recommended that economic cooperation within EFTA be intensified and that fisheries and agriculture be included in the agreement.

THE NORDIC ECONOMIC (NORDEK) PLAN

The NORDEK plan was the second major attempt to establish an economic union of the Nordic countries. To a large extent it was prompted by the abortive efforts to find an accommodation with the EEC. Following Charles de Gaulle's veto of British membership in 1967, the impression developed among the Scandinavians that it might now be considerable time before the whole situation was clarified and that they, the Scandinavians, should try to do something about it in the meantime. The NORDEK proposal was put forward by the Danish government at the 1968 session of the Nordic Council, where it was quite enthusiastically received. In April of that year the prime

---

*Iceland joined EFTA in 1970.

ministers, other members of the governments, and representatives of the Nordic Council met in Copenhagen, where they decided to instruct the experts to draft a treaty of expanded Nordic economic cooperation before the end of the year. The work went much more smoothly than it had in the previous effort, and by January 1969 the report was completed. On several points the negotiations had been preceded by contacts with the governments. Where the experts agreed, in a sense the result was a provisional agreement among the governments, made on condition that an overall agreement would be reached.

One of the most important points in the instructions given to the committee of experts, which was called the Committee of High Officials, was that the proposals included in the draft treaty should not create conditions in the Nordic countries that would make it more difficult for them to become members of, or associated to, the EEC later on.

Significantly, no noun was included in the name given to this effort of integration, NORDEK being an abbreviation of the Scandinavian equivalent of "Nordic Economic." This is related to the difficulties involved in the use of the word "union" when applied to anything political in Scandinavia, where the Norwegians in particular, but also to some extent the Finns, have had reason to dislike the term.

As in the earlier case, the social democrats from the four countries were, as a group, on the whole less hesitant to discuss the possibility of an economic union than were the nonsocialists.

Not only were the experts asked to stay away from proposals that could possibly create difficulties for the countries in the event of a membership in or association agreement with the EEC, but they were also asked to keep in mind the legislation, agreements, and policies of the EEC and wherever possible bring the Nordic measures close to this policy. By July 1969 the draft treaty was completed.

An important part of the NORDEK proposal was a common Nordic tariff, the purpose of which was to achieve a level of competitive and differentiated industry in Scandinavia that would be in a position to assert itself in an integrated Europe and on the world market. However, with regard to industrial goods a free market was already in existence for the Nordic countries as members of EFTA. Why then a tariff union? The answer seemed to rest on the belief that it was desirable to form a larger Nordic economic unit inside Western European integration in order to facilitate more rapid economic growth. In case entry into, or association with, the EEC did not come about, other forms of Western European cooperation would be likely; this would not necessarily bring about closer Nordic integration, it was argued.

The goal was to avoid the preservation of unsuitable and ineffective forms of production. The elimination of obstacles to trade, that is, of duties on manufactured goods, was not sufficient. The committee proposed intensified exchanges of economic information, consultation on fiscal policies, harmonization of different instruments of financial policy, and extended cooperation in the field of monetary policy, as well as liberalization of capital movements. Furthermore, regional policies were to be carried out on a cooperative basis, with access to funds from a Nordic financing institute in case of adjustment difficulties. A Nordic investment bank was called for that would be authorized to issue bonds in all Nordic currencies, in order to develop a common Nordic capital market. Common principles for bilateral trade policy were to be developed, and common measures against dumping and against other imports considered disruptive to the market should be undertaken.

Far-reaching structural changes in Nordic industry were called for, as well as common measures of economic policy intended to create favorable conditions for industrial development. The committee also proposed enlarged cooperation in such fields as automation, marine research, technical and economic information, management training, and power supply. Finally, common agricultural and fisheries policies were aimed at, with some details given about how they were to be implemented. The NORDEK plan also dealt with rules of competition, trade legislation, education, and research and development assistance. The above-mentioned outlines of enlarged cooperation were to be embodied in a treaty that would also set up the necessary institutions.

In its resolutions the Nordic Council had asked that the proposed treaty incorporate all the fields of cooperation and that the treaty itself aim at comprehensive economic cooperation. The council also requested that the proposals for this substantial enlargement of economic cooperation be presented to the parliaments of the four countries as soon as possible.

Some issues proved to be more difficult to deal with than others. One of them was related to certain aspects of the organization of the tariff union itself. There were some important differences between the tariffs of Denmark and of Norway on one hand and those of Sweden and to some extent of Finland on the other. The Danish tariff, in particular, had no duties, or in some cases very small duties, on such items as iron and steel, some plastic materials, and certain other chemical products. The Danes and Norwegians would have preferred to maintain their duty-free imports of those commodities, a point that was unacceptable to the Swedes. Some type of compromise concerning other aspects of the overall treaty would have to be worked out.

A second bone of contention was the problem of agricultural commodities. In this area it was natural for the Danes to want Nordic cooperation expanded to include as much agriculture as possible. The counterargument from the other Nordic countries was that their economic and social conditions would make it very difficult for them to reduce their protection speedily and to cut down employment in the agricultural sector as fast as would seem to be required to absorb the Danish supply, or so it was argued.

A third major issue dealt with the proposed fisheries policy. The difficulties were based on the right of Nordic fishing vessels to reload and to use transit transportation in the territories of the other Nordic states.

The fourth issue involved problems in reaching an agreement on particular aspects of financial cooperation. The delegations agreed to set up three funds and a Nordic investment bank, the purpose of which would be to finance projects that were of interest to more than one Nordic country. There was also agreement about the contributions to these funds, which were to be arranged according to the following formula: Denmark, 24 percent; Finland, 14 percent; Norway, 16 percent; and Sweden, 46 percent. During their first five-year period the three funds would receive a little more than the equivalent of $.4 billion, and the investment bank would receive a basic fund of some $200 million. The Swedish delegation was unwilling to accept larger amounts than those indicated and was unfavorably disposed to any prolongation of the five-year period suggested. The Danish, Norwegian, and Finnish delegations were ready to accept the proposed amounts, but they foresaw a larger future need for money.

Basically the experts' proposal was meant to constitute a combination of measures according to which the different states would gain and lose something, but in total find the arrangement favorable. Obviously, the final decisions would have to be taken on a very high level, and according to some principle very like what is called horse-trading.

Before going into the political fate of NORDEK, it might be interesting to examine more closely its structure as well as some of its underlying assumptions. (See Figure 3.) First, there was to be a council of ministers at the top, consisting of one representative from each country. Since all decisions would have to be taken unanimously, the scheme was devoid of any element of supranationality.

Second, there was to be a permanent committee of government officials occupying a central position in the whole system. This committee was to be charged with the preparation of all decisions made by the council of ministers and might have had the right to make decisions on minor items. The role of this committee might have been an important one, insofar as the same experts that had drafted the actual treaty would be its future members. Third, there were to be 10 special committees of cooperation that would be charged with tasks concerning different fields of work.

FIGURE 3

The NORDEK Plan: Proposed Decision-Making Machinery

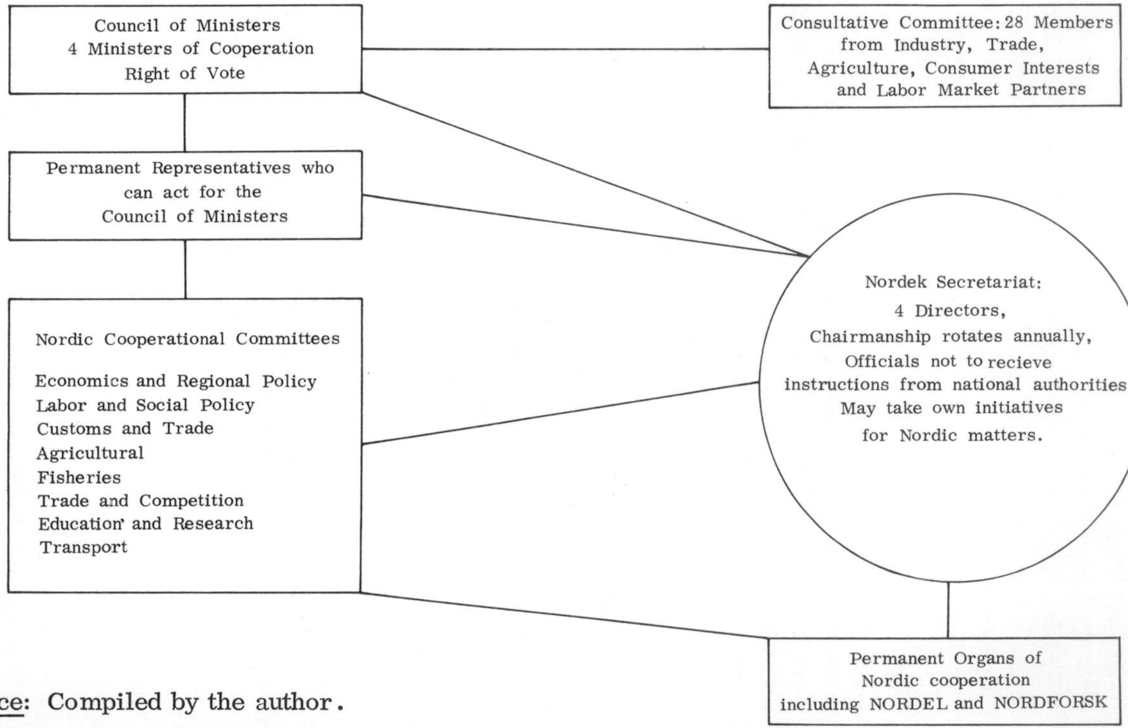

Source: Compiled by the author.

Annexed to this pyramidical structure would be a consultative committee, possibly modeled somewhat on the EEC machinery. This committee would consist of some 28 members representing industry, trade, agriculture, fisheries, consumer interests, and labor market partners.

Also there was to be a secretariat made up of four directors, which would have the right to present proposals to the different governmental institutions of NORDEK and to investigate such problems as they saw fit. Since the directors would not have any formal power, much of the influence of the secretariat would depend on the strength and personality of its board of directors, the chairmanship of which would rotate on an annual basis. The officials of the secretariat were to receive no instructions from national authorities, and the secretariat would take its own initiatives; in a sense its scope would resemble that of the EEC Commission.

No provisions were made for a court of justice or other judicial institution inside NORDEK. As I have stated, one of the basic principles was to avoid the element of supranationality, which may account for the omission of a court.

The role of the Nordic Council was a subject for further elaboration and negotiation. Generally speaking, it was assumed that no great changes would occur as far as the rights or functions of the Nordic Council were concerned. On the contrary, the council was to maintain its function of consultation and taking of initiatives and its right to raise such questions as it saw fit.

The NORDEK plan represented an attempt to formalize and solidify some of the already existing functional integration in Scandinavia and to present a machinery through which future decisions were to be made.

Several points in the proposed plan deserve scrutiny. The notion of a regional policy appears to have been only very superficially touched on. There are several problem areas that would seem to lend themselves to joint Nordic solutions, such as the North Cape, but there are other regions in which joint efforts would also be helpful.

The actual use of the different funds referred to above was not clearly specified, this point being perhaps related to the superficial treatment of regional policy.

No attempt to define a Nordic industrial policy appears to have been undertaken, although several fields of endeavor would naturally seem to present themselves. Furthermore, it was not clear how and in what sense private industry would be involved in the decision-making process, apart from the proposal of a consultative committee that would apparently be patterned after EEC.

More important, perhaps, was the fact that the whole report seemed somewhat one-sided with regard to overall planning and goals, the assumptions here seemingly resting more on narrower economic cost-benefit considerations than on larger social and economic issues. It is no secret, for example, that there is considerable difference on precisely this point between, say, Norway and Finland on the one side and Sweden on the other. The whole problem of centralizing forces as opposed to regional planning was not dealt with to a satisfactory degree.

Despite the weaknesses in the overall NORDEK scheme, the plan itself proceeded more or less according to its timetable. At the 1970 session of the Nordic Council, two recommendations were passed, one dealing with the implementation of the scheme and the other recommending participation by Iceland in the expanded economic cooperation. Two additional recommendations concerning Nordic economic cooperation in general and NORDEK in particular were passed by the Nordic Council, in 1970 and 1971 respectively.

In the meantime, developments were taking place elsewhere. On January 12, 1970, Finland had stated that she was prepared to continue the NORDEK negotiations so as to arrive at a treaty as soon as possible. She also stated that in case any of the Nordic countries, while the NORDEK talks continued or after they had been completed, decided to enter into negotiations with the EEC for the purpose of membership, Finland would maintain the option of dissociating herself from whatever parts of the NORDEK agreement would be affected. In 1970, during the 18th session of the Nordic Council, the Nordic prime ministers agreed to instruct the committee of high officials to have the treaty ready for signature by March 7, 1970, or as soon as possible thereafter, to be followed by ratification in the different Nordic capitals.

On March 24 the Finnish government decided not to sign the NORDEK treaty. The official explanation offered at the time was that the other Nordic countries were really preparing themselves to enter into negotiations with the EEC, which would put the entire NORDEK plan into a state of ambivalence. Thus it would not be in the interest of Finland to put her signature to it.

RECENT WORK

The Nordic Council has concentrated its efforts in the economic sphere to specific areas, the most important of which are industrial cooperation, border trade within Scandinavia, trade with Eastern Europe, agricultural cooperation, and fisheries and the export of fishing products, as well as matters relating to the North Cape and the Lapps. The creation of a duty-free market in industrial goods has led to an increase in production sharing and an exchange of technical and economic industrial know-how. Although the Nordic countries adopted different policies regarding their relations with the European communities, the free trade established by EFTA has by and large been maintained.

The Nordic countries have agreed to further develop their economic cooperation through concrete projects. As we shall see, education, research, harmonization of laws, culture, and communications are important areas in which cooperation is proceeding along firmly established lines. Further cooperation seems to be desirable in industry and in regional and environmental policy, as well as in the field of energy. Today there is intra-Nordic cooperation in the supply of electric energy. The power grids of Denmark, Finland, Norway, and Sweden are connected, and power producers are closely cooperating through an agency called NORDEL. A Scandinavian Fund for Technology and Industrial Development has been created, and its secretariat is based in Stockholm. Top priorities include projects concerning the environment, health, and transport.

During its first extraordinary session in Stockholm in the fall of 1975, the Nordic Council passed a recommendation asking that a Nordic investment bank be established. The proposal, which had been put forward by the Nordic Council of Ministers, had been debated for some time. For once, there seemed to be enough political agreement among the governments to push the case to its conclusion in the Nordic Council, and the matter was expedited relatively quickly. Its basic fund of 400 million SDR (Special Drawing Rights) was divided as follows: Finland, 64 million; Denmark, 88 million; Iceland, 4 million; Norway, 64 million; and Sweden, 180 million. Despite a relatively modest capital, especially viewed in relation to such capital needs as those of the North Sea energy activities, the bank could prove to be an important organ for further economic integration in the Nordic area. No doubt the Nordic Council will turn its future attention to activities flowing from the institution and to attempts to assure that maximum parliamentary influence is yielded on its activities.

NOTES

1. See in particular Frantz Wendt, The Nordic Council and Co-operation in Scandinavia (Copenhagen: Munksgaard, 1959), pp. 90-91.

2. For a discussion of the postwar economic problems of Norway, see Per Kleppe, Main Aspects of Economic Policy in Norway since the War (Oslo: Oslo University Press, 1960), and Eric Brofoss, "Survey of Economic Developments and of Economic Policies in Norway Since World War II" (Oslo: University of Oslo International Summer School, 1963).

3. For a discussion of this period and of some of the issues involving Britain and the rest of the functionalists, see Miriam Camps, Britain and the European Community (Princeton: Princeton University Press, 1964), p. 210.

4. See in particular Wendt, op. cit., pp. 165-232.

5. For a good discussion of the changes in Norwegian foreign policy orientation and images, see Tim Greve, Norway and NATO (Oslo: Norwegian Universities Press, 1963); Nils Orvik, The Decline of Neutrality (Oslo: Johan Grundt Tanum Forlag, 1953); Orvik, Trends in Norwegian Foreign Policy (Oslo: Norwegian Universities Press, 1962); and Halvard Lange, Norsk Utenrikspolitikk Siden 1945 (Johan Grundt Tanum Forlag, 1952).

6. See Wendt, op. cit., p. 178.

7. Per Häkkerup, "Nordic Cooperation and the World Around Us," speech to the Danish Norden Association annual meeting, Aulborg, Denmark, June 13, 1964.

8. Among them Stanley Anderson in The Nordic Council, A Study of Scandinavian Regionalism (Stockholm: Svenska Bokförlaget Norstedts, 1967), p. 137.

9. Knut Getz-Wold, "Norge, Norden og markedsproblemene," Nordisk Kontakt, no. 10 (1963), p. 581.

10. See "Effects of EFTA on the Economies of its Member Countries," EFTA Bulletin 10, no. 1 (January-February 1969).

11. Ibid., p. 11.

12. Ibid.

13. Ibid., p. 14.

CHAPTER 7

INTEGRATION AND LAW

BACKGROUND

The first Nordic legal conference, a private arrangement, took place as early as 1872. The participants were practicing lawyers, university law professors, and government officials. The aim of the conference was to achieve the greatest possible uniformity in legislation.[1] Legal meetings have been held on a regular basis every third year since then. One of the subjects discussed was the need for uniformity in bills-of-exchange legislation.[2] Proposals were tabled in the Norwegian, Swedish, and Danish parliaments, and they were adopted and given royal assent in all three countries on the same day, May 7, 1880.[3] This was the first joint Scandinavian law and the beginning of legal cooperation in Scandinavia.

The first joint governmental civil law commissions were created by 1901. Uniform legislation followed that affected contracts, transactions, and sales of goods.[4] Legal cooperation continued to expand, and by 1910 it included legal activity outside the sphere of economics and finance, such as joint family law commissions, the purpose of which was preparation of draft legislation in several fields of law, concerning marriage and guardianship, for example, as well as dealing with minors. Finland and Iceland did not participate actively in this type of legal cooperation; in fact, they remained outside such cooperation until after World War I. Finland took a particularly active part in this work from 1930 onwards.[5] As yet there were no formalized procedures or fixed lines for Nordic legal cooperation.

Following the end of World War II a special Nordic committee for legal cooperation was set up (1946), composed of two representatives from each of the Nordic states. Its main tasks were to examine

Nordic legislation that was relevant to legal cooperation and to recommend specific action concerning this type of cooperation. The committee appears to have been less effective than expected,[6] and in 1960 a system of "contact men" was set up instead.

FORMS AND LEVELS OF LEGAL INTEGRATION

Legal cooperation within Scandinavia is carried out on three main levels: governmental, private, and parliamentary.

On the governmental level there are regular meetings among the Nordic ministers of justice. These meetings are prepared by the so-called contact men. Each country appoints its undersecretary of state or a correspondingly senior person in the ministry of justice to act as a contact man regarding the ongoing work in Nordic legal cooperation. The contact man follows all existing and planned work of this type and keeps contact with his counterparts in the other Scandinavian states. This contact is often informal, such as by telephone or by irregular meetings. The contact man plays a key role, insofar as he is the central figure around whom far-reaching cooperation is carried out on the ministerial level. He attends the regular conferences of the Nordic ministers of justice, which have been held regularly since 1953. The contact man may also suggest which legislative questions should be subject to joint Nordic action to bring about maximum legal harmonization. When a bill is introduced in one of the parliaments, investigations are undertaken to ascertain whether or not similar or identical legislation can be carried out in the other Scandinavian states. By 1972 legal cooperation on the governmental level had been further formalized through the council of ministers.

On the private level the meetings initiated in 1872 are still carried out once every third year. These meetings enable legal practitioners and officials to maintain close contact across the borders. The participating professional jurists constitute an important pressure group for continued legal cooperation, if and when required. So far, however, legal cooperation in Scandinavia seems to be advancing satisfactorily.

It is at the parliamentary level that the Nordic Council aims its efforts regarding legal cooperation and coordination. The council may be active at several stages of legislation. First, it may make particular recommendations concerning specific actions to be taken. It may propose legislative measures in a wide field on a Scandinavian basis. Its power of initiation will normally be used to produce proposals or recommendations, which are directed to two or more Nordic governments. (See Chapter 2.)

Second, the Nordic Council may be active at a later stage during the process of legislation. It may, for example, express itself on some matter while specific formulations are being prepared in the ministries of justice. More importantly, according to the Helsinki Treaty the Nordic Council has a right to be heard on specific matters. (See Chapter 5.) Third, the governments may transfer to the council the main points on some new bill in order to solicit the opinion of the council about it. This will of course enable the governments to increase their knowledge of the trends of opinion in the different Nordic parliaments.

The legal committee of the Nordic Council, the membership of which varies from session to session, is a permanent committee that meets at fairly regular intervals between the sessional meetings. It prepares legal questions to be considered at the forthcoming sessions and works closely with the ministries of justice and the contact men.

TOWARD A COMMUNITY OF LAWS

We have already noted that Scandinavian laws are based upon largely similar principles and that legal cooperation among the states is quite well organized. There are frequent meetings on different levels between legislators and legal administrators. The Nordic Council is active at different stages throughout the legislative process, and it plays an important role in several ways. The governments make use of the Nordic Council for information and advice concerning parliamentary trends, and the council is well aware of this. The council is even formally equipped with certain rights of consultation, which have only partly been enforced. It would seem that more could be made of the clauses of the Helsinki Treaty than has so far been attempted. (See Chapter 13.) However, although cooperation in the legal field is well organized and quite advanced, much could be done to solidify the achievements to which the Nordic Council has dedicated its efforts.

The council is committed to maximum integration in the legal area, and its aim is a community of laws. In order to create similar interpretations of the joint Scandinavian laws, the council has been pressing for the publication of Scandinavian law reports. For example, in 1957 it recommended that the governments investigate the possibility of publishing reports that would indicate how statutory provisions were interpreted by the different national courts. The reports should also, the council suggested, include decisions that would be of mutual interest in fields in which joint action might be taken. As a result a ministerial meeting took place in Oslo in February 1958, at which it was decided that such reports should henceforth be published, in accordance with the wishes of the Nordic Council. Published on a quarterly basis, the reports were started in 1958.*

Nordic cooperation within the field of family law has been going on since the beginning of the century. Similar marriage laws, for example, were developed during the years 1913-29. Recent trends indicate different national developments with regard to marriage as a social institution, which might affect the efforts at coordination in this area on a Nordic basis.

The Nordic Council has concerned itself with a wide area of legislation that covers citizenship, adoption, family and names laws, and children's legal rights, and the council has made a series of recommendations concerning these, beginning in the mid-1950s. The council has also recommended joint action in the fields of copyrights, trademarks, installment plans, aviation, and environmental control, to mention but a few. Legislation has followed in many of these fields, sometimes as a direct result of the recommendations of the council and at other times partly influenced by the sentiments it has expressed.

It is of course difficult to ascertain the exact extent to which the council has been directly responsible for initiating specific legislative actions, since the process involves several different levels of decision making and the interpenetration of bureaucracies. However, one of the main tasks of the Nordic Council has been to identify areas and specific problems for which joint action can successfully be sought. There is little doubt that the council has been important. Practical results have been achieved in the fields of social legislation, for example, and of legislation dealing with travel and communications. (Social legislation is discussed in Chapter 9.)

The initiative of facilitating the movement of persons within Scandinavia was first taken by the Nordic Parliamentary Committee, the work of which has been continued by the Nordic Council since the beginning of the 1950s. As early as 1954 the council recommended that the existing "movement certificates" should be taken up for reconsideration. Following the war, basically for security reasons, the regulations covering the rights of persons to move freely about in Scandinavia were rather restricting. However, by the mid-1950s many people, and this included the Nordic Council membership in particular, thought that bureaucracy had gone too far. Gradually the postwar powers of the administrative authorities in question were decreased, and traffic was allowed to flow more freely. For example, the Nordic Council recommended in 1957 that the rules about the

---

*The reports were to be published and printed in Norway and to have a Norwegian chief editor and Nordic subeditors. It was decided to divide the expenses equally among Norway, Sweden, Finland, and Denmark.

obligation of citizens to inform the authorities about their addresses when visiting other Nordic countries be abolished. Following a report in 1961 the Nordic Council was satisfied that sufficient action had been taken.

With the increasing movement of people within Scandinavia and with the larger numbers of Scandinavians spending time in countries other than their own, several problems arose. Since the states operate dissimilar systems of national service, there was the problem of "double service," that is, of individuals being drafted into the services of different countries at different periods in their lives. The Nordic Council wanted to eliminate this bureaucratic nuisance, and it made a representation to the governments that brought about a solution to this problem by mutual agreement.

Increased travel within Scandinavia has had one predictable unfortunate side effect. There has been an increase in the amount of crime committed abroad by citizens of all the states. The only way to try to curb this tendency is by increased cooperation in criminal justice. The Nordic Council turned its attention to this matter and advised that the rules of extradition should be brought up to date. According to the council, the police and law courts ought to be given wider authority both to examine suspected persons and to hear witnesses at the request of police or courts in other Scandinavian countries. (See Chapter 8.) In January 1964 an act came into effect that provided for cooperation on a Nordic level with regard to imposing penalties. This also covers persons on suspended sentence or probation. Persons on probation, having received suspended sentences or having been conditionally discharged, can now be transferred from one Nordic state to another.

The Nordic Council has been constantly working to simplify the rules that govern the acquisition of citizenship for Scandinavians in countries other than their own. Changes in citizenship still have advantages for the individuals concerned, although on the surface these changes seem to be a superficial if not contradictory concern for the Nordic Council.

The successful introduction of the Nordic labor market has made it necessary to discuss what steps can and should be taken to ensure freedom of establishment for Scandinavians throughout the region. The harmonization of business laws, especially those of corporations, and the institution of joint rules about the right to operate a business in another Scandinavian country have been dealt with on a Nordic basis for some time. Steps have also been taken to investigate the possibility of agricultural subsidies on a Scandinavian level, regardless of the nationality of the recipients, and for the integration of laws covering coastal traffic and transportation. To begin with, Nordic integration in this area has resulted in simplification of the transit trade. Special agreements have been drawn up, such as the agreement between Sweden and Denmark enabling either country to load or unload goods bound for or arriving from the continent in the other country.

In its Recommendation No. 7.1953, the Nordic Council requested that the governments consider the possibility of continuing to make practical, concrete measures that could create equality among citizens of the Nordic states. It further requested the governments to report such measures as had been undertaken to the council. In their report to the council the governments made it clear that the purpose of this recommendation had been fulfilled in Sweden with regard to financial support for farmers and partly in Denmark concerning laws regulating support for investment in agricultural production. The Danish laws covering tenement for agricultural workers also put Danish, Finnish, Norwegian, Swedish, and Icelandic citizens on an equal basis. As for loans to younger farmers, there are no limitations or restrictions based on nationality in Denmark.

Of equal or possibly greater importance was the council recommendation of 1961 asking for the establishment of a contact unit for agricultural questions. This was carried out, and the unit in question held its first meeting in March 1962. A similar contact unit for fisheries questions was set up in 1963, following discussions among the Nordic ministers of fisheries in 1962.

The Nordic Council had for some time recommended the earliest possible introduction of an integrated system of patent laws, whereby patents taken out in one Nordic country would be valid in the whole region. On the initiative of the council, the governments set up a committee of patent experts, and a report was published in 1963.[7] The Nordic Council has been working for the establishment of a Nordic board of appeals, which would have the power to judge appeals on patents from any of the Scandinavian states.

Because of economic developments on the continent, the Nordic Council considered it to be important that the governments examine the possibility of creating uniform legislation concerning joint stock companies, as well as of establishing equality before the law for Nordic citizens acting as the founders or managers of such companies. A recommendation to this effect was made in 1961. Although at that time entry into the EEC had different priority among the Nordic states, the council found it necessary to impress upon the governments the need to check on legislation in the EEC. A resolution concerning this was passsed by the council in 1962. In 1965 the Nordic Council was informed that an expert committee had been set up, whereupon the council considered that sufficient action on the matter had been taken.

At the 1973 session, in its report to the Nordic Council concerning Nordic cooperation, the newly established Nordic Council of Ministers presented a program for legal cooperation. Since then a large part of its efforts has been directed toward coordinating the wishes of the Nordic Council with those of the Nordic Council of Ministers.

Further work in Nordic legal cooperation proceeded according to Recommendation No. 1.1974 of the council concerning a program of action to supplement the reports by the council of ministers. At the Reykjavik session in 1975, the presidium of the Nordic Council asked the council of ministers to implement, as soon as possible, equivalent laws concerning county and local elections, based upon principles that had been developed by a working group of the council of ministers. The direct result of this has been that some of the problems are partly solved surrounding local elections or affecting Scandinavians who are settled on a working basis in countries other than their own.

In important areas within family, criminal, and procedural law there are almost identical laws in existence throughout Scandinavia. Increasing trade among the Nordic countries has led to the need for similar or even identical rules covering various aspects of such trade. Legal integration has also been carried out, partly as a result of, but also in order to facilitate, industrial cooperation. Important laws affecting contracts, purchases, installment buying, instruments of debt, commercial agents and commercial travelers, insurance contracts, bills of exchange, and checks have been made almost identical, at least in Denmark, Finland, Sweden, and Norway. Much remains to be done on a Nordic basis, however, particularly in such fields as structural modernization, which requires national agreements.

To conclude, the integrational process in the legal sector has been carried far, giving the states visible results of their efforts. Generally speaking, the work of the Nordic Council has been successful in this area, and a community of laws seems to be in the process of being created. The most important question for the future will be how to maintain and strengthen this type of community while also maintaining different relationships between the individual Nordic states and the EEC. In several ways legal harmonization has been carried further among the Nordic states than among any other group of states anywhere, the European Economic Community included. Conflicts between EEC legislation and Nordic legal agreements may occur in the future in joint stock company legislation, bankruptcy cases, and one or two other areas. Until such a time, the Nordic states will have to try to clarify their own positions and make agreements among themselves that will be consistent with their mutual interests and also their individual national or regional well-being. The Nordic Council will have some worthwhile tasks to carry out in this field.

NOTES

1. See Frantz Wendt, The Nordic Council and Cooperation in Scandinavia (Copenhagen: Munkgaard, 1959), p. 54.

2. Ibid., p. 55.

3. Ibid.

4. See Hans Hakkerup, "Nordic Cooperation in the Legal Field," speech to the Consultative Assembly of the Council of Europe, September 20, 1963.

5. Wendt, op. cit., p. 55.

6. See Herman Kling, "Legislative Cooperation among the Nordic States," speech to Nordic Council Conference for International Organizations in Europe, Hasselby, Sweden, June 2-4, 1965.

7. Nordisk Udredningeserie, no. 6 (1963).

CHAPTER

8

INTEGRATION AND COMMUNICATIONS

EARLY WORK

Nordic cooperation in the field of communications and traffic matters goes back to the middle of the nineteenth century. As early as 1840 the adherents of the pan-Scandinavian idea had put forward a proposal for common postal services.[1] Although this proposal was not adopted, extensive cooperation among the postal services has developed. For example, the first trilateral postal agreement among Norway, Denmark, and Sweden was set up as early as 1869. By 1874 the three states had decided to initiate a postal union, and 60 years later this union included all five Nordic states. The uniformity of rates, however, had been abandoned in the 1930s during the Depression. The Nordic Postal Association was established after World War II, and annual postal conferences took place among the member states on a regular basis. In addition to matters dealing with current Nordic postal problems, the Postal Association discussed questions regarding the Universal Postal Union.

During the last 40 years or so, regular telecommunicational conferences on a Nordic level have been held. A Nordic telecommunicational union has existed since 1937. All five states are members of this union, which has had quite an important effect. One of its main functions has been coordination of the work in telecommunications among the Nordic states. In addition, questions dealt with by the International Telecommunicational Union and other international organizations in this field have been put on the agenda of the Scandinavian organization. Telecommunicational cooperation and coordination has been extended to such fields as broadcasting and television. Special plans for joint ventures in Nordic television have been implemented under the auspices of Nordic Television (NORDVISION),[2] and further coordination of efforts is planned. A few years ago a Scandinavian Committee on Telesatellites was set up with Sweden, Denmark, and Norway as participants.

The Scandinavian Association of Railwaymen, which included representatives from Sweden, Denmark, and Norway, was set up in 1874.* Finland joined this association in 1924. Its task has been the technical and administrative development of the railway systems on a Nordic basis. Regular meetings of railway administrators and experts have taken place, and some working groups and committees have been set up.

A Nordic association for the coordination of road technology has been in existence since 1930. This organization is of a technical nature and works through semipermanent committees. In addition to this, there is frequent contact among the road administrations of the Scandinavian states.

Attempts at coordinating aviation go back as far as 1930. Postponed because of the outbreak of World War II, these negotiations were taken up again in 1946. The most important single result was undoubtedly the creation of the Scandinavian Airlines System (SAS), which is jointly owned by Sweden, Denmark, and Norway. Sweden holds 3/7 of its ownership, and Denmark and Norway 2/7 each. Half of the shares in each country are held by the state, the rest being in private ownership. Under the terms of the agreement, which was signed on February 8, 1951, three different national aviation companies assigned the operation of all routes the parties could agree to open to one jointly owned trust company. The total capital of SAS was about 210 million Danish kroner, half of which was subscribed by the participating states' governments. The governments also agreed to underwrite to a certain extent, any operating losses, an agreement initially given for 5 years duration but later extended. The company is run by a board of directors representing the three parent companies, headed by a chairman who is elected by each of the three countries in turn.

TRAVEL LIBERALIZATION AND COMMUNICATIONS

Passports for intra-Nordic travel were abolished in 1929. Instead a system of easily obtainable travel permits was introduced

---

*Iceland is not a member because she has no railways.

among the Scandinavian states.* By 1940 controls were tightened again, and both passports and visas were reintroduced in all the Scandinavian states. Except in the case of Finland, which sided with Germany against the USSR during World War II, visas were removed after 1945. Passports, however, were maintained for a long time for all of Scandinavia, as were detailed and cumbersome customs and currency regulations. There was a traditional reluctance on the behalf of police authorities to give up their control over the citizens, once this control had been imposed. At the same time, the desire to travel abroad increased, as did popular frustration with the strict attitude toward travel exhibited by the authorities. By 1951 the public disapproval of these conditions was so strong that something had to be done. Criticism of the authorities' policy was expressed, for example, by the Norden Association. Subsequently a joint parliamentary committee was set up to look into travel rules and restrictions; it met for the first time in November 1951. By the following spring the Nordic Parliamentary Committee for Freer Communication, as it was called, recommended a return to pre-1914 conditions as quickly as possible. This meant full freedom from identity papers on all intra-Scandinavian frontiers.

On July 2, 1952, the passport requirement was abolished for all Scandinavians on travel within Scandinavia. At the same time the governments decided to allow Scandinavian citizens to visit freely within the region for a period of three months. From 1955 this agreement, which was implemented six months after the abolition of passports on inter-Scandinavian travel, also included Icelandic travelers. The parliamentary committee deserves credit for its hard and consistent battle against governmental restrictions and postwar bureaucracy. It should be noted that foreigners still had to produce passports for intra-Scandinavian travel, both when entering the region and when crossing national boundaries within it, although the passport requirement was abolished for Scandinavians. The work of abolishing the passport requirement was taken up by the Nordic Council, which also directed its attention to a host of other problems connected with travel, traffic matters, and communications.

There was close cooperation between the Nordic Parliamentary Committee for Freer Communication and the Nordic Council until the work of the committee was completed. By 1956 its efforts had led to several important results in the fields of travel and communications.

---

*Neither detailed certificates nor pictures were needed, and the charge was 25 öre (equivalent to five cents). They expired at the end of six months.

The Nordic Council recommended that the committee submit a final report, in which the problems that had not yet been solved would be summed up. This report was then submitted to the Nordic Council in 1957, and the document served as a basis for the efforts of the Nordic Council in this field of cooperation.

The Nordic Council had recommended that a Nordic Communication Committee be set up as soon as possible and given the mandate to work for the same ends as its predecessor. This committee was set up in 1957. It existed for a period of seven years, during which it played a useful role in dismantling obstacles to free traffic and communications in Scandinavia. It was terminated in 1964 because of changes in the working methods of the Nordic Council. From then on the committees of the Nordic Council were to meet on a permanent basis.

Much useful work in bringing Scandinavians closer together has been carried out by both the Nordic Council and by its predecessor, the Nordic Parliamentary Committee for Freer Communications. The abolition of laws calling for passports and travel documents was, as we have seen, already initiated and partly carried out before the Nordic Council had been set up. Much remained to be done, however. It was considered desirable, for example, that the control of passports within the Scandinavian region be abolished altogether, whether or not the person in question was a Scandinavian or a citizen of some other part of the world. The Nordic Council passed recommendations to this effect in 1953, 1954, and 1960. By May 1, 1958, all passport control for non-Scandinavians, after initial entry into the region, was removed. However, permits were required for those foreigners wishing to stay for more than three months within Scandinavia, which for this occasion was considered as one geographic unit. For Scandinavians there are, as we have seen, no permits whatsoever for either work or travel across national borders within Scandinavia.

There has been extensive coordination in customs matters. For example, shortly after the war there were a total of 55 customs offices between Norway and Sweden. The Nordic Council believed that these should somehow be pooled, both to further integration in several ways and to save money and work. It therefore recommended in 1956 that the customs services be integrated and carried out on a joint basis. As a result there have been drastic cuts in the number of intra-Scandinavian boundary stations, and some of their functions are now carried out jointly. Norway and Sweden, which have the longest common boundary, have reduced the number of customs stations along it to 22. Trains and buses crossing from one country into the other are inspected by officials from one country only. Similar improvements have been made between Sweden and Finland. The Nordic Council has also recommended that people without goods to declare be allowed to cross the boundary anywhere. Some of the Nordic Council's recommendations corresponding to the above-mentioned development have been Nos. 9.1953, 6.1956, 11.1957, and 3.1960.

The Nordic Council passed several useful recommendations concerning postal matters and telecommunication. A general recommendation concerning coordination in this field was put forward at its first session in 1953. The following year the council recommended that an internal postage rate be applied to letters, and later to parcels, within Scandinavia. This recommendation was reported back to the Nordic Council as successfully implemented, as were later recommendations concerning internal rates for telegram fees within Scandinavia, reduced teleprinter and telex fees, and reduced rates for intra-Scandinavian long distance calls. The respective recommendations bringing this about were Nos. 6.1954, 15.1955, and 11.1957.

TRAFFIC LAW AND SAFETY

Increased intra-Scandinavian travel and traffic has made it necessary for the states to attempt to maximize coordination of their traffic regulations. The Nordic Council was actively involved in trying to change the Swedish left-hand drive to conform with the right-hand drive of the rest of Scandinavia. Several recommendations were passed, and by 1967 the Swedes declared, whether or not as a result of these recommendations, that they were ready to make the change. This meant that the greatest obstacle to traffic conformity and safety within Scandinavia was removed, although several smaller obstacles remained.

A general harmonization of traffic rules and regulations has been promoted by the Nordic Council since 1955. The council received a symposium of all existing traffic regulations in Denmark, Norway, Sweden, and Finland at its annual session in that year. Much of the discussion was taken up with suggestions of ways in which the Scandinavian railway tariffs could be integrated, to make the four countries into one unit in this respect. The Nordic Council asked the governments to submit reports concerning progress in this field and to inform the council about all aspects of railway cooperation. During the following three sessional meetings the Nordic Council received the reports as requested. Only minor results were achieved, however, such as extension of the validity of return tickets for inter-Scandinavian railway travel to three months and simplification of the rules for group travel.[3] By 1964 a unitary system of railway tariffs had been introduced on a probationary basis.

The Nordic Council has paid great attention to traffic safety research from the beginning of its work. The council has passed recommendations of a general nature concerning this field of cooperation and has also dealt with some specific issues, several of which have been successfully implemented.

A general coordination of road-building plans between Scandinavia and the rest of Europe was recommended by the Nordic Council in 1958. Although in this respect no initiative has been taken so far, several large road and ferry projects have been undertaken in the Scandinavian region.

Proposals for joint action with regard to sea traffic and safety have produced good results. For example, the Nordic Council suggested in 1959 that the rules and markings for sea traffic be standardized. Following this recommendation, an agreement among Finland, Sweden, Denmark, and Norway was signed in 1962, with specific actions to be taken by July 1, 1965.

In 1959, following a thorough discussion two years earlier, the Nordic Council recommended that regular cooperation be established among the Nordic states with regard to icebreaking, a costly but necessary business. A need for cooperation in this field had existed in the Nordic states for a long period. The demand varies somewhat, and because of the Gulf Stream it appears to be smaller for Norway than for Denmark, for Sweden, and particularly for Finland. Regular icebreaking is required between Sweden and Finland, in order to maintain coastal traffic as long as possible during winter. As a result of the council recommendations, an agreement was signed in December 1961 among Finland, Sweden, Denmark, and Norway.

The Nordic Council also paid attention to the problems connected with lifesaving in the North Sea. It recommended in 1957 that cooperation be initiated with regard to sea and air safety in this area. Two years later the recommendation was declared successfully implemented by the Nordic Council. A combined lifesaving and meteorological Norwegian vessel was placed in the North Sea, jointly financed by Sweden, Denmark, Norway, and the Federal Republic of Germany. The annual cost, to be divided equally among the participants, was estimated at 200,000 Norwegian kroner.

Much preliminary work concerning joint road projects has so far been carried out on the initiative of the Nordic Council. The practical results of this have been sparse, however. A generally phrased recommendation concerning road connections in the North Cape area, which the Nordic Council produced in 1958, yielded meager results. Subsequently the Nordic Council changed its strategy and began concentrating on specific suggestions. Pointing out that there were three roads connecting northern Norway and northern Sweden that were good enough to be kept open all year round, the council proceeded to recommend in 1963 that the governments work out a plan for jointly carrying out this task. The recommendation led to a joint Norwegian

Swedish report in January 1965 that analyzed three road projects on which joint action could be taken, suggesting that the end result might be expected, subject to governmental approval, by 1974.

Two of these projects were temporarily postponed by the Norwegian government, one, Kiruna-Abisko-Narvik, because of military considerations, while the third project, Arjeplog-Graddis-Storfjord, was accepted in 1965.[4]

SUBREGIONAL INTEGRATION

Subregional integration within Scandinavia is mainly found in the North Cape (see Chapter 6) and Öresund. The latter is a region including parts of Denmark and Sweden. In Denmark it covers parts of Zealand, the island on which Copenhagen is situated; and in Sweden it covers the southern parts of the western and southern coasts.

In addition there has been some coordination of the local and regional policies of neighboring counties, especially in the case of Sweden and Norway.[*] Individual projects such as road building and hospital and institutional schemes, as well as joint access to resources that involve two or more Nordic states, must be included in this category. Subregional coordination in the form of joint efforts by neighboring counties across boundaries in Scandinavia is of growing importance. However, much remains to be done to maximize these efforts. Grand schemes for joint action do exist within the field of regional planning, especially in the case of Öresund, but also to some extent concerning the North Cape area.

The Nordic Council has passed several recommendations asking for different types of joint action with regard to the North Cape. For example, in 1958 it recommended joint exploitation of natural resources in this area (No. 23.1958), the prerequisites to which were jointly built and developed road projects (No. 23.1958) and airline connections (No. 21.1958). Foreseeing the successful implementation of these recommendations, which only occurred in part, the Nordic Council also recommended that steps be taken to further the North Cape as a tourist attraction (No. 14.1959). Although there has been rather meager success in the primary economic development of the region, there has been success with regard to road and airline connections. Questions pertaining to the North Cape are also discussed at some length by the Norden Association, under the auspices of which the so-called North Cape conferences have been held on a regular basis.

---

*In Sweden these policies are called *län*; in Norway, *fylker*; and in Denmark, *amt*.

Some work of regional importance is also carried out within the private sector.

Regional coordination in the North Cape region has also involved dealings with the Soviet Union, which has a joint boundary with Norway in the north. The Norwegian-Soviet border was kept open for a time during the summer of 1965, and Scandinavians were allowed to cross into the USSR at Boris Gleb without visa, although they had to surrender their passports to the border guards during their visits. Alcohol could be purchased cheaply by the visiting Scandinavians. Some Norwegian contact was made with the governor of Murmansk. No similar traffic of Soviet citizens into Scandinavia occurred.

Of considerably greater importance, perhaps both from an intermediary and a long-term point of view, is the Öresund region. The idea of a permanent connection between Sweden and Denmark which would tie the Scandinavian peninsula to the European continent, has existed since the end of the nineteenth century. A Swedish-Danish commission has for some time been studying a project involving the building of a bridge across the waters at Öresund. For several reasons it seems that the final decision will take some time. Since the project is a huge and costly one, with estimates of $200 million or more, the stakes are rather high. There are several alternatives for the connecting link, one of which is connected to the grand plan of the Saltholm Airport. Because of this, the various interests involved naturally tend to complicate matters. One of the alternatives put forward has been a tunnel under the water.

A permanent connection in this region would be of vital interest not only to Denmark and Sweden, but also to Norway and the rest of Scandinavia. For this reason the Nordic Council has been actively involved in the Öresund project.

OVERALL EVALUATION

For the communications sphere as a whole, the role of the Nordic Council has been important and decisive. In part the expansion of organized Nordic coordination in this field is a direct result of the institutions and working methods of the council. The steady stream of resolutions passed and reports presented has formed the basis for continued piecemeal coordination. Partly because of this, and following naturally from the groundwork laid by the parliamentarians, attempts have been made to institutionalize the work and put it on a firmer basis. For example, in 1971 the council recommended that the governments set up a Nordic committee of high officials on a permanent basis to deal with questions regarding transport (No. 14.1971); the recommendation was successfully implemented. A council of traffic safety was also instituted in 1971, with special committees for research on traffic safety, for traffic legislation coordination, and for the solving of particular problems connected with the whole sector. This has resulted in an increase in bilateral cooperation as well.

A treaty of cooperation among the five Nordic countries in the field of transport and communication came into force on March 1, 1973. This treaty, which is parallel to the treaty of cultural cooperation, is based on the Helsinki Treaty. It deals with land, sea, and air transportation as well as with postal matters and telecommunications. It does not, however, include problems of road safety or international maritime and air transport policies. The treaty aims at strengthening and further developing the existing cooperation in these fields by promoting research, establishing uniform legislation and regulations, encouraging technical standardization, coordinating transport policies, and preparing common action at international conferences and in negotiations on transport and communication matters. This collaboration must, however, take due consideration of the other international obligations of the countries.

This treaty, and of course all the preparatory work that went into it, have brought about increased collaboration in air traffic in the North; liberalization of the rules of charter flights; and further cooperation regarding the network of transnational highways, tourism, and matters related to Öresund. Joint meetings have taken place between the Nordic Council of Ministers (the traffic ministers) and representatives from the Nordic Council for the purpose of discussing aspects of the practical implementation of the treaty and also of further integration in traffic and communication.

NOTES

1. See Frantz Wendt, The Nordic Council and Cooperation in Scandinavia (Copenhagen: Munksgaard, 1959), p. 74.

2. See Thor Störe, Nytten av Norden (Oslo: Foreningen Norden, 1969).

3. See Nordisk Udredningsserie, no. 8 (1962), p. 221.

4. See "Enkelte mellomriksveier mellom Norge og Sverige," Nordisk Udredningsserie, no. 3 (1965); "Mellanriksvag Kiruna-Nord Norge," Nordisk Udredningsserie, no. 3 (1957).

CHAPTER

9

INTEGRATION AND SOCIAL POLICY PLANNING

BACKGROUND

In the social field cooperation among the Nordic states began at the executive and administrative levels. It was, and still is, characterized by a functional orientation that has sprung from concrete and practical needs in the more or less natural intercourse of these closely related neighboring peoples. This kind of cooperation was already a fact when the Nordic Council first met in 1953. However, although it was both widespread and frequent, social cooperation among the states was neither coordinated nor centrally organized.

Governmental and private organizations responsible for the daily administration of social security, preventive medicine, labor inspection, and other welfare activities have felt the need for a closer and more regular contact and for discussion of common problems. This need expressed itself at an early stage. In 1907 the first regular cooperative arrangements for health insurance funds in Denmark, Sweden, and Norway were initiated. In 1909 the directors-general of the public health services in the Nordic states began to cooperate in planning elaborate legislation for the inspection of foodstuffs and to regulate other matters within their fields of competence. The previous year it had been decided that meetings of the state accident insurance representatives of the three above-mentioned countries were to continue on a more permanent basis, that is, every third year, and that these meetings were to take place in the national capitals of Sweden, Denmark, and Norway in rotation.

After World War I social cooperation became wider in scope, and representatives of the ministries of social affairs met at regular intervals. Since 1926 the Nordic ministers of social affairs have met every second year. A general social insurance congress has been held every third year since 1935. Following the setting up of the International Labor Organization (ILO), cooperation among the Nordic states in the social field increased even further. Each year since 1947, Denmark, Sweden, or Norway in turn has translated into its national language the report submitted by the director-general of the International Labor Office to the International Labour Conference. The Danish, Norwegian, or Swedish edition is then distributed in all three countries.

By 1953 the Nordic governments had established two permanent bodies of cooperation in the social field. These were the Nordic Committee on Social Policy, covering social security, social care, and child welfare, and the Nordic Labor Market Committee, which dealt with questions connected with the embryonic Nordic Common Labor Market. Bilateral reciprocity agreements in social security legislation were already in existence before 1952.

It was up to the Nordic Council, as the first comprehensive body for governmental cooperation, to carry this work further in accordance with the wishes of its interparliamentarian membership. The council works in the three main areas of the social field, in social policy making, in the Nordic labor market, and in health and hospital matters. The council works to strengthen the already existing net of cooperation among the member states and also to propose new action.

Although, as we have seen, the Nordic ministers of social affairs had been meeting on a regular basis before 1953, there were no meetings on such a basis for the government members responsible for health services and hospitals. For this reason the council recommended that such joint meetings be started on a Nordic basis. By 1958 this recommendation had been implemented.

Upon the request of the council the Nordic governments also carried out a recommendation of closer cooperation within the World Health Organization (WHO). The council had suggested preparatory meetings for the Nordic representatives to WHO, and such meetings have been held since 1956.

As we have noted, the council has set up five permanent committees to prepare matters for its agenda. Like the other four committees, the committee on social policy meets both during and outside the council sessions. Normally it meets about three times a year.

It should be mentioned here that since 1962 the Nordic ministers of social affairs have been meeting regularly every second year. The minister of each country prepares a survey of developments in the social field during the previous year, which is then discussed by the participants. In addition, the ministers and collaborating experts discuss particular matters within the whole field. At the 1963 meeting, for example, there were four specific topics of concern: security of income during illness; the waiting period for additional retirement pensions; vocational training of adults; and help schemes and housing problems for the old. These meetings also supervise the activities of subordinate and other bodies, the most important of which is the Nordic Committee on Social Policy.

SOCIAL POLICY AND PLANNING

As Heikki Waris has pointed out, in the Nordic states the concept of social policy differs somewhat from the German, English, and French conceptions. The Scandinavian concept is broader and more inclusive than the German Sozialpolitik, since the latter does not include social work (Fursorge) or housing policy. Also, Nordic social policy is more specific and limited than the French concept of politique sociale, or the somewhat loose English term, social policy.[1]

Social welfare statistics for the Nordic countries have been published in English for more than 20 years, as well as in the Scandinavian languages. Tables 2 and 3 show the main categories that make up Nordic social policy and the distribution by country. Apart from describing the actual spending, the table demonstrates the difference in emphasis among the Nordic states, which has been one of the problems faced by the Nordic Council in its attempt to integrate these services.

The primary task of the council in the social policy field has been to collect and consolidate the existing intra-Nordic agreements into a general convention on Scandinavian social security. In 1953 the council recommended that the governments take up this work and set up groups of experts to work under its direction (No. 6.1953). A draft convention, signed by the Nordic ministers of social affairs in Copenhagen in 1955 and ratified by all five governments, took effect on November 1, 1956. (See Chapter 2.) The convention was to be applied with a minimum of administrative regulations and machinery.

Sweden has introduced general supplementary pensions that also include retirement pensions, which are in principle graded according to previous payments of contributions, which again vary with income. In Sweden the general supplementary pensions are higher than in the other Scandinavian states. Taken together, for example, the two types of old-age benefits correspond in principle to two-thirds of the previous earnings of the pensioner during the 15 financially best years of his or her life. Although the Swedish arrangement does not come under the 1955 Nordic social convention, all those who live on a permanent basis in Sweden and receive income from work in that country are entitled to the benefits of the scheme. According to the convention of 1955, the citizens of one Nordic country living in another

TABLE 2

Social Security Expenditures, 1973/74
(in millions of national currency units)

Type of Expenditure	Denmark	Greenland	Finland	Iceland	Norway	Sweden
Health	10,493	78.5	3,066	4,137	7,080	18,265
Health insurance and corresponding arrangements	3,133	—	877	3,677	2,196	6,053
Total in cash	1,312	—	311	171	847	3,177
Public health and hospital services	6,030	—	2,077	388	4,459	11,122
Care of mentally deficient	807	—	112	17	268	723
Dental care	523	—	—[a]	55	157	367
Occupational injuries and workers' protection	441	0.9	266	178	104	308
Occupational injuries insurance	401	0.9[b]	261	138	87	253
Workers' protection	40	—	5	40	17	55
Unemployment	1,172	1.4	561	56	296	2,638
Unemployment insurance	854	—	175	48	182	638
Employment services	99	1.4	42	8	69	332
Retraining of unemployed	209	—	107	—	—	630
Public work for unemployed	10	—	237	—	45	1,038
Old age, disability	15,131	23.2	4,920	2,891	8,089	16,681
Basic pensions	10,715	18.7	2,316	2,667	6,902	11,372
Old-age pensions	7,407	14.5	1,585	1,877	4,543	7,188
Disability pensions	3,050	4.2	680	682	1,947	1,865
Widows' pensions	258	—	51	108	412	705
Supplementary pensions	110	—	2,223	137	739	2,941
Rehabilitation and employment of partially disabled	742	—	73	68	114	377
Old age homes and pensioners' dwellings	2,856	3.9	293	19	213	1,145
Homehelp services for the aged or handicapped	708	0.6	15	—	121	846
Family welfare	5,513	27.4	1,003	1,944	1,972	7,371
General children's allowances	2,110	3.7	371	1,138	1,344	2,369
Housing supplements	258	1.3	51	—	15	1,188
Child pensions	207	3.6 (Child pensions and Maintenance advances)	53	243	201	167
Maintenance advances	140		18	139	43	343
Care of mothers and babies	472	1.6	64	123	86	510
Total in cash	290	—	61	93	69	498
Day nurseries, nursery schools	1,568	14.4[c]	168	175	73	1,315
Homehelp services (for housewives)	96	—	34	26	60	288
Holidays for housewives and children	12	—	7	22	2	5
Public child welfare	650	2.1	95	78	140	521
School meals	—	0.7	142	—	8	665
Public assistance	410	4.9	177	128	173	600
Social assistance	300	3.3	144	125	135	563
Other assistance	110	1.6	33	3	38	37
Compensation for personal injury during military service or in wartime	93	—	426	—	323	25
Total social services	33,253	136.3	10,419	9,334	18,037	45,888
Estimated cost of tax reductions for children	—	—	169	720	90	—
Total expenditures	33,253	136.3	10,588	10,054	18,127	45,888

Note: Figures are partly provisional.
[a]Included under public health and hospital services.
[b]Paid compensations.
[c]Includes children's homes.
Source: Yearbook of Nordic Statistics, 1975 (Stockholm: Nordic Council and Statistical Secretariat, 1976).

TABLE 3

Finance of Social Security Expenditures, 1950-73
(in percent)

Country	Central Government	Local Authorities	Employers	Insured Persons (contributions and special taxes)
Denmark				
1950	57	28	3	12
1960	59	23	3	15
1973	65	17	4	14
Finland				
1950	50	19	24	7
1960	42	24	24	10
1973	26	18	46	10
Iceland				
1950	37	30	9	24
1960	51	24	9	16
1973	81	9	8	2
Norway				
1950	28	40	8	24
1960	24	33	17	26
1973	19	18	39	24
Sweden				
1950	57	28	5	10
1960	43	29	6	22
1973	33	30	24	13

Source: Yearbook of Nordic Statistics, 1975 (Stockholm: Nordic Council and Statistical Secretariat, 1976).

are automatically entitled to the same benefits as the citizens of the country in which they reside. Like all other nonnationals who stay permanently in a Nordic country, they have the right to medical care and prosthetic and other aids.

As for health insurance, the principle was introduced by the 1955 convention that a member of a health insurance plan in one Nordic country should automatically have the right to medical care during a temporary stay in another country. A special agreement of 1956 lays down detailed regulations for the transfer of membership during temporary stays. Finland introduced compulsory health insurance in 1964, which makes it possible for her to take part in this aspect of Nordic integration.

THE NORDIC LABOR MARKET

Continuing the work of the by then defunct Nordic Parliamentary Committee on Freer Scandinavian Communications, at its first session in 1953 the Nordic Council passed some resolutions dealing with mobility of labor. In its recommendation No. 9.1953, the council requested that the governments abolish the system of working permits for Nordic citizens within Scandinavia. This was successfully carried out, and by May 22, 1954, the system of permits was abandoned and an agreement to this effect was signed by all the countries involved except Iceland. Several tens of thousands of workers have since taken advantage of the initial agreement and the fact that the introduction of the labor market was followed closely by the Nordic Social Security Convention in the following year. The most important exception to the general rule of free labor mobility is in the case of workers who are engaged in some activity that is dependent on public authorization. In this particular field, as we shall argue, the role of the Nordic Council has been very important.

The Nordic Common Labor Market is based upon the principle that the governments of the four countries shall endeavor to maintain full employment and that they keep one another informed of all plans to that end. The governments of Sweden, Denmark, Finland, and Norway have set up a joint body, the Nordic Labor Market Committee, the major task of which has been to study labor market developments, manpower movements, and statistics and to set up guidelines for coordination of employment services.

The committee deals with placement, vocational guidance, manpower training, and shortages of skilled manpower as well as with the special problems on the labor market of women, of young people, of the aged, and of refugees. It has also dealt with problems connected with regional planning. The Nordic Labor Market Committee meets once a year, or at times more frequently.

Seminars have been organized, with coordination of training and adult education as the main objective. Possible reforms in the statistical registration of labor from other countries have been discussed. There are some differences among the countries with regard to statistical information, and not all the countries have equally good statistics covering the residents of other Nordic countries who are working in their territory. The point has been made in the committee that the Nordic states define labor market policy, social insurance, and assistance schemes in somewhat different ways and that more uniform definitions would be advantageous.

Most important in this context, clarification has been requested in relation to labor market policies in general. At present, it seems, the common labor market has been accepted as far as free movement of labor is concerned, but without an accompanying common labor market policy. Furthermore, there are important differences with regard to regional and social planning among the Nordic states, which would have to be reconciled before full integration in this sector may be said to have occurred.

Although too much should probably not be made of this point, I would nevertheless briefly focus on one major difference between two elements of regional planning that in the final analysis confronts the Nordic Committee. In Sweden there have been considerable movements of labor from the northern part of the country to the middle and southern parts, movements that have often been officially encouraged for the sake of relieving shortages of labor. In Norway, on the other hand, a somewhat different policy has been followed more or less consistently. Rather than moving workers out of the northern areas to industrial centers in the middle or south of the country, Norway takes direct measures to encourage the larger percentage of the population of northern Norway to stay on in that part of the country. Similar examples of this kind of thinking exist, for example, in Britain. Also, attempts have been made to take industry out to such areas, often at high cost, to maintain a more or less balanced population, although about 12.5 percent of the total population lives in the three counties north of the Arctic circle. It has been considered important strategically to maintain a relative density in comparison with the Murmansk area in the neighboring Soviet Union. It is also considered important for social and cultural reasons. In addition there is a reluctance, in Norwegian administrative thinking as well as generally, to promote too much the growth in the large population centers. The reasons may even go deeper than that. For example, the opposition to cultural centralization that is expressed in several segments of Norwegian political opinion has a basis that may be partly romantic and partly rational. Here at any rate are some of the basic difficulties, or realities, with which the Nordic Labor Market Committee eventually has to come to grips.

The Nordic Common Market Convention applied primarily to persons employed in the private sector. Neither civil servants nor professional people were included. The Nordic Council, therefore, decided to work for an extension of the labor market to include categories that had initially been excluded. In a proposal to the 1959 session, the council suggested that a free labor market for professional people would result in a more effective utilization of such manpower and that therefore it ought to be carried out. Professional education, according to the Nordic Council, differed too little among the countries for the right to practice these professions to be restricted along national lines. This was also the case in many areas of law, in which the council had worked hard for the introduction of similar and in some cases identical laws in all the states. The council then suggested that the governments abolish all present obstacles to a free market for professional employment and create the freest conditions possible.

In addition to this general declaration of intent, the Nordic Council adopted a step-by-step method of functional integration. Nevertheless, it proved to be more difficult to establish a labor market for the professions than had at first been expected by the more active Nordist members of the council. For example, a common market for dentists and physicians was the subject of at least three different recommendations (Nos. 14.1954, 7.1957, and 2.1960) before the council approved the results. By 1965 the scheme was being implemented by Sweden, Denmark, and Norway, but Finland reported that she would need at least two more years to carry out the legal work considered necessary. Having completed their studies in one of the three countries in which this common market is in use, Nordic citizens may under certain conditions practice in any of the countries. The conditions referred to are usually limited to specific social and medical additions to the medical or odontological curriculum. This, however, poses little difficulty, since the legislation in this field is similar to start with, and legal integration makes it increasingly so. Iceland has not taken part in this work.

As a rule the labor market is entirely free throughout the region for most categories of employment. None of the countries extend privileges to their own citizens. The Nordic Council is constantly trying to extend the general Nordic labor market by introducing numerous specific categories of employment of a nonmanual nature. Medical personnel and dentists are now successfully integrated with regard to employment within Scandinavia, and the council is attempting to incorporate veterinary surgeons, psychologists, librarians, officers in the merchant marines, accountants, druggists, and teachers.

Some of these categories seem to be easier to integrate than others. In some areas there has been little integration, or none at all. For example, the council has so far been almost entirely unsuccessful, for no fault of its own, at integrating Nordic school teachers into the general labor market. After several years, very little progress has been made in this field.

This shows, I think, the inherent difficulties under which the council is still working. School teaching is seemingly a neutral field; the difficulty of integrating it shows the extent to which the national states, or rather the national administrations, continue to be the decision makers. By renewed efforts, by reintroducing the matter in a different context, by keeping up the pressure, and perhaps by making a different recommendation altogether, the Nordic Council may succeed in bringing about integration among teachers at a later stage.

HEALTH AND HOSPITALS

The top medical officials of Scandinavia have been meeting more or less regularly since 1929. As in many other fields, however, the participants have failed to undertake any coordinated efforts. The importance of its early tradition has largely been the exchange of information, which by itself aided in the formulation of a common Nordic policy to be applied within the World Health Organization.

In 1953 the Nordic Council requested a careful examination within the whole field of health and hospitals. The purpose of this would be to submit, by the next session if possible, a complete list of the problems existing in this field concerning which joint Nordic action could or should be taken. This, as we have seen, has been a favorite way of approaching the different areas in which the council is now working. By choosing this approach, the council has managed to further legitimize much of what it does in the minds of many groups. The list was submitted at the following session in 1954, as requested. The report from the governments contained detailed data from a number of subgroups, within the wider field of health and hospital matters, in which joint action was thought to be useful and/or necessary.

The council then proceeded to investigate the report, on the basis of which it adopted eight recommendations addressed to the Nordic governments. For example, the council wanted better and more thoroughgoing cooperation among the Scandinavian hospitals. When visiting any of the Nordic states, any Nordic citizen should be entitled to the same hospital benefits as the citizens of that state. The council also urged cooperation with regard to the exchange of medical specialists. This would, the council suggested, be very useful in the case of epidemics. The resolution (No. 10.1954) has to some extent been carried out through the extensive general social security convention of 1956. Since December 1956, Denmark, Norway, Iceland, and Sweden have also had an agreement covering the transfer of sickness benefits for people changing their addresses from one country to another. A committee that had been set up to investigate the problems connected with boundary medical services submitted its report in 1958. Since then there has been some harmonization of social and medical legislation, whereby boundary physicians in both Norway and Sweden may practice on either or both sides of the boundary according to need.

OVERALL EVALUATION

Within the social field, questions of the environment and the Nordic labor market have been discussed frequently and have received a good deal of attention. Insofar as the Nordic Environmental Convention and the Convention for the Protection of the Baltic Marine Environment were introduced in 1974, that year may be considered an important one for environmental policy.

Since the end of World War II a major goal in the social sector has been to turn the Nordic states into one unit with respect to the social rights and responsibilities of citizens throughout the area. A citizen of any Nordic country should be allowed to travel freely throughout the region, with the absolute minimum of administrative interference, to take work where he or she wants, and to make full use on an equal basis of social services, medical and hospital facilities, and pensions and social security. Largely because of piecemeal successive work by the Nordic Council, among other groups, this goal has largely been achieved. Through the Labor Market Convention and the Social Security Convention, the Nordic states were the first European group of states that developed a community in this field.

In addition, the gradual harmonization of social legislation in many important areas has cemented this unity together, partly by conventions and partly by microintegrative efforts carried out by the Nordic Council, the importance of which cannot easily be overestimated in this entire field. The fact that total harmonization of all social legislation has not, and probably will not, be achieved should not be allowed to overshadow the particular successes that have been achieved.

Furthermore, absolute harmonization may in fact not be necessary if the goal is to maintain some element of diversity in unity, which is manifestly the case. We touch here on an important point. The question is not, as several of the integration theorists seem to assume, how to go on integrating indefinitely, seemingly under the assumption that steadily advancing integration is always superior to limited or piecemeal integration.

Since I have argued that there is an interconnection of institutions, men, and methods, presumably the problem is one of finding the point at which the maximum of useful and welcomed coordination is achieved. In other words, it is important to find the point of diminishing returns as far as integration is concerned.

To a large extent the social sector is a success story; but it is nevertheless curious to note how the natural connections among the various areas of integration seem to have been deliberately downplayed. Take the stillborn NORDEK proposal, for example. In this general economic and social scheme for Scandinavia, large areas of local and regional planning were seemingly ignored. Although there have been, as we have seen, some important differences between Norway and Sweden, for example, with regard to regional planning, the successful implementation of NORDEK would almost certainly have led to strong concentrations of both capital and population in two or three large regions in Scandinavia, including Stockholm-Mälaren, Öresund, Gothenburg-Oslo, and possibly southern Finland. This would have created some problems that NORDEK in its proposed form might have been largely unable to handle.

The Nordic Council paid some attention to these problems, as well as to the related ones arising out of the possible expansion of the European Community to include some or all of the Nordic states. It would seem that the present trends of development could possibly lead to a situation in which the Nordic part of this enlarged community would play the role of a somewhat depressed outer area, in terms of productivity and concentration, if the trend was allowed to go on unchecked. The question of whether the Nordic countries will be able to protect their social policy and legislative structure and their common labor market in the face of different forms of membership or association agreements with the EEC depends to a large extent on the evolution of the EEC itself, as well as on developments within Scandinavia.

To a lesser but far from unimportant extent it would also partly depend upon the degree to which the Nordic statesmen could muster some sort of consensus, ideally through institutions of their own design that were both credible and sufficiently important politically. The future importance of the Nordic Council, for example, will depend upon the outcome of these developments, as well as on the ability of the politicians to act in agreement.

NOTE

1. See Heikki Waris, "The Social Policy of the Nordic Countries," paper read at the Hasselby Conference, Stockholm, Sweden, June 2-4, 1965.

CHAPTER

10

INTEGRATION AND CULTURE

EARLY WORK

One of the strongest unifying forces in Nordic integration has probably been the common cultural background of the peoples inhabiting the region. There seems to be a fairly widespread feeling among many of the inhabitants that for various reasons they belong to the same cultural group.[1] Culturally, to a larger extent than in almost any other field, the Nordic countries are in fact developing the characteristics of what could become a community. It remains to be seen, however, to what extent this is more than just a vague feeling of cultural proximity. What is more important is the question of whether this spirit of cultural community feeling in fact has a cementing effect on Nordic integration. More specifically, what, if any, would be the concrete manifestations of the above-mentioned cultural characteristics?

First, the social and economic conditions are, as we have seen, quite similar. People feel that they share the same values and aims in many instances, such as on some of the issues concerning welfare economics and politics.[2] There is agreement on the main goals but not necessarily of the methods of achieving them.

The ideals of legal justice and parliamentary democracy, for example, are nearly identical in the Scandinavian states, according to national leaders and foreign observers alike. The roots of cultural similarity go back far into history. With the exception of the 90 percent of the Finns, whose mother tongue is Finnish, and the Icelandics, all the Scandinavians speak a similar language. The religious similarities are also obvious to the observer. All the Nordic churches are Lutheran. Their break with the Catholic Church occurred at about the same time, in about 1530.

These similarities have no doubt been of great importance both historically and culturally; to deny this would be foolish. However, two main observations should be added for the sake of clarifying the Scandinavian case. First, cultural affinities, or the sense of belonging to a cultural community, were not related to formal political union. That is to say, the feeling of belonging to a cultural union or community has never been stronger than since the five states all achieved their national independence.[3]

Second, much of the important work of cultural cooperation has been organized and carried out on a private basis, rather than on a state level. Cultural cooperation is so comprehensive and many-faceted that it is next to impossible to draw the entire picture of it all. Several large organizations that are broadly based and that meet on a regular basis are actively involved in working for intensified cultural unity in Scandinavia. Some congresses meet at regular intervals, dealing with a variety of questions involving many aspects of cultural life. Specific organizations and agencies dedicated to certain tasks, including those of education, research, art, and cultural programs, are in existence. The most important of the larger organizations of this type may include the Norden Associations, the League of Norden Associations, the Nordic Council for Fine Arts, and the Council of Nordic Composers.[4]

A change took place in Nordic cultural cooperation following the end of World War II. At the 25th sessional meeting of the Nordic Interparliamentary Assembly in 1946, the delegates suggested that a permanent coordinating organization for cultural questions be set up. Meeting in the fall of that year, the ministers of education recommended that the Nordic governments set up a commission the function of which should be to further Nordic cultural cooperation, particularly for the fields of academic and scientific matters, education, and adult education and the arts. Six members from each of the countries should be appointed, to deal with the following three main sections: academic and scientific matters; educational questions; and adult education and art. By 1948 this commission was fully constructed, and it held its first meeting in Stockholm during February of that year.

The Nordic Cultural Commission became a consultative organization. Its three sections were set up as Nordic committees. The delegates from each country also formed national groups, with two parliamentarians to take part in every group. More important, the commission itself was given the right of initiative. It became responsible to the Nordic governments, which could ask it to investigate certain questions, and it has submitted regular reports to the Nordic Council since 1952.[5] The council publishes these reports in its own minutes, and it has referred questions to be examined to the Nordic Cultural Commission.

The Nordic Cultural Commission worked on a number of questions concerning cultural affairs, education, and research. The scope of its activities was wide, and the results were good. Marine biology, for example, benefited from the work carried out by the Nordic Cultural Commission, as did several other subareas within the field of culture and research.

Research in marine biology has been going on in Sweden since 1877, in Norway since 1892, and in Finland since 1901. Denmark has had no previous marine biological institution. By 1945 it was clear to the Scandinavians that their own research was falling very much behind that of the great powers.

The only way to combat this trend and prevent Scandinavia being left entirely out in the cold would be by integration. For this reason the cultural commission set up a committee to investigate the possibilities of the above-mentioned kind of integration. The committee started its work in 1954, and it submitted its proposals for comprehensive cooperation in marine biological research in the following year. It was unrealistic to assume that each of the Scandinavian states would be able to train experts for each and every subfield of marine biology. This would be too expensive an undertaking for the individual countries, and would be wasteful in terms of financial resources, man-hours, and personnel. It would work better on a Scandinavian basis. The Nordic Kollegium for Marine Biology, consisting of the leaders of the already existing marine biological stations throughout Scandinavia, was set up in 1956. After a trial period of a few years, the plans had been adopted, and Nordic marine biological research was fully integrated. Each country concentrates its efforts upon one or more special areas of research, so as to prevent overlap and to have as sensible as possible a division of labor among the participating countries. The Swedes, for example, emphasize anatomy and morphology in their work, as well as analysis of the micro plant life of the ocean bed. The Danes concentrate upon forms of animal life on the sea bottom, and the Finns dedicate their efforts toward particular questions of oceanography. The Norwegians, for easily understandable reasons, undertake research on the economics of fishing and fisheries, as well as the impact of these categories of activities upon the overall economy. All results and findings are immediately made available to the Scandinavian region as a unit. In addition, a comprehensive educational exchange program of marine biologists has been initiated, in such a way that experts in this field will receive parts of their education elsewhere in Scandinavia.

Despite such examples of success, the Nordic Cultural Commission received some criticism at the beginning of the 1960s to the effect that its organization was ineffective. The Nordic Council therefore suggested in 1962 that the commission enter into fresh discussions with various departments in order to work out new rules for its activity. The council took the view that the commission should become an effective organization for coordination of national as well as inter-Nordic and regional aspects of regional policy. The commission should also be given wider authority as a government organization, and improvements should be made both financially and in regard to personnel.* It should also be given the right to use the investigatory machinery of the ministries or departments in question and be entitled to the assistance of experts if it so desired. The new statutes of the Nordic Cultural Commission took force from January 1, 1964, in accordance with the above-mentioned suggestions by the Nordic Council.

If, as I have asserted, close cultural cooperation is a natural prerequisite for solidarity and successful cooperation in other fields, it is easy to see that the Nordic Council should devote great attention to this field; and so it has. It has divided its efforts among the following main categories of cooperation: research, education, and cultural exchange. In addition, the council has undertaken several individual projects, such as the awarding of annual prizes for music and literature. It has also paid attention to the role of Iceland in Nordic collaboration and has taken upon itself the task of spreading information about Scandinavia abroad.

RESEARCH

Research, particularly in the natural sciences, makes great demands on both financial and human resources. Therefore, the Nordic Council, since its first session in 1953, has been trying to establish the widest possible cooperation among the Nordic states in this field, with a clear view of integrating as many functions and services as possible. One of the most comprehensive demands originating in the Nordic Council was incorporated in a recommendation passed in its 1961 session, in which it proposed that the governments, working with the Nordic Cultural Commission, should produce a plan for extensive cooperation in education and research during the next three years. More important, perhaps, was a request that the governments work out an order of priorities for tasks to be undertaken and set up a permanent coordinating organization, the function of which should be to plan a systematic division of labor for Scandinavia as a whole within the whole field of research and scientific education.

---

*Each national group should consist of three top civil servants with influence and responsibility within their own departments and six representatives of cultural life in each of the countries.

This was asking for too much. When they reported the recommendation back to the Nordic Council at its 1964 session, the governments rejected it as impractical. Instead they suggested a different approach involving educational planning based on cooperation among the ministers of education, maintenance of certain joint institutions, and a limited division of labor concerning specific subjects and specialties. In other words, the decisions were still to be taken on a national level, but with extensive cooperation among the ministers and some task sharing and joint planning.

The Swedish Minister of Education, Ragnar Edenman, suggested a different type of approach to the problem. First, the planning of higher education in Scandinavia ought to be based upon cooperation among the ministers of education. Second, the central subjects of education should be built and structured on the national level by making use of already existing institutions and also by investing in new ones, such as universities and special colleges. Nordic cooperation should not prevent a comprehensive national building of education, to be carried out as swiftly as possible. Edenman made the following distinctions with regard to Nordic cooperation projects:

1. There should be joint institutions in one of the Nordic countries, such as the school of journalism in Arhus, Denmark, where courses have been given since 1957 for journalists from Norway, Denmark, and Sweden. Another example is the Nordic Institute of Marine Law, situated in Oslo.

2. These should be joint institutions for the study of different subjects at different Nordic universities and graduate schools. For an example he mentioned the Nordic School of Home Economics, where subjects were studied in Oslo, Arhus, and Gothenburg respectively for a Nordic degree.

3. There should be a division of labor whereby certain subjects and disciplines would be taken as specialties at different Nordic schools, such as Celtic at the University of Oslo; history of medicine at Copenhagen University; and special pedagogics at Jyvaskyla, Finland. A chair of criminology was created in 1964 at Stockholm University, as well as a chair of modern Chinese languages, both of which were expected to be of great importance to the whole of Scandinavia.[6]

The Nordic Council then switched its emphasis to certain fields that it considered particularly useful for cooperative and integrative efforts. Some of these fields were criminology, Arctic medicine, alcohol research, marine biology, oceanology, technical research, agricultural research, transport economy, consumer research, animal husbandry, and air and water pollution research.

The Nordic Council arranged a conference in Helsinki in 1965, dealing with problems in Scandinavian research and with research projects. The participants were governmental and organizational representatives, individual researchers, and leaders of various Scandinavian research institutes. The conference dealt with tasks, resources, and planning, as well as with the profitability and viability of the already existing projects and institutes.

The Nordic Council showed an early interest in cooperation for the peaceful use of nuclear energy. At its fourth session in 1956, the council recommended that the governments appoint a committee to investigate possible projects for nuclear cooperation. This recommendation was successfully implemented, and in 1957 the council recommended that a Nordic institute for theoretical nuclear physics be set up. This recommendation (No. 19.1957) was reported back to the council, which concluded that it had been carried out to its satisfaction, and an institute called the Nordic Institute of Theoretical Nuclear Physics (NORDITA) was set up on a temporary basis and connected with the University of Copenhagen. This was the beginning of the Nordic Institute of Theoretical Nuclear Physics, headed by Nils Bohr of Denmark. Its budget for 1960 was as follows:

Country	Amount (in thousands of Danish kronen)
Denmark	150
Finland	140
Iceland	5
Norway	115
Sweden	240
Total	650

In the meantime the Nordic Council had successfully widened the field of nuclear cooperation to include several aspects of nuclear energy production. A committee proposal for the setting up of a joint Scandinavian body for nuclear cooperation was unanimously endorsed at the fifth session of the Nordic Council in Helsinki in 1957. The council added a provision for the extension of nuclear cooperation to include industrial production of reactors and equipment. This was successfully carried out. By 1973 the budget of NORDITA was 4.5 million Danish kroner.

Another area of successful work by the Nordic Council has been that of criminology. At its 1959 session, for example, the council recommended that a joint research institute of criminology be created on the basis of reports submitted to the council at its request. The recommendations were successfully implemented, insofar as a Nordic Research Council on Criminology was set up and held its first meeting in Oslo in the fall of 1961.

An example of useful research work by the Nordic Council is furnished in the field of marine law. By 1959 the council had recommended that a Nordic institute for marine law be set up and that it be based at the University of Oslo. The education ministers, when meeting in Helsinki in March 1961, discussed this recommendation, and they agreed to set up this institute, which has been in existence since 1962, headed by a Norwegian professor.

Several of the Nordic states have national research councils. Since 1947 a Nordic council for research has been in existence, dealing with research in the natural sciences, in some applied sciences, and in engineering. Nordic Research (NORDFORSK) has also been actively involved in arranging seminars, conferences, and exchanges of scholars. The Nordic Council has, for understandable reasons, paid some attention to NORDFORSK. As early as 1957, for example, the council proposed that NORDFORSK be allowed to budget research money regardless of national considerations. NORDFORSK has also produced reports at the request of the council.

EDUCATION

The field of research is closely related to that of education. Successful cooperation in research depends to some extent on cooperation in, and coordination of, programs at the preresearch level in the educational systems of the countries involved. Subsequently two goals have been kept clear. First, basic education is considered to be of equal value in all of the Scandinavian states, with the practical consequences fully accepted.

Second, the Nordic element in education is maintained. This does not imply excessive Scandinavian nationalism; rather it means an emphasis on the joint cultural experiences of the past. The Nordic Council has passed several recommendations dealing with instruction in Nordic languages and literature in the elementary and secondary schools, and most of these recommendations have been successfully implemented.[7] The council has also been working for more radio programs about Scandinavia, aimed at schools, and for educational tours and exchanges of teachers as well as pupils. As early as 1953 the Nordic Council recommended that Scandinavian students be allowed to write part exams, such as Christmas and Easter exams, anywhere in Scandinavia and be given credits for the same in their home countries. At a conference organized by the Nordic Cultural Commission in 1957, plans were drawn up for Scandinavian recognition of subjects such as botany and history, exams which could be taken anywhere. This trend has continued.

In order to enable Nordic students to spend any period, long or short, at universities or teaching institutions outside their own countries, the council has been working toward the institution of student loans and scholarships to be made available by the Nordic governments. One of the results of the council's work in this field has been the so-called incentive scholarships, several hundreds of which were made available by the governments to students furthering their education elsewhere in Scandinavia.

The question of exchanges of university lecturers was taken up by the Nordic Council as early as 1953. This problem had been studied by the Nordic Cultural Commission since 1947. There has been some success in this area, but the obstacles are surprisingly hard to remove. Although the Nordic countries have all adopted programs of frequent exchanges of lecturers, the open labor market of university employees has not yet materialized.

The Council has been successful in forming a Scandinavian labor market for people with medical training, but doctors are in demand throughout Scandinavia, as are dentists, which explains why this kind of integration has been easier to carry out. The council has been trying to institute the same system of open employment for nurses, midwives, veterinarians, druggists, and pharmacists, to mention a few, with little direct success so far.

The council has directed its attention toward graduate education in several fields. For example, in 1956 it recommended that a Nordic program of instruction for journalists from all over Scandinavia be set up at the University of Arhus in Denmark. The need for such a program was evidently realized by the governments, and the recommendation (No. 2.1956) was reported back to the council as successfully implemented. A school of journalism was set up in Arhus in 1958, offering an annual course of three months for students from all over Scandinavia. The participants in these courses are generally seasoned Nordic journalists, although there are some newcomers to the profession among them. The council has also recommended that special stipends be made available to the participants at the school.

With the help of WHO, a course in further education in the field of public health has been given in Gothenburg since 1953. Following a recommendation from the Nordic Council in 1954, investigations were made for a proposed Nordic institute of public health. Formal decisions were made by the governments in 1962, and a chair of public health was created within the new institute.

Finally, the council has successfully worked for the setting up of a center for the Nordic folk high school movement, that is, a cultural center for teachers, journalists, and youth leaders, as recommended in 1954 (No. 18.1954). The governments have contributed to the folk high school in Kungälv, Sweden, to the extent that it now serves as a focal point for the Nordic folk high school movement. Several conferences covering a wide variety of topics are held on a regular basis at this school, thanks to the initial pressures by the Nordic Council and the joint financial efforts by the governments.

CULTURAL EXCHANGE

The work of the Nordic Council in this field falls roughly into three categories: cultural and artistic exchange among the Nordic states; joint Nordic representation abroad; and direct involvement in cultural exchange and planning of joint projects. Children's books and educational films are now imported freely from one Scandinavian state to another, thanks to the work of the Nordic Council during the first few years of its existence. The council has also been responsible for an increased exchange of Scandinavian stage performers and other artists, as well as for increased cooperation regarding musical performers. A recommendation asking for joint Nordic representation in the arts at the Biennale Exhibition in Venice in 1955 led to the construction of a joint pavilion there that has been used since 1962. A scheme for a joint international edition of some 80 volumes of Nordic prose and poetry has been more difficult to carry out, and no action has come of it.

The Nordic Council participates directly in cultural cooperation, partly as a result of its own resolutions. In a recommendation by the 1961 session (No. 1.1961), the council proposed that an annual prize for Nordic literature be set up. This recommendation was successfully implemented, and the prize has been awarded annually since 1962. A similar prize has been awarded for a Nordic musical composition each third year since 1963.

One of the most interesting projects in cultural integration has been the creation of the Nordic Cultural Fund, which is jointly administered with a budget of some 5 million Danish kroner. The cultural fund, which is financed by the governments of the Nordic states, disposes of the money on its own authority, according to criteria of Nordic "cultural importance" that it decides upon by itself.

Like the other committees of the Nordic Council, the cultural committee, which is made up of 13 Nordic parliamentarians, meets at regular intervals throughout the year. Besides considering proposals made to the council and submitting recommendations for consideration by the council, the cultural committee has also taken the initiative with regard to the arranging of conferences and the issuing of publications. Examples that could be mentioned in this connection are the conferences at Biskop Arnø in Sweden in 1966 and in Copenhagen in 1968. The topic of discussion at the 1966 conference was

Nordic cooperation within the field of radio and television. The 1968 Copenhagen conference was dedicated to the question of the ends and means of cultural activities. Artists, persons involved in cultural work, scientists, and politicians from all the Nordic countries took part in the 1968 meeting. The direct feedback from both conferences included publication of the discussions and proposals that had been put forward.[8]

In addition to the cultural fund and the semiregular conferences in the field of culture, broadly speaking, and more specific areas such as research, education, and exchange of information, there is a network of bilateral funds among the Nordic countries. Nordic cultural cooperation is no longer regarded as additional to the economic cooperation and to cooperation in other fields, but rather as an essential prerequisite for successful efforts in the other sectors of social interaction.

Whether this point has been seized upon and utilized sufficiently in a political sense remains to be seen. In one sense the whole cultural field of Nordic cooperation seems curiously underplayed as a mechanism for bringing about closer unity. The dual nature of cultural closeness and active day-to-day cooperation is not fully understood by many of the observers who write about Scandinavian integration. It is often either underplayed or taken for granted by them. Again, the cultural infrastructure is supposed to be performing tasks or solving particular difficulties out of some nearly automatic principle. Neither of these ways of looking at the cultural field is correct. I shall return to this point later on.

The Nordic cultural community may well be emerging as an entity born out of geographic proximity, cultural similarity, similar and in some cases identical goals of development, and active collaboration across borders. However, this community is not self-sufficient, insofar as it looks upon itself in contrast to, or as an alternative to, European or global cooperation. An interesting statement that substantiates this view can be found in the common manifesto of the League of the Norden Associations of 1966, expressed as follows:

> If agreement is obtained in the near future on extensive economic co-operation designed to create a stronger community in Europe, the Nordic countries must also participate in such co-operation. We have the future in common with the other European peoples. We should therefore go to meet Europe. But we must do it in a closely co-operating North. Only in this way shall we be able to contribute to the development of Europe, jointly furthering at the same time our own economic interests, maintaining our social and political ideals and developing our form of civilization,

> everything within the larger framework and in a fruitful community with the other states and peoples of our Continent. And only a closely co-operating Europe will be able to give a valuable contribution to the development of the world.[9]

The Nordic countries do not want to be self-sufficient in the sense that they actively try to block out cultural influences or impulses from abroad. A few limited efforts of this type have been attempted within the national framework of Scandinavian states, apparently with little success.[10] The Nordic countries also do not wish to be alike. The most useful contribution that can be made by Nordic cultural cooperation would be the attempt to bridge the gap between the individual Nordic countries and the rest of the world.

I have argued that the cultural dimension of integration in Scandinavia provides a backbone of support for integrative measures in different fields of activity. Some of this effect comes naturally because of various proximities and similarities in background. However, it is exactly in this field that some of the less obvious but very real obstacles to integration lie. Past experiences of occupation, of power politics, and of superimposed unionism, coupled with natural differences in power and capacities, have given rise to suspicions of each other's motives among the Scandinavian countries. The background experiences of joint institutions have taught the Scandinavians that problems can often be solved better jointly; but familiarity may breed contempt, and it may be argued that to some extent this has taken place in Scandinavian relations. Suspicions can be based on insight, but they are just as often based on fear. For that reason suspicions are not always easy to remove, especially in older people, who may often know more, but are also often more prone to suspicion.

During the press debate about the NORDEK plans, the strongest opposition to the idea of a customs union as a basis of the project seemed to come from people, at least in Norway, who referred to the past union with Sweden and seemed to remember this clearly, or who had been told about it by their parents. Of course there were both political and purely economic arguments for or against this or any other union involving Norway and Sweden; but we are concerned with the psychology involved, which affects our concept of a cultural community and its viability.

Nevertheless, pressures exist within any community. They can even act as a cementing force by spurring groups or individuals to increase their activities and contributions, thus upgrading the general level of system activity, production, standard of living, interpersonal relationships, and the like. What matters is how ostensibly open the system is, how fair it is, and how easily demands and requests can be processed through the machinery of government and administration. Although the pressure of individual or aggregated suspicions increases the activity of an open society, it also tends to increase the speed with which some of those suspicions prove to be unfounded or exaggerated. The quicker they are killed off, the better for all concerned. Should they prove to be justified in some sense or other, then only genuine openness in the system will prove itself by eliminating the causes of the suspicions.

The upshot of this is that there may very well be a cultural community with pressures caused by deeply engrained suspicions on the part of some of the components of that community. If this community is sufficiently open, it can be activated toward solving problems and settling differences. The Nordic countries are well on their way toward constituting such a community.

During its 18th session the Nordic Council passed a recommendation (No. 21.1970) asking for the preparation of a Nordic cultural agreement prior to January 1972. Immediately following the Nordic Council session, the respective Nordic ministers of education and culture, whose portfolios vary somewhat, set up a working group to draft such an agreement. The proposal of the working group was presented in December 1970[11] and discussed during the 19th session of the Nordic Council in February 1971. After some debate, agreement was reached on the final form of a cultural agreement, which was signed in Helsinki on March 15, 1971; ratified by December 8, 1971; and in force by the beginning of 1972. An organizational committee, set up in April 1971 by the Nordic ministers of culture and education, was empowered to work out supplementary arrangements, which were submitted to the newly formed Nordic Council of Ministers for its approval.

THE SECRETARIAT FOR NORDIC CULTURAL COOPERATION

The cultural agreement, which took effect on January 1, 1972, was to some extent a summation of the results that had been achieved in different areas of the cultural sector, as well as a statement of intent to continue work along these lines. It was the first sectoral agreement within the framework of the Helsinki Treaty. Agreements are traditionally originated by the governments, but in this case the agreement came into being through, and was based on, continued cooperation among Nordic parliamentarians. The fact that the agreement was arrived at in this fashion is at least to some extent an illustration of the active and good contacts maintained by the Nordic Council with the respective ministries.

Within the framework of the cultural agreement, the leading organ is the Nordic Council of Ministers, which according to Article 9 of the agreement is the decision-making body. As we have already seen, the organization of the council of ministers is such that, although most cases will be within the fields of education and research, other ministers may also take part if necessary. Immediately below the council of ministers is the Civil Servants Committee for Nordic Cultural Cooperation, consisting of one member and one substitute from each country. This committee is charged with the task of coordinating Nordic cultural cooperation, preparing the agenda for the council, and carrying out the tasks given it by the council. The committee took over some of the tasks that had previously fallen to the Nordic Cultural Commission, which is now defunct.

There is also a joint secretariat for Nordic cultural cooperation set up in Copenhagen, the primary duties of which are to assist the council of ministers and the civil servants committee and to work as a secretariat for such consultative committees as are set up by the council of ministers. Since decisions by the council of ministers require unanimity, there is no element of supranationality in existence on the governmental side of Nordic cultural cooperation.

The Secretariat is, appropriately, divided into three sectors, which are education, research, and other cultural activities, each having a section chief and consultative committees. The secretariat is charged with giving the Nordic Council such factual information as is required, as well as with carrying out other tasks of a similar character.

The three central committees have somewhat different agendas because of the division of labor mentioned earlier. The Committee for Educational Questions concerns itself with consultation among the different national authoritative organs. If necessary this committee will be divided into subgroups. The Committee for Research Questions deals with questions of research principles and priorities. The Committee for Additional Cultural Activities concerns itself with the broader spectrum of the various projects and ideas in existence in the cultural sector at large and attempts to evaluate their relative importance. The cultural agreement does not detract from the functions of the Nordic Council; rather, it specifies with regard to financing and budgetary matters that the appropriate organs within the Nordic Council be given the opportunity to debate these matters.

To conclude, there have been two fairly important results from the cultural agreement, in particular with reference to the crash drive toward Nordic integration and to the parliamentary role played in it by the Nordic Council. First, the agreement, which in itself is very much a result of parliamentary pressure by the council, emphasizes the importance of the cultural community to the Nordic peoples, with particular and fairly detailed reference to education, research, and the cultural sector at large.

Second, the agreement may enable the Nordic countries to increase the effect of their total efforts with regard to the cultural sector. By pooling national resources in these areas, if this can be achieved, and by administering them on a Nordic level, money may be saved and better results obtained. The question on which the latter results depend is of course the extent to which the agreement will be utilized to the limits of its capacity. The cultural area is one in which other sectors are important and the interrelationships among them are seen. For this reason it is important that the Nordic Council be given all necessary assistance, that it be aided rather than hampered in its broad multisectoral approach to integration. In the cultural field this seems to be the pattern of the future.

NOTES

1. Frantz Wendt, for example, argues this point. See in particular The Nordic Council and Cooperation in Scandinavia (Copenhagen: Munksgaard, 1959), especially Chapter 2. American writers have, as a rule, tended to accept this view with little or no qualification. See for example Stanley Anderson, The Nordic Council: a Study of Scandinavian Regionalism (Stockholm: Norstedt's, 1968), and Amitai Etzioni, Political Unification: A Comparative Study of Leaders and Forces (New York: Holt, Rinehart and Winston, 1965).

2. Several U.S. textbooks on Scandinavian affairs tend to emphasize this point. See also Wendt, op. cit., and K. B. Andersen, "The Nordic Countries as a Cultural Community," speech to the Third Conference organized by the Nordic Council for International Organizations in Europe, at Hindsgavl, Denmark, September 29 to October 2, 1969.

3. See Wendt, op. cit.

4. For a detailed discussion of the various types of organizations working in the field of Nordic cultural cooperation, see Hans Sølvhøj, "Nordic Cultural Cooperation," speech given at the Hässelby Conference, Sweden, June 2-4, 1965.

5. See Nils Andren, "The Nordic Cultural Commission," The Norseman 15, no. 6 (November-December 1957).

6. See Olof Wallmen, Nordiska Radet och Nordisk Samarbete (Stockholm: Norstedt's, 1966).

7. See Nordisk Udredningsserie, no. 12 (1965).

8. See Nordisk Udredningsserie, no. 21 (1969).

9. League of Norden Associations, Common Manifesto (Stockholm: the League, 1966).

10. Ibid.

11. Nordisk Udredningsserie, no. 20 (1970).

CHAPTER

11

CONSEQUENCES FOR NATIONAL POLICIES

THE PATTERNS OF POLICY MAKING

This chapter is concerned with the relationship between the Nordic Council and the national bureaucracies. I will examine the patterns of policy making and try to establish to what extent, if at all, these patterns are determined or influenced by the Nordic Council.

Furthermore, I shall examine closely the relationship between the council and the national bureaucrats, especially those who have been actively involved with Nordic cooperation in general and with Nordic Council work in particular, and who have participated in some regular capacity in the implementation of the proposals of the Nordic Council, working them into national policies.

It would seem that this procedure implies two tasks. First, it will be necessary to consider whether the two types of bureaucracy referred to are interlocked, and if so to what extent. Second, I shall examine the impact of the Nordic Council on individual national bureaucrats in their roles as decision makers. Do they perceive the council as an important and useful instrument of cooperation? Do they think that its organization and methods function well? Do they find any particular faults with the way in which the work is carried out? Do they consider the council to be capable of increased coordination of policies? More important perhaps, are they themselves in favor of the goals and methods of the council? What do they perceive these goals to be?

The Nordic civil servants have contact with one another in several different ways. As we have seen, there are already a number of permanent bodies of collaboration and coordination, such as the Nordic Cultural Commission, the Nordic Committee for Social Legislation and Policy, and the system of contact men for Nordic legal cooperation. In addition to these, several committees and working groups are set up on a special basis, with members from two or more Nordic states, depending on their functions and purposes. Such committees and groups may include members of national as well as regional or even local administrations. As in the case of politicians, members of the professions, members of organized labor, and the like, the national bureaucrats have contact with one another through a finely meshed net of communication that is spread out over the whole Nordic region. I shall discuss the possible future implications of this later. At this point I shall examine the direct contacts between the Nordic Council and the national bureaucrats.

A relatively large number of national civil servants participate in the annual meetings of the council in the capacity of experts. The expert group of the council, like the ministerial group, has tended to increase over time, and numbers 100 or more. The experts may be there throughout the plenary session, but they often stay only part of the time. Some of the elected members have complained privately about the number of experts and observers, the latter of which are only a handful, as compared to the number of parliamentarians, basing their criticism on the fact that the council was meant to be an inter-parliamentarian body, which is what it is. On the whole this view has been voiced by a small group only, and this kind of criticism may be unavoidable. The whole administrative and bureaucratic apparatus of the Nordic Council compares very favorably with those of other international organizations.

The experts are present at the annual meetings to enable the council to consult them about implementing its recommendations.[1] The views of the experts are almost always heard at the committee stage. In addition to this comes the informal contact within the council among experts, ministers, and parliamentarians. This procedure is useful, since the experts who are present are usually the same persons whose practical task it becomes to carry out what the council decides. On the other hand, this arrangement could hamper or restrict extensive collaboration. This might be the case in areas that are slightly, but not in an important sense, controversial. In other words the search for the realistic solution may at times result in the choice of an overcautious option. Of course, much depends on the matters in question and on the persons involved in them.

The civil servants attend the plenary meetings of the Nordic Council to take note of the speeches and subsequent debate. They also participate in the committee stage, according to paragraphs 1(c), 1(d), and 1(e) of the directions for committee work, in which their capacity is one of assisting the elected members. The experts' role is a larger one than that of simply assisting, however, although the formal decisions are of course made by the elected members, the parliamentarians.

There has been some discussion about the specific role that the bureaucrats should play at this stage.[2] Should the experts be allowed to try to induce committee members to reach specific decisions in conformity with the desires of particular departments or should they be used strictly as called upon, to assist, and perhaps be left out of the committee stage at the point when the committee reaches its decision? It seems difficult to formulate precise rules for this, according to persons who have been actively involved in Nordic Council affairs.[3] It is important to note in this particular context that the national administrators participate in cooperative measures originating in the Nordic Council at a very early stage.

Not only do the parliamentarian committee members of the Nordic Council seem to wish to "delegate" decision-making power to the experts, but to some extent the elected members also rely on the bureaucrats to formulate the language of the committee's proposals.

The attendance of experts in the committee stage varies somewhat, depending upon the nature of the work. As noted by one observer of the Nordic Council,[4] the committee with the lowest rate of ministerial attendance has been the one with the highest proportion of attendance by civil servants. It is not really surprising that the standing committee on communications has depended heavily on the assistance of national bureaucrats, as has the Standing Committee on Social Policy.* The standing committees for cultural affairs and for legal and economic matters have had approximately equal participation by ministers and experts.

The procedure at the committee stage is as follows. (1) A matter is introduced to the committee members. (2) The experts are heard on the matter. Questions may be asked of them, and replied to. (3) An informal discussion is held by the elected committee members, and a decision is arrived at. (4) There is voting by a system of straight majority. In case of a tie the vote of the committee chairman decides the matter, according to Section 13(4) of the Rules of Procedure for the council. In the actual drafting of the proposal, as we have seen, the national bureaucrats may often be called on.

There has been a noticeable absence of dissent in the committees. Stanley Anderson found from his study of 534 committee proposals in 9 years that there were only 15 reservations, or less than 3 percent.[6] Furthermore, four of these had been submitted by a single dissenter; eight were offered jointly by two dissenters; two were submitted by three dissenters; and only one was submitted by four dissenters.[7] It would seem that unanimity is attained according to the principle of

---

*According to Stanley Anderson, the committees were 90 percent and 80 percent dependent upon civil service assistance, respectively.[5]

the lowest common denominator. Could it be that the presence of national bureaucrats not only endangers the chances that the decisions will be made by the parliamentarians, as Løchen has argued,[8] but that this system would also actively restrict cooperation that would otherwise have come about? I shall examine this point more closely later. The influence of the bureaucrats may at times have been a supplementary factor making for such restriction, to the extent that such restriction may be said to have occurred.

This is important, because it may hold part of the answer to the question of why Nordic integration seems to have shunned particular institutional forms and why some types of integration have in fact been retarded.

Following the committee stage, the completed proposals go for a second reading, that is, for debate and final vote in the plenary council. The bureaucrats play a very passive role at this stage, whereas the elected council members and the ministers may speak in the order in which they have asked for the floor. The experts also do not take part in the voting or final disposition of the proposals. They return to their own national administrative duties later, in some capacity or other, to be concerned again with these very matters they helped to prepare in the Nordic Council.

Following the introduction of the year-round operation of the standing committees of the Nordic Council, the national bureaucrats' chances for contact with and influence on the members of these committees must have increased. In order to see to what extent the bureaucracies are interlocked, I now turn to this matter.

INTERLOCKING BUREAUCRACIES

The bureaucracies of which we are talking are the bureaucratic apparatus of the Nordic Council itself, a fairly modest one by most criteria, consisting of its presidium and its central and national secretariats, as well as the national bureaucracies (the central administrations) of the member states. To this should be added the council of ministers, its secretariat (Oslo), and the cultural secretariat (Copenhagen). The latter two may be sketched as in Figures 4 and 5. Both are traditional intragovernmental types of institutions.

Because of the multifunctional character of the Nordic Council, different parts of these bureaucracies will be brought into contact with the council and with one another. I have already described the ways in which civil servants have contact with one another, through inter-Nordic committees, in special committees or working groups, and through informal and often personal communication. At this point I shall focus attention on the relationship of the civil servants

FIGURE 4

The Council of Ministers Secretariat (Oslo)

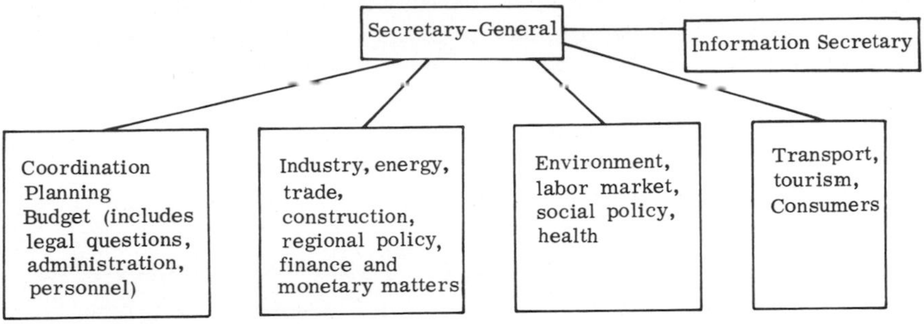

Source: Compiled by the author.

FIGURE 5

The Secretariat for Cultural Cooperation (Copenhagen)

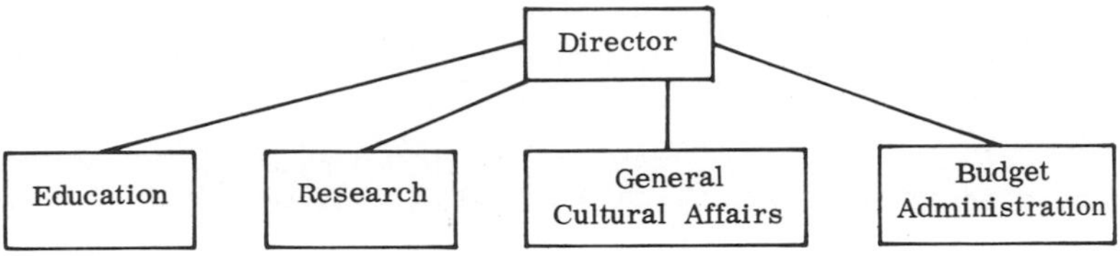

Source: Compiled by the author.

to the Nordic Council as decision makers. It would seem that the success of the efforts of the Nordic Council will in part depend upon the ways in which its proposals are implemented by the civil service sector. This in turn will depend at least partly upon the opinion civil servants have of the council and upon how important and realistic they consider it to be in Nordic collaboration as a whole.

There are several factors worth looking at when considering whether or not integration is or will be successful. One of them is clearly the opinion of the individual decision maker concerning the machinery or instrument of integration, in this case the Nordic Council. It is important to know whether the active national bureaucrats have a high opinion about the organization in question and its methods, organization, or aims, or whether they consider its proposals, suggestions, or commendations as badly planned, unrealistic, or introduced in the wrong way or order. If in the process of analyzing this it is found that some, several, or many of the proposals that are put forward or aims or goals of the organization are perceived by the national servants as contrary to their own beliefs, certain of the setbacks of the organization or its failure to achieve its aims may possibly be understood.

In order to obtain answers to the above-mentioned questions, I carried out conversations with some of the civil servants who had been actively involved in the work of the Nordic Council and put questions to them about their opinion concerning the Nordic Council and its importance as an instrument of integration. (See Appendix B.) The questions I asked them were similar and sometimes identical to the questions I asked of a group of parliamentarian members of the council who had participated in its work for the last few years and to the questions put to cabinet ministers who had participated in the annual meetings of the council.

The civil servants had all participated in council sessions and/or had been active in the implementation of council proposals after these had reached the national administrations. The questions were divided into three parts. One part had to do with the Nordic Council in a very general way and with the proposals originating from it. The second part was related to the working of the council, as seen from the point of view of the civil servants, and with its public image. The third set of questions dealt with supranationality, which for several reasons seemed to be perceived as a rather controversial issue in all three groups. To some extent this question also dealt with the future of the Nordic Council.

I approached 42 civil servants from different Nordic states, all of them actively involved in Nordic Council work; 36 of them replied to my 22 questions. There was little difference in their national positions. The differences as I shall show later on, were in the categories of Nordic Council participants and decision makers, that is, the parliamentarians, the ministers, and the civil servants. In a narrow legal sense one could argue that only the parliamentarians in the Nordic Council are its decision makers. For our purposes and in a wider sense, all three categories are decision makers, since all of them are responsible, formally as well as informally, for the initiation, formulation, and implementation of decisions coming from the council.

On the whole, the civil servants considered the proposals of the Nordic Council to be useful. However, more than one-third of the group was uncertain whether the proposals were, on the whole, realistic. Furthermore, more than two-thirds of the civil servants thought that the proposals could have been better prepared or planned.

Less than half of the group (15) wanted the council to concentrate on fewer and more important tasks, and there were as many responses opposed to this as there were uncertain responses (9 of each). Three bureaucrats preferred not to answer the question. When they were asked which tasks the council ought to concentrate its efforts on, the affirmative respondents became less firm. Some of them thought that these tasks should be the central tasks, a further unspecified category. There was agreement in this subgroup that the Nordic Council might add to its status by weeding out unnecessarily trivial matters. Two of the respondents stated that in this case the council should be left to decide what was important. Some of the bureaucrats thought this question was related to, and would be determined by, the possible implementation of the NORDEK Treaty. If an economic union came about, then the Nordic Council ought to be given full decision-making powers.

Some of the respondents explained that the trouble with the Nordic Council in this respect was one of communications. The council should restrict itself to introducing the same matter only once. Examples were given to illustrate ways in which certain detailed matters were either already being dealt with as a part of another recommendation or were being examined simultaneously in some different context. Two of the civil servants stated that much of the trouble had to do with the fact that Nordic Council members were simply badly informed about some matters. Nevertheless it was felt that the council constituted a very valuable (the Icelandic verdict was "indispensable") forum for debate and collaboration among Nordic parliamentarians.

The civil servants thought the ministers should be more active in the Nordic Council (22), but only 14 of the 36 experts considered it necessary for the government members to introduce more matters to the council. For some of these experts, then, increased government activity in the Nordic Council must have implied something else. In fact, 11 civil servants were opposed to the idea of more governmentally based recommendations and 8 respondents were uncertain. Nearly as many (12) were uncertain as were in favor of more cooperation and collaboration between the parliamentarian members and the ministers prior to the tabling of proposals before the Council (14). There was considerably stronger agreement against extending the right of vote to the ministers (24), with no more than 2 experts preferring this. The council was big enough without being too big, and its sessional meetings were long enough for the work load.

A somewhat sensitive question referred to whether or not the membership of parliamentarians in the Nordic Council ought to vary more. Some of the parliamentarians themselves thought that it ought to. Only 3 of the civil servants agreed with this, and 18 were against it; but 12 civil servants were uncertain on this question, which was a pretty straightforward one.

The civil servants thought that a central secretariat might mean an improvement for the council (22 to 5), and they also believed that there was enough interest among their own parliamentarians in the Council (24 to 6). However, 19 of the civil servants did not think that the public relations machinery of the council was sufficiently developed, and 21 of them thought that this machinery did not function well enough. In fact, only 2 seemed to be impressed by the public relations function of the Nordic Council. There was not enough popular support for the Council (5 to 22), but there was no agreement at all among the respondents about whether the aims of the Nordic Council should be redefined and clarified. Slightly fewer (10) thought this should be done than were against it (11) or felt uncertain (11).

Some of the civil servants who were in favor of a redefinition and clarification wanted this to be done to "do away with some of the romanticism involved." Asked what they perceived the aims of the Nordic Council to be, the civil servants, to no surprise, produced varied answers. Some of them, in fact only very few, thought that they could, that is, ought, not answer this question in their professional capacity, an interesting point if it refers to some sort of an allegiance to the council rather than to the governments in question. A few civil servants said that the council itself should find out what it was supposed to be doing and aiming at.

Others thought that the aims of the council were to further Nordic cooperation in all fields or to create the basis for increased integration in the social, economic, legal, and cultural spheres of activity. There was a need to codify such activity, according to two of the civil servants who wanted redefinition and clarification.

I had asked them if they thought that the Nordic Council, since it included so many important politicians participating in its work on a regular basis and since it seemed to play an important role in Nordic politics in general, could possibly become a Nordic parliament at some stage. The civil servants were divided on this question; 14 thought it could, whereas 16 did not think so. Only a few (5) of them were uncertain. It could mean, and I shall come back to this later on, that the civil servants had already formed their opinions firmly, one way or the other, about whether the Nordic Council could or should become such a body. If, as I have suggested earlier, civil servants who are performing important tasks or who are in important positions concerning the carrying out of these tasks do not want the Nordic

Council, or a similar body, to be given increased, perhaps even supranational, decision-making powers, the chances are that this will not come about. This lack of action would follow despite the fact that everybody involved might seem to be in favor of increasing Nordic collaboration.

Not surprisingly, 17 civil servants were opposed to giving the Nordic Council supranational powers, while only 6 thought that it should be given such powers. It would have been interesting to know which way the scales would tip in the group of 10 civil servants who were uncertain on this point.

The portion of replies of uncertain was also large in the following question, pertaining to whether or not there were particular problems in any of the countries that might be easier to solve or settle with a supranational council. There were 14 uncertain civil servants and an equally large number who thought that there were no such problems in existence in their particular countries. On the other hand, by those who replied affirmatively it was stated that several such problems did exist and that there were additional technical problems that could be brought into the sphere of activities of the Nordic Council.

Half of the civil servants thought that the council had too slow and awkward machinery for efficient solving of the problems with which it was supposed to deal. However, 9 of them did not agree with this evaluation and 7 civil servants did not reply to the question.

All the experts answering these questions were active in Nordic Council matters. In some cases they had been working on related tasks for several years. Since they, as we have seen, are actively involved throughout the life span of a recommendation and at times also prior to the formulation of such a recommendation, it seems clear that their opinion about the methods and work of the Nordic Council will weigh quite heavily. The council, on its side, is often concerned about bringing the experts from the different national administrations together for discussions and working sessions. Apart from more narrowly defined conferences for certain experts involved in specific fields of Nordic collaboration, there have been large conferences arranged under the auspices of the Nordic Council in which bureaucratic personnel from the different administrations have participated. Following the introduction of the system of contact men for legislative collaboration, the Nordic Council arranged a conference for contact men in Denmark in September 1966. Two years later the scope was widened by a two-day conference for top civil servants in Sweden. The Nordic Council secretaries-general, academics, and politicians also participated in these conferences. This practice is still followed.

THE IDEOLOGY OF COOPERATION

As is the case with democracy, nobody seems to be against Nordic cooperation. The party positions, or interests within the party as expressed publicly, may vary somewhat depending on the issues involved; but no party spokesman, including the late C. J. Hambro of the Norwegian Conservatives, has come out against Nordic cooperation. Since this type of cooperation, as we have seen, is both extensive and in certain fields intensive as well, the future would appear to be promising for continued efforts along already established lines, and it would also seem likely that new lines will be drawn. Since more collaboration is already planned; since the Nordic Council, which is a few horses' lengths ahead of other organizations in Nordic matters, acts as a catalyst; and since an increasing number of politicians and bureaucrats find themselves involved in this type of work, it might be thought that all is well in Nordic cooperation.

However, there are certain problems connected with this ideology of cooperation. First, the fact that different decision makers express themselves in favor of Nordic cooperation in its many different aspects does not necessarily mean that they are fully aware of, or even interested in, the full implications of these goals, let alone willing to carry them out. If anything, the near unanimity of opinion in favor of further cooperation (integration being a somewhat dirty word in several circles) may be deceptive. It may be a veiled inertia. I shall discuss this point at a later stage, when dealing with the particular shortcomings of Nordic integration.

However, it might be useful to stress that the hostility toward political merger that we found within certain Norwegian groups, initially the Center Party, the Christian People's Party, and a segment of the Liberal Party, has and will probably continue to have a braking influence on the integrative process. Also there is an element of Norwegian rationalism, which is in opposition to what it considers strong cultural centralization, that must be taken into account in assessing the durability and direction of the integrative process. A secular decline in the support base for this sector of opinion could prove to be an important factor in the long run, and certain changes could come about. At present, however, this does not seem likely.

NOTES

1. Einar Løchen, "Arbeidsformeme i Nordisk Rad og Europaradet," in Nordisk Kontakt, no. 8 (1963), p. 441.

2. See, for example, Stanley Anderson, The Nordic Council: A Study of Scandinavian Regionalism (Stockholm: Norstedts, 1967), p. 113.

3. According to Anderson, op. cit., p. 80. My own findings substantiate this view.

4. Ibid.

5. Ibid., p. 81.

6. Ibid., p. 84.

7. Ibid.

8. Løchen, op. cit., p. 441.

CHAPTER

12

IMPACT ON DECISION MAKING

GENERAL IMPACT OF THE NORDIC COUNCIL

As we have seen in Chapters 6 through 11, the work carried out by the Nordic Council in various fields of integration has influenced the national policies of all the participating states. Since the Nordic Council, as we have seen, is not the only organization working for unity and integration in the region, it is difficult to measure the degree to which this integration and unity have come about specifically because of the work of the council. It may well be that had the Nordic Council never been set up, there would still have been attempts at integration. Some writers argue that the process of integration has more to do with general historical processes of change than with specific attempts carried out and institutionalized in the shape of customs or economic unions, whether in the case of specific types of integration[1] or in more general cases. It is awkward, not to say impossible, to refute such an assertion, insofar as it involves historical nonevents, things that have not happened. The Nordic Council (or EEC or GATT) does exist; therefore cooperation, coordination, and integration said to be connected with or derived from it must be examined on that basis. One might reverse the argument and ask whether or not the particular organization was created by the forces of integration rather than the other way around; but in a sense this is the chicken-and-egg paradox and should be recognized as such. A close analysis of both sides of the paradox may help us understand the phenomenon.

Clearly the institution in question has an impact upon integration, even if it in turn is partly caused by that process, or some part of it, itself.

If this manner of looking at the phenomenon is correct, there is an impact made by the ongoing natural, historical, and/or social processes on institutions, and an impact on these processes by the institution. If this is so, what interests me here is the influence of the institution on the national environment, by which in this context I mean on the main decision makers, at least by law, that is, the cabinet members and parliamentarians. I would like to know what kind of impact the Nordic Council has had, and still seems to have, on these two groups.

IMPACT ON CABINET MINISTERS

During the plenary sessions of the Nordic Council, the speeches made by the ministers are looked forward to with considerable interest by politicians and by the news media. Although it is true that the government members have not introduced a large number of cases to the Nordic Council, they have been the originators of some fairly large and important matters, such as the NORDEK plan.

How do government members view the Nordic Council in terms of organization, methods, and aims? Do they consider the council an efficient organization, or are they critical of its structure and methods of work?

Of the 18 ministers I approached, 16 cooperated with me in providing answers to my questions. For comparative purposes I asked the same questions of a group of 38 parliamentarian members of the Nordic Council, partly in writing and partly through personal conversation. Of the parliamentarians, 31 replied, on the understanding that their identity would not be revealed. (See Appendixes A and B.) At this point I will give the conclusions of this survey, taking first the ministerial group.

Since the ministerial group included present members of the Nordic governments, among whom were several of the prime ministers, of the ministers of foreign affairs, and of the ministers of economics, and since the answers were obtained on the understanding that the respondents should remain unidentified, it is not fair to give a national breakdown here. The data base is also too small to permit generalizations concerning differences of opinion among the states. Suffice it to say that the national positions did not vary greatly (nor did I expect them to do so), but that there were some differences of opinion between this group and the group of parliamentarians, as well as between them and the group of civil servants, to whom similar questions had been put. Before a comparative analysis of the replies is attempted, I shall examine the conclusions from the ministerial group in more detail.

Organization

I had asked the ministers whether or not the organization of the Nordic Council was good, generally speaking; whether its annual sessions were long enough; and whether contact between the ministers and the parliamentarians was good, both between and during sessions.

Less than a third of the ministers thought that the organization was generally good, although in their elaboration the majority described it as satisfactory. On the whole the ministers thought that the sessions were long enough and that there was sufficient contact between ministers and parliamentarians, both during and between sessions. The majority thought that there was enough interest in the Nordic Council in their own parliaments but that the interest within their own populations at large was insufficient.

Two points are worth noting. First, one-third of the government members thought that they should have the right to vote in the Nordic Council, which was intended to be, and to all intents and purposes still is, an interparliamentary organization. At the same time only 6 of the 16 government members thought that their groups ought to be more active in the work of the council. Generally speaking the ministers felt that the organization of the council was satisfactory but that more ought to be done to advertise its activities and the role it plays in inter-Nordic affairs.

Methods

I wanted to know whether or not the ministers thought that the Nordic Council should concentrate its efforts on fewer and perhaps more important matters and whether the government members themselves should be more active, that is, whether they should introduce more matters or raise additional issues in the council. I also asked whether they thought the Nordic Council was too cumbersome to function well. Finally, I asked whether a central secretariat would mean an improvement in the working methods of the council and whether they thought that the organization should be equipped with supranational powers.

The majority thought that the Nordic Council ought to concentrate on fewer and more important tasks. When asked what these should be, the members of the group mentioned economic affairs such as the NORDEK plan, regional planning, work on industrialization problems, environmental control, and general social planning. Only 6 of the government members though that their group should be more active in Nordic Council work, and only 4 out of the 16 respondents thought that the governments should introduce more matters to the council.

Half of the group felt that the Nordic Council was too slow and cumbersome in its methods, and some suggestions for improvement were made; but it was added that in certain cases this was necessary for "democracy" and that it could not very well be otherwise if the council were to continue to function according to democratic principles. Opinions were split on the question of whether or not a central secretariat would be a good idea for improvement of the working methods of the council, as well as for its organization. Since this survey the presidium and the council of ministers have come to have their own secretariats, located in Stockholm and Oslo respectively, in addition to which the cultural secretariat has been set up in Copenhagen.

Aims

My last category of questions dealt with the aims of the Nordic Council. Here I thought it would be useful to ascertain whether or not the respondents felt that there was a need to redefine and clarify the aims of the organization. In a subsequent question I asked them to specify what, in their opinion, the aims of the council were. Then I went on to inquire whether the Nordic Council was creating greater unity among the Nordic states when it participated in such organizations as the European Free Trade Association (EFTA), the Council of Europe, and the United Nations, and whether the council was capable at that time of furthering Nordic integration. Finally I asked the respondents whether they thought there was sufficient popular support for the council within their own countries.

Nearly half the group saw no need for a redefinition and clarification of the aims of the organization. However, four were uncertain on the matter, and three of the members preferred not to answer the question. Their opinion was split on whether the Nordic Council really meant anything in terms of increased Nordic unity within such other international organizations as EFTA, the Council of Europe, and the United Nations. Membership in the Nordic Council was fully compatible with both full and associate membership in the EEC, according to the majority. Concern was expressed in favor of safeguarding Nordic unity and cooperation, regardless of the outcome of the negotiations for EEC entry. Only six of the members thought that the Nordic Council was capable of further Nordic integration at that time, and only two ministers were prepared to consider equipping the council with supranational powers. There was not enough popular interest in the Nordic Council, according to five government members; but two thought that there was sufficient interest, five were uncertain, and four preferred not to reply.

On the whole the cabinet members seemed to think that the Nordic Council had shortcomings in both organization and methods of functioning. There were differences in opinion about what the aims of the council were, or should be, but evidently not enough to merit a redefinition and elaboration of those aims.

A few of the respondents felt that the importance of the Nordic Council was primarily to be found in dealing with the "lesser" matters. On the other end of the spectrum, some of the members thought of the Nordic Council as an embryonic parliament of Scandinavia, filling an important future need. This faction thought that the council should be made supranational. None of the respondents seemed to be basically opposed to the council or to consider its functions of very little use. There was a lot of paper work, some government members thought; but the council compared favorably in that respect with the Council of Europe, as was pointed out by those who had practical experience of both organizations.

Some government members, when asked, specified that although a central secretariat for the Nordic Council would probably not mean an improvement in methods and organization, this situation might be changed, and a secretariat might even be required, if Nordic collaboration were intensified. This change could come about if the NORDEK plan were accepted and fully implemented by the states. Some changes in the organization of the council were expected to follow from the implementation of the findings in the Fagerholm Committee Report, the results of which were looked forward to.

IMPACT ON PARLIAMENTARIANS

Let us turn now to the 36 parliamentarian members of the Nordic Council, whose replies were obtained in the same manner as those of the ministers, that is, partly through conversation and partly through correspondence, and who were asked the same questions.

Organization

The parliamentarian group, like the government members, felt that on the whole the annual sessions of the Nordic Council were long enough. Within this group, four parliamentarians, all from different countries, did not think that the session meetings were long enough. Several of the members (7) did not think that the time of year was the best chosen, or were uncertain about this (4), but there was general agreement, except for two members, that the time chosen was probably the only one that would be acceptable for all national delegates.

The majority (24) thought that there was sufficient contact between the ministers and the parliamentarians during the sessions, as had the government members, but less than half of the parliamentarians (15) thought there was sufficient contact between the sessions.

These parliamentarians, who had all been members of the Nordic Council within the past three years, were practically united against extending the right to vote to the government members (30 to 1). As opposed to the government members, the parliamentarians thought that the governments should be more active in the work of the council, but this opinion was held by a very slender majority of 13 to 12, with five members uncertain or of no expressed opinion. There was hardly any difference between the two groups in opinion about whether the political parties had sufficient representation in the council. In both cases the majority was satisfied with the present size of the Nordic Council membership.

The government members had thought that there was sufficient parliamentary interest in the Nordic Council in their own countries (11 to 3, with 2 uncertain), but the answer by the parliamentarians differed. Nearly two-thirds of them felt that the interest in the council of their own parliaments was insufficient (19 to 10, with 2 uncertain or of no expressed opinion).

There was also agreement between the majorities of the two groups that the machinery of the council was sufficiently utilized between the sessions, although seven parliamentarians stated that it was not used enough and five were uncertain. Some of the parliamentarians felt that in this respect the problem was one of introducing enough important and realistic questions to the council, and some examples were given to which I shall later return. There was a tendency, as some members pointed out, to produce too much paper, irrespective of its importance. On the other hand the critics seemed aware of the fact that this was almost unavoidable if the council was to function in its originally intended manner as a truly democratic interparliamentary body to which anyone could bring matters for attention.

Compared to the government members, who were somewhat split on the issue, a two-thirds majority of the parliamentarians felt that the organization of the Nordic Council could generally be described as good. From the six members who thought such a description unjustified and the four members who were uncertain about the relevance of this claim, there was some criticism that may be worth noting. Several of the Norwegian parliamentarians thought that there was a need to strengthen the Norwegian secretariat. These were members of different parties. It was not clear, except in two cases, whether this process of strengthening referred to an increase in personnel or an improvement in methods. These two members stated outright that the Norwegian Secretariat did not function satisfactorily.

Methods

As with the government group, the parliamentarians felt (by a relatively smaller majority, 18 out of 31) that the Nordic Council ought to concentrate on fewer and more important tasks. The respondents who were uncertain about this felt that perhaps the council should be able to do both, that is, consider important matters as well as a variety of smaller matters, but they thought that this might be a difficult thing to do. It was generally felt that the council spread itself too thin, but there were opposing views about what could or should be done to change this. On the whole the government members had not been in favor of playing a larger role in the council by introducing more questions. The opinion of the parliamentarian group was split; 12 thought the governments should introduce more matters and 12 did not, the rest being either uncertain (5) or of no expressed opinion (2).

Slightly less than half of the parliamentarians though that the council was too cumbersome in its working methods (14), but as many as 11 members had not, for the purpose of answering in this context, made up their minds one way or the other. Only two members preferred not to answer the question.

Nearly half the parliamentarians (15), as opposed to less than a third of the government members (5), thought that a central secretariat for the council might mean an improvement. Some of the parliamentarian respondents stated that a central secretariat would be a good thing by itself, but that this would not necessarily mean an improvement since the problems lie elsewhere, such as in the contacts among the ministers, in the whole working procedure, in the will to collaborate politically, or in other, often combined, areas.

The majority of the parliamentarians, as of the government members, were against giving the council supranational powers or uncertain on the matter (14 and 3 respectively), but nine parliamentarians, or nearly a third, of different nationalities and parties, saw a need for this. About half of the members in favor of supranationality felt that the Nordic Council should be given such powers only in specific areas in which the need was said to exist by these members. The other half stated an unspecified belief in supranationality for the council that would, if accepted, be of considerable importance to the future forms of Nordic politics in general, because of the multifunctional character and parliamentary base and emphasis of the council.

Aims

According to approximately half the group (14), there was no need to redefine or elaborate the aims of the Nordic Council. Only nine, or nearly a third, thought that this ought to be done. When subsequently asked to specify what they thought these aims were, the answers varied somewhat, ranging from "as much discussion as possible" on joint problems, through "maximum harmonization," to replies that the council was meant to be an instrument of integration. In this part of their answer the government members emphasized cooperation, while the parliamentarians saw the aims of the council as having to do with harmonization or even integration, although it was not entirely clear as used in this context what the differences in these terms were.

The majority of the parliamentarians (17), as opposed to the government members (only 5), thought that the Nordic Council contributed to unity by the participation of the Nordic states in other international organizations. A few of the parliamentarians who had had experience of other organizations of the above-mentioned type stated that the Nordic Council was important in this respect, pointing out which features of the council they felt were particularly useful.

More than two-thirds of the members of the group thought that Nordic Council membership was fully compatible with either full or associate membership in the EEC. None of the members thought that these memberships would be mutually exclusive.

The majority of the parliamentarians was not certain that the council with its present powers would be capable of increasing Nordic integration, 12 members stated outright that they did not think the council would be capable of this. This is interesting in view of the reply by the same group to the question of whether it thought the Nordic Council should be given supranational powers, to which only 9 members answered that they were in favor and 12 members that they were against. If the parliamentarians participating in the work of the Nordic Council are in favor of further Nordic integration, it would be interesting to know how they expect this to come about, if not by means of the council.

Neither the parliamentarians nor the government members thought there was enough public support for the Nordic Council in their own countries. Both groups pointed to a need for full utilization of what was described as the public relations apparatus of the council, which, some stated, should be built up or improved. On the other hand, it was also pointed out that the Nordic Council was more efficient in certain important areas than several other international organizations.

NOTE

1. See for example Nils Lundgren, "Customs Unions of Industrialized Western European Countries," in Economic Integration in Europe, edited by G. R. Denton (London: Weidenfeld & Nicholson, 1969), p. 54.

CHAPTER

13

NEED FOR ORGANIZATIONAL REFORM

SUPRANATIONALITY

As we have already seen, the major theorists of regional political integration have paid close attention to the concept of supranationality, stressing its importance both as a part of the process of integration and as a mechanism necessary to trigger off such a process. For example, already in his earlier formulation of the concept of spill-over, Ernst B. Haas saw the need to involve an element of supranationality, vested with some group, committee, or commission, to get the whole process of integration started.[1] Once it had gotten off the ground and important sections of the economy were included, there would be a tendency for decisions taken supranationally to influence other sections of the economy, the need to take further decisions would arise, and so on. Some of the initial decisions would influence other decisions within the political system, the many parts of which are connected and interact. This would all come about when the initial element of supranationality had been set up and plugged into the political system, and when decision makers, partly as a result of the influence of this element, had developed a sense of allegiance to new, or to dual, centers of authority, whichever might be the case. In later reformulations of his concept of the spill-over, Haas took some of the more mechanistic assumptions out of it. However, the importance of supranationality in the whole argument remains firmly based, both in Haas's theorizing as well as in integration theory in general.

To Amitai Etzioni, the term supranational referred to interstate systems having centers in which decisions binding the member states are made and in which the identification of the politically conscious citizens with the common units (the nations) is high and of what he called the secular-historical type.[2] Etzioni was very much aware of the importance of supranationality in the process of integration or, as he called it, of unification.

Of Karl W. Deutsch's two types of integrated security-communities, the pluralistic and the amalgamated, only the latter needed supranationality. Deutsch used as his example of the former, "Norway-Sweden today."[3] For the first type to become the second type, one might well argue that the element of supranationality would have to be brought into action as the process takes place through conquest or coercion.

I have argued that, external pressures aside, the slowness and caution observed of Scandinavian integration arise from two main internal factors. First, part of the answer may be found in the historical and political background of Scandinavia. The top dog (Sweden and Denmark) versus underdog (Finland and Norway) hierarchy throughout history and the unions that have been based on it have acted as a brake on later integration. The historical and psychological effect of this has been a problem of over-familiarity, which certainly breeds suspicion, if not contempt.

Second, in Scandinavian integration, or at any rate in that part of it in which the Nordic Council parliamentarians, ministers, and civil servants play an important role, the two questions to which I referred earlier have in fact been discussed at some length and have been raised simultaneously. The two questions were: How does one go about integration? and What exact type of political community do we want, and why do we want it? If it is true that posing both questions and discussing the ramifications of them at an early stage might slow down the work of theorizing about integration, it would clearly also tend to slow down work on the practical aspects of integration. This is not the full answer, of course, but it is part of the answer, and one that may have tended to be postponed or avoided, both in theory and in the practical politics of integration.

Institutional differences aside, what I am assuming here is that if there were agreement of opinion in favor of injecting supranationality into Nordic integration, such supranationality would eventually follow. I say eventually because of the complexities involved. Also the nature of the central administration and public services in the Scandinavian countries is such that a combination of the complexity of the issue and the special features of institutional behavior could conceivably delay the implementation of supranationality for some time, even if politically conscious citizens were generally in favor of it. I know of no opinion poll in Scandinavia that in fact has shown that politically conscious Scandinavians have been in favor of supranationality. Therefore the argument is somewhat hypothetical, but nevertheless it is important, since the relationships among the different types of decision makers in Scandinavia, the politicians, civil servants, experts, and government members, is sufficiently informal and sufficiently based upon mutual understanding and interest to allow this type of situation to occur.

It might be asked what the chances would be for the introduction of supranationality in Scandinavian integration. Is it realistic to assume that the Nordic Council will be equipped with supranational powers of decision making within the foreseeable future? I asked the group of civil servants, parliamentarians, and ministers of the different Scandinavian states a direct question concerning this. In comparing the responses from these groups, I found agreement in opinion against supranationality, but with different margins of both agreement and disagreement. (See Table 4.)

Among the parliamentarians a larger percentage was in favor of extending powers of supranationality to the Nordic Council than there had been in either of the other groups. Since the parliamentarians who were asked had all been actively involved as elected members of the Nordic Council, some of them for a number of years, the figure is less optimistic as far as the chances for supranationality in Scandinavian integration are concerned. It may well be, for example, that, if it becomes adopted, the element of supranationality will be injected by way of Scandinavian participation in a wider scheme of collaboration, in the same way that, during the postwar period, free trade happened to Scandinavia by way of EFTA rather than prior to it.

The civil servants are important in much of the work of the Nordic Council, and they are in fact partly responsible for the success or failure of that organization. It is they who actively implement the proposals passed by the council. Except in politically sensitive issues, of which there have been some but not many, the civil servants have some control over the recommendations. As experts, for example, they have the ears of the ministers, in particular, and also of parliamentarians. When called upon to report or pass expert opinion on a certain measure, the civil servants can theoretically delay or actually hinder the implementation of recommendations. This system also allows ministers or parliamentarians to pass on to the civil servants decisions for one reason or another they do not want to make themselves. Although this is probably not frequent practice, the condition for it exists.

The same number of civil servants who wanted a supranational Nordic Council also felt that there were special problems existing in their own countries that could be solved more easily if this came about. However, several civil servants who were involved in Nordic Council work refused to answer the question, saying that they saw it as contrary to their duties. This is a pity, in a way, since many of the civil servants I asked, the overwhelming majority in fact, saw no such inherent contradictions. It would have been particularly interesting

TABLE 4

Attitudes toward the Nordic Council among Government Officials

	Yes	No	Uncertain	No Response	Total
Question: Do you think the Nordic Council should be given supranational powers of decision making?					
Civil Servants					
Number	6	17	10	3	36
Percent	16.7	47.2	27.8	8.3	100.0
Parliamentarians					
Number	9	13	6	3	31
Percent	29.0	41.9	19.4	9.7	100.0
Ministers					
Number	2	10	3	1	16
Percent	12.5	62.5	18.8	6.2	100.0
Question: Are there special problems in your country that could be solved more easily if the Nordic Council became a supranational organization?					
Civil Servants					
Number	6	14	14	2	36
Percent	16.7	38.9	38.9	5.5	100.0

Source: Compiled by the author from a survey conducted in Oslo, Stockholm, and by mail of 83 officials and politicians connected with the Nordic Council during 1970. Subsequent correspondence, discussion, and personal interviews in 1972 and 1975 substantiate these findings.

to obtain the responses from the reluctant civil servants. We might then have been able to verify the claim made by Bertil Ohlin in 1965 that there is a group of people for whom Nordic cooperation is seen as a complication of their customary tasks and for whom the present rather loose procedures constitute a smoke screen behind which they may conceal themselves when little is accomplished regarding a certain matter.[4] For some individuals, but far from any whole group, this may apply.

PARLIAMENTARY CONTROL

Whether or not the claim made by Ohlin is true, it seems to me, based upon my own findings, that there may be a need for improvement in Scandinavian integration. The public may be in favor of, or opposed to, further integration, and politicians may produce arguments for or against supranationality as a useful instrument in Nordic integration, but the argument for improvement seems to rest elsewhere.

There is the question of consistency. If a claim is made for a certain goal and a plan or a model for the future is set forth and accepted by a large group of people as desirable, then there is a need for them to be aware of and to accept the implications of, such a goal or plan. Since goals, like plans or models concerning the future, are liable to change, this would necessarily involve some often painstaking self-scrutiny from time to time.

Even nations involve themselves in such internal stock-taking. At times this is forced on them by the pressure of events or by the external system. A need for a defense arrangement, for example, might be the outcome of such self-scrutiny or of the setting up of certain political institutions with regulatory or initiating powers. Both NATO and the EEC originated to a large extent because of the pressures from external forces and the demands of regionalism.

Once the stock-taking has been made and the self-analysis carried out, it must be acted upon. If the majority of the politically conscious citizens of Scandinavia have decided that it is in favor of a particular set of ideals for the future, then it is up to these citizens, through their elected leaders, to see that the ideals are achieved. It is not easy to carry out ideals fully, but they must at least be attempted.

If the Scandinavians feel, as they seem to, that there are certain characteristics of their own type of society that are well worth preservation and protection, they should do something serious about it. The Scandinavians want to maintain their mixed private-public enterprise system and their welfare states, a point on which there seems to be hardly any disagreement at all. They also want to maintain economic growth, democratic institutions and traditions in all areas, and an efficient security system. Membership in plural or different systems may create difficulties in achieving the latter goal, but so far things have gone quite smoothly for the Scandinavians.

Referring briefly to the cut-off points used by Etzioni when discussing regional political integration, namely the preunification, unification, and termination stages of political integration, it may be possible to argue that in the case of Scandinavia interests are often tied up in the preunification and unification stages to the extent that the termination stage may not even be achieved, although this is a goal that has been stated by several of the actors. As far as theory is concerned, the problem is perhaps also that insufficient attention has been paid to disintegration. The notion of a termination stage is thus difficult if not impossible to conceive. In the case of Nordic integration, this makes the application of integration theory more difficult, but also more interesting. I shall return to this point later.

However, consistency is required to achieve the results stated in the goals or to do away with unnecessary claiming of goals that probably will never be achieved. The reason for this may be an inherent contradiction between the stated goals, such as the contradiction between Nordic unity and the actual interests and motivations that are tied up in the stages prior to unification.

In addition to the goal of a security community, however, the ideal of successful political integration requires rationalization and modernization of the political machinery if it is to be achieved. Modernization may consist of giving authority to regions, perhaps new regions that cut across national boundaries, but it certainly will not be a process of simply increasing the size of the political machinery or of just adding to it by the setting up of new, smaller machineries.

In all likelihood the problem is one that is common to all political integration, regardless of type or area. The need for consistency widens and becomes, not surprisingly, a need for control both of institutions and of relations among individuals.

Central to this whole problem and to its understanding and possible solution is the question of parliamentary control. In Scandinavia this relates to the actual control that is exercised by the parliamentary element over the type and direction of the integrational process. By expansion of the apparatus surrounding Nordic integration and by the addition of a series of intragovernmental organizations, committees of experts, and so on, the possibility arises that the parliamentary input to and control over decision making may become watered down.

Several Nordic politicians have become aware of this problem during recent years. The point was well put by the Norwegian parliamentarian Guttorm Hansen, who during the general debate in the Nordic Council in 1973 expressed concern over the possibility that the new Nordic institutions might be dominated by the civil servants at the expense of the democratically elected council members.[5] He feared a conflict of interest arising out of the fact that the civil servant would face situations in which allegiance toward his or her own country and department would weigh heavily against the Nordic interest. Hansen requested that the presidium of the Nordic Council consider the whole question of strengthening the parliamentary element of the work of the council, if need be by revision of the Helsinki Treaty.

The problem of the declining power of the elected or parliamentary element versus the increasing power of civil servants, experts, and bureaucrats is of course a central one, not only within the field of regional integration but in governmental decision making in general. As such it deserves close attention, especially in a setting in which the role of the civil servant looms large and in which the tradition of a powerful bureaucracy is a phenomenon of the recent past.

PROPOSED METHODS OF REFORM

Having discussed the need for improvement in Scandinavian integration, we arrived at the conclusion that this may be of some importance with respect to both institutions and methods. The need, as we have seen, is one of consistency regarding the theory and practice of integration and of an element of control regarding the methods and machinery used. Our next task will be to try to suggest what kinds of reforms may be needed and how these may be brought about.

One of the main goals of Scandinavian integration is the rationalization and modernization of the political machinery. The need for administrative reform would seem to be fairly obvious, since society changes under the impact both of new technologies and new modes of thought.

So far the demand for administrative reform has primarily been made on the national level and directed to the national centers of decision-making. In the future there may be a need for authority to be granted to some higher center of decision making and to be given to certain types of local or regional institutions within it, depending primarily upon the particular problems at hand. More than this, there seems to be a need to decide on the main question of the powers of government as a whole; that is, the question is one of governmental intervention and coordination. This question is unavoidable in the discussion of internal politics, and there is very little reason to assume that it can be ignored in the discussion of integration among states.

The claims for administrative reforms, which, I am arguing, will be taken from the national to the international level, are based upon different assumptions as well as upon different primary value positions. To different degrees, most of them contain elements of truth. This is so even at this time, when public dissatisfaction with what government does or does not do in relation to individuals or to particular groups in society is very widespread indeed.

The problem is fundamental, which is the reason why I take it up in this context. It raises the question of the relationship between the size of the administrative machinery and its efficiency. That efficiency will of course be interpreted somewhat differently by different people, depending upon what their own basic values are with regard to what governments should do in directing and controlling, or "guiding," the lives of individual citizens. The more the demands for control, intervention, and "guidance" are pressed, the larger the need to expand the administrative machinery seems to become, and the larger government becomes, the less efficient it seems to be. The more the State intervenes directly, the poorer its performance of the primary function of control. Conversely, the more poorly organized the actual work of the government is, the greater its need to depend upon civil servants becomes, and the more the results will be generally improvised. It may well be convenient, both politically and otherwise, to shift the work load, or particular pieces out of it, to the bureaucrats. However, it is not ultimately in the interests of either the politicians or the civil servants that such policies be followed.

Here, as nearly everywhere else, the problem of general administrative reform is at the base of the contradictions and difficulties in Nordic integration. This problem must be faced squarely and solved on the national level in Scandinavia before any improvement will follow in either methods or institutions. As we have seen, the role of the civil servants looms large in Nordic integration. Most of the negotiation of the NORDEK project, for example, was carried out by teams of civil servants, even during those stages at which people looked to the governments for direction and decision.

Much of the day-to-day conduct of affairs arising out of the Nordic portfolio has been left to the civil servants, even though the overall coordination of Nordic policies rests elsewhere, as in Norway in the prime minister's office. Much of this daily routine is carried on in addition to other duties, which at times take preference to the Nordic matters.

Perhaps the need is for a professionalization of Nordic affairs in the administrations of the different states. Possibly a more formal institutionalization of powers and duties is in order.* The trouble with this, of course, is that it seems to be contrary to something very important that has already been built up in Scandinavian cooperation: the informal gemeinschaft-oriented relationships among the countries.

An informal contact based upon frequent consultation and mutual dependence is of the utmost importance for successful political integration; but more than this is needed. The following policy could be useful, and to the extent that it is now partly being executed, it could be intensified. A coordination of efforts, aims, ideals, and proposed methods for unity in Scandinavia must be carried out. This is already partly done, but it is still too fragmented for continued successful integration to take place. The Helsinki agreement, a watered-down treaty if there ever was one, spells out the progress so far and outlines the aims for continued Nordic integration. The trouble has been that the Helsinki Treaty has not been fully implemented, especially those sections that deal with the right of the Nordic Council to be consulted on certain matters. There is really no reason why this should not be carried out, since it rests upon agreement among all the partners to the treaty.

The importance of the Helsinki Treaty seems to be twofold. First, it points out in clear terms what has already been achieved in Nordic cooperation, indicating the importance of some of these matters and making it clear that the underlying interests of all the countries is to maintain the results of the cooperation so far achieved. Second, but in a weaker form, the document could possibly serve as a blueprint for future action. There would, however, be a need in this case to do one of two things, either to change the treaty in such a manner that the provisions recommending consultation with the Nordic Council on important matters would be stated in terms of "should" rather than "ought," or to consistently use the treaty in such a way that "ought" becomes "shall," that is, that the Nordic Council is in fact consulted whenever the governments of Scandinavia discuss important matters. This calls for such massive political good will from all quarters that it would perhaps be too idealistic to count on it to happen. For that reason I think that the first line of action, a change of the treaty, would be required, over and above its amendments.

---

*From this point of view the establishment of intragovernmental organizations, such as the council of ministers and the cultural secretariat, may be a step in the right direction.

There is sufficient basis for understanding among the countries, and the treaty is already there to justify making the changes necessary to make the council a viable instrument for strengthening the Scandinavian community as it exists at present, if that is what the Scandinavians want. The initiative for this should preferably come from the parliamentarian quarters with which it would be expected to originate. It should be raised again, if need be, by the Nordic Council, which has the potential, although seldom used, to influence or even harrass governments into action. The important matter here is that if the Nordic Council would devote its energies toward this end, it could rely to some extent upon the mass media to amplify some of the pressures. The fact remains that elite parliamentary opinion is represented within this council and that if it could muster a consensus across party groupings and national considerations, as it has done before, much could in fact be done to break down inertia elsewhere in the political system, if this is the true reason for the feebleness of the Helsinki Treaty. In this case the Norden Association and the youth organizations working for Nordic unity should also rally to the assistance of the Nordic Council. As we have seen, the infrastructure is fairly well built up in Scandinavia. The problem of the Norden Association is perhaps that it represents too many circles, and that in this case its aims could be interpreted too widely and diversely to guarantee the necessary type of action.

As originally conceived, the Helsinki Treaty did have the "should" clauses to which I refer. Why, I wonder, was the agreement watered down? Why were these sections of it partly ignored in important earlier discussions of Nordic affairs among the governments?

Gustaf Petren's claim that Article 36 has not yet been implemented still stands unanswered. His allegation of the tendency to secrecy whenever a certain type of information is required from the governments by the Nordic Council[6] has, I think, enough potential political dynamite to be taken up, perhaps not by such a multifunctional and heterogeneous body as the Norden Association, but by a smaller, more action-directed organization, possibly the youth group of a political party or, ideally, by an alliance of such youth groups. This is material worthy of being incorporated into a program for political action. The fact remains, however, that at present Scandinavia has no such action committee or group committed to Nordic integration in specific terms, although the need for it seems to exist.

This takes us back to our initial concern with the need for administrative reform. Perhaps it is not enough to have politicians who express themselves in favor of continued Nordic integration in all fields. Perhaps it is not enough that the Nordic Council, represented by the best-known and most active politicians, meets on a regular basis, working to further Nordic unity wherever possible. If anything further is to come out of this grandiose exercise of good motives and occasionally eloquent debate, it may be necessary to modernize the Nordic Council, to make it smaller perhaps or to vary its membership, in order to make it a more responsive and responsible organization. By the latter statement I do not mean that the individuals meeting in the council lack responsibility, as persons or as parliamentarians; but I do mean that there is a need for this organization, just as many international organizations, to be made subject to the same types of criteria of evaluation (or control, in one sense) as are applied on a national level. For example, does the size and cost of the machinery compare to its efficiency?

As its own members admit, the Nordic Council obviously needs to concentrate its efforts on fewer and more important matters. If these are to be satisfactorily implemented, the organization needs more power, as is also fairly well comprehended. If supranationality is out of the question, then at least the Helsinki Treaty must be fully implemented and if need be amended to satisfy this demand. There is much that the Nordic Council can do, both in general and in order to increase its own stature.

It is not always a question of "lack of political will" by the governments, although this is important, that prevents the council from fulfilling its duties. The public relations aspects of the council could be improved, a point generally agreed upon. More important, the council is very much its own public relations machine, as is a normal parliamentarian assembly. If it works efficiently, which on the whole it does, the public image will improve.

If enough politicians feel that the Nordic Council is not given a fair say or is not taken seriously enough or even consulted where it should be, they should do something about this. They ought to turn either to the public by the mass media or, if the claim is more serious or deep-seated than that, to other political channels. If need be, they should make it an important point in their own political programs.

At present there seems to be a tendency among some of the council members to complain privately and do little about it or to reconcile themselves to the fallacious belief that everything concerning the Nordic Council is decided by the governments (with their "lack of political will"), and that nothing can be done about this state of affairs by the ordinary elected council members. Where such tendencies exist, the temptation of inertia is always at hand, which is at least as dangerous in politics as in other human activities.

Recent developments may have borne out some of these opinions. The amended Helsinki Treaty may mean some improvement, particularly in conjunction with the role of the Nordic Council of Ministers and the other intragovernmental agencies recently set up. More importantly, perhaps, the need for parliamentary control and public openness in documents and negotiations pertaining to Nordic integration has been recognized and partly pressed by the Nordic Council. Work is under way to improve the balance in numbers of civil servants and bureaucrats in relation to parliamentarians. A strengthening of the presidium secretariat of the council in Stockholm has also been discussed, and this should definitely be an improvement in the overall picture.

Finally, the council decided to set up a budgetary organ consisting of ten members (the five chairmen of the permanent committees of the Nordic Council plus one additional member from each) for full participation in the setting up of the joint Nordic budgets. This may prove beneficial.[7] If the Nordic Council could assure full participation in this and guarantee a maximum of openness and the freest possible flow of information, much could be done to improve Nordic integration. The council cannot do all of this by itself, obviously, but it has some power of initiation and control over the whole exercise, as I have shown. This, needless to say, ought to be utilized fully.

NOTES

1. Ernst B. Haas, The Uniting of Europe: Political, Economic and Social Forces (Stanford, Calif.: Stanford University Press, 1958).

2. Amitai Etzioni, Political Unification (New York: Holt, Rinehart & Winston, 1965), p. 331.

3. Karl W. Deutsch, The Analysis of International Relations (Englewood Cliffs, N.J.: Prentice-Hall, 1968), p. 194.

4. See Bertil Ohlin, speech to the Hasselby Conference, Stockholm, June 2-4, 1965, published in Nordisk Udredningsserie, no. 9 (1965).

5. Nordic Council, minutes of meetings, general debate, February 18, 1973.

6. Gustaf Petren, statement to the Nordic Civil Servants' meeting at Storlien, Sweden, September 2-4, 1968, in Nordisk Udredningsserie no. 9(1969).

7. See Nordisk Udredningsserie, no. 16 (1975).

CHAPTER

14

CONCLUSION

INTEGRATION THEORIES RECONSIDERED

I began by examining the key concepts and hypotheses of some of the main theories of regional political integration, applying these to the study of Scandinavian regionalism and to the central role played in it by the Nordic Council. Some of my findings were then used in assessing the theory of integration, and suggestions were put forward concerning the "fit," or value of the theories to the Scandinavian case and vice versa.

The time has come to try to answer some of the initial queries and to reconsider our hypotheses in the combined light of theory and practice. Finally, the remaining task will be to consider whether the Scandinavian case is helpful for the study and understanding of political integration in general and to try to determine to what extent these theories and hypotheses give a better understanding of Scandinavian regional integration in particular, as well as stand up to the test of this case study.

According to theorists in general, and to Deutsch and Etzioni in particular, the fact that important similarities exist among the Scandinavian states should be useful and important to integration itself, and to understanding of it.

The view that "favorable background conditions" mattered a great deal was widely shared, although the importance attached to this varied among the theorists. We found that favorable background conditions were important in terms of shared community values and that they had been underestimated in some of the literature on political integration.

This was particularly true of the role of "identitive" powers, such as dedication to certain methods of collaboration and to the ethic of consultation that we found in existence among the Scandinavians. It was also true in the sense of "utilitarian" powers, which were underestimated. In part, and for reasons that do not seem obvious, these were underplayed in the Scandinavian case, not only by theorists but by political practitioners as well. Whether or not this was done deliberately remains to be seen.

The importance of similarities, which has been taken for granted, is a more difficult and somewhat awkward question. Familiarity, in this context, has bred some suspicion and distrust. Both from a historical and a psychological point of view, the evidence is too important to be ignored.

The Scandinavian states, we found, constitute a stable union according to the criteria developed by Amitai Etzioni.[1] However, as we have shown, they are more than that. They are on their way to becoming an integrated, nonamalgamated pluralistic security-community, to utilize the somewhat wordy but accurate terminology of Karl W. Deutsch.[2] The most important modification of this view must be made when we consider the impact of external systems. Scandinavian integration is apparently not capable of developing on its own in the economic sphere, which is an important dimension of integration. Attempts at creating an economic union in Scandinavia in the postwar period have all failed, though some observers continue to believe that this can be achieved.

Great Britain and the other EEC countries are much too important for the Scandinavian states and for Denmark in particular. Of particular significance in this context, perhaps, is the Swedish neutrality policy, which has prevented that country from considering the option of full membership in the EEC, although this option may well have been attractive in economic terms. The Swedish policy of neutrality was developed for political and strategic reasons. Full membership in EEC would mean actively placing the Swedish economy under the partial or even full direction and influence of a group of states that could be considered a bloc; this would violate the principles of Swedish neutrality. The political content of the stated aims of European integration as pursued by EEC would, in Swedish opinion, interfere with the rights of self-determination and the social and economic planning of Sweden.

The Norwegian and Danish decisions to apply for full membership in EEC were in both cases dictated by the need to follow Britain and the need to avoid falling outside the large market grouping that would result from the successful entry of Britain into EEC. From an economic point of view it may well be that Sweden can benefit from participation in the EEC enterprise, despite her position of neutrality.[3]

The Finnish case is, for obvious reasons, a very difficult one, but it has not prevented the Finns from trying to establish contact in order to negotiate an arrangement with the EEC.[4] If the impact of external systems is important for Scandinavia in general, this is overwhelmingly the case for Finland. For example, there is now sufficient evidence to suggest that the Finnish announcement that broke off the NORDEK talks in 1970 was in part caused by Soviet suspicion of the project.[5] It is more difficult to trace the impact of external systems on the other Nordic states in specific cases, but there is little doubt that it exists.

It is also very difficult to state how much of the present success of unification has been brought about by the Nordic Council, since it would be necessary to assume what would have happened had the Nordic Council not existed. However, I have shown what results the council has had in the different dimensions of integration, in terms of what it has been trying to achieve and also of what types of recommendations have been successfully implemented. The records of the Nordic Council show that approximately 60 percent of its recommendations have been partly or fully carried out or are in the process of being carried out. About 24 percent are under consideration, and the remainder have been rejected for various reasons that I have discussed.

At this stage it might be useful to reemphasize that the structure of the Nordic Council has proved to be important in two respects. First, as we have seen, it allows for the representation of all the different political interests, to the extent that these interests are articulated in the form of political parties with a certain minimum of national representation. In this respect the Nordic Council compares favorably with both the Council of Europe and, prior to 1970, with the European Parliament.

Second, the structure of the council allows for close contact between parliamentarians and ministers throughout the annual sessions. The unicameral nature of the council and its seating arrangements are such that they allow the ministers to be present and to express themselves throughout the plenary parts of the session without participating in the voting procedure that follows the committee stage. It also permits frequent mixing of ministers and parliamentarians across national as well as across party lines. This point has been underplayed by theorists who have discussed the Nordic case of integration, including Stanley Anderson and Amitai Etzioni.[6] Foreign political practitioners who have had the opportunity to participate as observers in the sessions of the Nordic Council, however, are acutely aware of built-in advantages that this structural feature of the council offers.[7]

As we have seen, the support base for the Nordic Council is broad and the perception of the aims of the council is diffuse, even as far as the participating members are concerned. This is both good and bad. A certain ambiguity about what the organization is supposed to achieve in direct and detailed terms is sometimes helpful, insofar as this contributes toward the creation and maintenance of a wider support base than would probably have been the case if the aims were to be set out precisely and in great detail from the beginning. It is difficult to know exactly what will be achieved before an organization has been operating for a certain period of time. In the case of institutions that are intended to integrate or unify, the difficulty is increased. This is seen quite clearly in the case of the EEC. This particular organization is qualitatively different from many other organizations in that it has a built-in time dimension for change as the Treaty of Rome is implemented. This is not the case with the Nordic Council, in which no supranational element exists, though it is in the embryonic stage in some fields.

The ambiguity becomes a hindrance when the aims of the organization are questioned at a time when little agreement about the nature of these aims exists among the main political decision makers. The goals of an organization depend upon the motivations and expectations of the people whose interests depend on, or are touched by, the functioning of the organization. To be more specific, it is no good for Sweden and Denmark to express publicly their desire for greater Scandinavian unity and integration, through the Nordic Council or in other forums, if at the same time these countries are pursuing policies that are clearly and unashamedly nationalistic. The decision not to allow Finnair the right of regular landings at Kastrup airport, the center of Scandinavian air traffic, on its Helsinki to New York route* was one such case in point,[8] as was the problem that Loftleidir, the Icelandic airline, ran into a few years back.[9]

It could be argued that this has to do with the distance between ideals and political reality, but that does not quite answer the question. It is clear that there is a discrepancy of some sort, and it is not conducive to the furtherance of support for any organization that policies that are seen to be in contradiction with some of the basic aims of that organization are permitted to be carried out. It is useful for the Nordic ministers of transport to meet frequently, and that informality is the order of the day among them, but that does not necessarily help solve the problems with which large sections of the national populations are often faced. In fact, the whole support base of the organization will depend upon the manner and speed with which

---

*Finnair was allowed three weekly landings during the summer term, temporarily for one year. The problem involved Loftleidir's right to set its own prices, although it touches on more complex matters relating to international agreements in aviation.

such practical problems are dealt with. As I have shown, support for Nordic collaboration and unity is broad, and more importantly it is based upon some quite firmly held beliefs about the usefulness of maintaining unity and diversity through collaboration as well as about the importance of the shared community values that are seen to exist. A lack of consistency between ideals and practice could quite seriously jeopardize the credibility of such ideals or of their public spokesmen, as well as complicate future attempts at collaboration. More importantly, it has the sinister effect of eating away at the network of small mutual dependencies, and it might seriously affect the mutually successful prediction of behavior that is required for successful long-term integration.

A solution to the problem posed above may lie in the authorization of greater powers for the Nordic Council, possibly of the supranational type; in a firmer implementation of the amended Helsinki Treaty; in the politicization of the Norden Association and in particular of the Confederacy of the Norden Associations; and in the necessity of incorporating certain specific aims within the political program of some party or combination of parties.

It is hard to see how this may come about, when as we have seen, opposition to unity and integration is found within the very organizations that are said to further these aims and when much of this opposition is tied to particular interests both within the national groups and within the political structures in Scandinavia. The outcome of the conflict depends to a large extent upon how speedily and to what extent political modernization is brought about. Although there is an inner link between institutions and methods, there are also situations in which these are opposing elements.

THE IMPORTANCE OF MICROINTEGRATION

I have used the term microintegration to mean integration that is carried out in small matters. An example would be the amending of some aspect of national laws to bring them into harmony. Several such amendments regarding a particular type of law in different countries may lead to the same law being in operation in all of them and possibly even enforceable on a cross-national level, if the various steps of microintegration have been taken to that extent. The concept is a useful one, since it directs our attention to the fact that many such steps, taken in the successive order in which they need to be taken, could very well lead to important changes, although we may not be aware of this at any given time. It is a concept analogous to that of spill-over, but it carries no claim of automaticity.

Another example of microintegration would be a decision taken in the context of integration on a seemingly unimportant level. By itself it may not impress us as being of great importance that, say, Tröndelag (Norwegian) and its neighboring Swedish county, in accordance with some resolution passed by the Nordic Council, decide to intensify their efforts at collaboration, to initiate a joint road project or to share the costs of administering some small local task. The right of the citizens of one country to use a neighboring hospital in a different country, if it happens to be the closest one or the one that is best equipped to carry out certain functions, is also a small step.

Another example is the right of the public to use certain footpaths, beaches, and lakes, regardless of what sides of the national coundaries these paths, beaches, and lakes are situated on. A successfully carried resolution calling for a standardized labeling system for drugs and for the right to obtain medicines in one country on a prescription originating in another is a further example of such a microintegrative step. By themselves these may seem to be of peripheral interest, but seen in connection with one another, within a larger framework, the importance should be quite clear. This is nothing but a type of fragmented or bit-by-bit functional integration, originating to a very large extent in the activities of the Nordic Council.

On the basis of our examination of the structure and methods of the Nordic Council, and within the theoretical framework developed so far, there are certain conclusions that we can draw from the above. In a typical session the Nordic Council will commit itself to some 20 to 30 microintegrative goals in the form of recommendations on issues ranging from joint systems of stereophonic broadcast and improvement of bits of road to cooperation in environmental planning and comprehensive and diversified economic cooperation. Some of the smaller tasks will be carried out easily enough. It may even be tempting to say that they might have been carried out without the help of the council, although this again would be difficult to prove. The council has developed the practice of reintroducing a matter, small or large, in different contexts, with different phrasing, or in the form of different recommendations if it thinks that something may be achieved by doing so, although the initial reaction from the national administrations may have been one of rejection. Furthermore, it should be added that a matter that seems insignificant in the context of Scandinavian integration may not necessarily appear that way in a larger framework. Several social and cultural tasks that have been successfully achieved by the Nordic Council would be examples of this if seen in a wider, for example European, framework. Also, it is not certain that goals that the Scandinavians see as desirable, such as several of the claims regarding cultural integration and joint environmental planning, would appear that way to a larger audience of states and populations. In other words, what seem to be small, insignificant, or obvious (or a combination of these) may not necessarily remain so when the frame of reference is widened or changed.

The larger tasks, such as the NORDEK project and more specifically its central element of a Nordic Economic Union, remain subject to the pressures of external systems. In this case the Nordic Council can constantly remind the governments about the agreements they have previously arrived at, and it can make clear to the national administrations the pressures in favor of such recommendations as those relating to NORDEK and similar schemes that still exist in the national parliaments, among backbenchers and opposition members alike, and within the general populations. This task is a slow and arduous one, and it is one in which the shortcomings of the Nordic Council in its present organization show up. However, this does not detract from the general utility of the council and from its important role as an initiator of integrative measures.

It now seems that our first two main hypotheses, Hypotheses 1 and 4 (see Chapter 1), which state that (1) "recommendations dealing with noncontroversial issues have little effect on political integration," and (4) "since the methods of the Nordic Council are informal and its measures are not binding, the impact of the organization on political integration is minimal" do not hold. Hypothesis 1 must therefore be substituted by either 2, which states that "micro- or low-level integration is a major and perhaps necessary factor favoring unification," or 3, which states that "issues that are considered noncontroversial may not necessarily remain so in the future or in some different context, with the result that recommendations dealing with them may in fact become useful for political integration." Hypothesis 4 must give way to 5, which states that "for some dimensions of integration, the less such formalized institutions as binding guidelines and timetables, rules of conduct, and penalty clauses are applied, the greater is the chance of successful long-term unification," or 6, which states that "economics is probably not one of these dimensions," or to both, at least in the Scandinavian case of political integration.

As for a wider application of Hypothesis 2, for example, we found that the difficulties attached to its operationalization centers on the word "necessary," which could only be solved by a precise definition of "micro" or "low-level" within a given context. As we have seen, differences in opinion may occur at this point, but without necessarily detracting from the explanatory value of Hypothesis 2 as such. I will return to the remaining hypotheses shortly.

SUPRANATIONALITY AND INTERGOVERNMENTALISM

"For successful integration to be triggered off and maintained, supranationality must be introduced." This familiar argument, used previously in connection with the European Communities, may be true, but it is somewhat inconclusive. Much depends upon what fields of integration one is considering. The granting of certain supranational powers to an agency is a crucial task, but it does not guarantee integration, let alone maintain it, at least not in the context of contemporary democracy. Political integration, as foreseen by the founders of the European Community, for example, can only be realized in one of two ways. One of these is by genuine abdication of certain powers, for present or future use, by the national governments. The full implementation of the Treaty of Rome, according to its original intentions, without the compromises that tend to undermine these intentions or make them obsolete, would be one such way. This is not exactly what we are witnessing in Europe today, although it does not mean that the battle for the above type of integration has been completely lost. The other way such a change could come about would be through some spontaneous, although not necessarily quick, movement from below. It is possible, if not too idealistic, to assume that education and opinion formation have crucial roles to play in such a process and that they can in fact initiate such changes.

In contrast to the type of integration pursued by the EEC, the preference in Nordic integration, as we have seen, has been to set up particular agencies for specific fields in which the needs for such bodies, according to the decision makers, can clearly be seen to exist. One example is the jointly administered cultural fund, whose budget and importance in cultural matters is seen to increase year by year.

Not even the ambitious, but now shelved, NORDEK project envisaged any supranational element with overall powers of decision making. The institutions called for in the plans were surprisingly close to what one thinks of as the classical forms of intergovernmentalism of the past. However, the ambitiousness of the NORDEK project was in the scope of its activities rather than in the methods by which it was to carry them on.

This of course brings us to an interesting suggestion, which was made earlier concerning the whole undertaking of Nordic integration. To what extent is it true, if it is, that the formal weakness observed in Nordic integration, particularly in the Nordic Council, is its actual strength? So far the evidence suggests that the claim is partly true. That is to say, this way of posing the question makes us aware of an alternative and possibly more fruitful way of examining Nordic integration. Rather than looking for its strength through the institutions alone, one could profitably examine it from a different angle, as I have tried to do, that is, by looking at the results and methods first. This does not take care of the whole problem, which is enormously complex, but it is of considerable help.

LESSONS FROM THE NORDIC CASE STUDY

At this stage of our analysis several interesting conclusions may be derived from our findings. As with most regional groupings, there is very little within the regional integrational processes of Scandinavia that is completely self-contained. However, there are clearly certain elements in Nordic integration that deserve particular attention, since they may be of general use and importance in any political integration. I shall try to isolate these phenomena and then discuss their general usefulness.

It may be a good idea to compare the results of the EEC integration with those of the more than 100-year-old Nordic collaboration efforts. Article 3 of the Treaty of Rome calls for the following:

> (1) The elimination of customs duties and quantitative restrictions for export and import among the member states, as well as of all other measures with equivalent effect;
> (2) The establishment of a common customs tariff and a common commercial policy toward third countries;
> (3) The abolition of the obstacles to the free movement of persons, services, and capital;
> (4) A common agricultural policy;
> (5) A common transport policy;
> (6) A system ensuring that competition shall not be distorted in the Common Market;
> (7) Co-ordination of the economic policies of the Member States in order, among other things, to remedy disequilibria in their balance of payments;
> (8) The approximation of their respective legislations to the extent necessary for the functioning of the Common Market;
> (9) A European Social Fund to improve the employment opportunities of workers and to contribute to the raising of their standard of living;
> (10) The establishment of a European Investment Bank to facilitate the economic expansion of the Community through the creation of new resources; and

> (11) The association of overseas countries and territories with the Community with a view to increasing trade and to pursuing jointly their efforts towards economic and social development.

The result of this complex of integrational measures may be referred to as an economic community.[10] In several of the above-mentioned areas the EEC have achieved the stage that the Treaty of Rome calls for. In other areas, however, this is not as yet so. It also remains to be seen whether the European Economic Community can become a genuinely supranational organization, with the kinds of power its founding fathers hoped for.

Now let us compare Nordic integration with the integration achieved by the EEC countries. The first interesting fact we find is that the Scandinavian countries appear to be more integrated, even economically, than any other group of independent states in the world.

By examining such a central and important area as the labor market, we find that the Scandinavians have achieved a real community. They have in fact gone further than the stage called for by the Treaty of Rome. The same applies to the area of social policy and legislation. (See Chapter 9.) As for the field of legal harmonization, the Nordic countries have gone further than the EEC, insofar as they have achieved a unitary system of laws covering sales, agreements, part payments, debts, insurance, commissions, trade agents, commercial travelers, powers of attorney, bills of exchange, cheques, patents, and life insurance. In patent legislation, integration has reached the point at which a joint Scandinavian authority for patent laws has been planned. Other areas in which intensive coordination is being carried out are company legislation, marine law, laws of pattern, arbitration law, and laws covering employees' right to their inventions. In addition, the Nordic countries have common rules for important parts of public law, family law, law of due process, and punishment. In these fields the results of Nordic integration compare favorably with those of EEC integration. In fact, in some of them it will take the better part of a generation for the EEC to reach the level that has already been achieved by the Scandinavians.

The sector of communications is also relatively highly integrated in Scandinavia. It is only a matter of time before the whole region will have identical traffic rules and regulations. The Nordic countries have recently created a joint organization for cooperation in research into traffic problems and safety. Scandinavia is a postal union and is in the process of becoming a telegraph union. Three Scandinavian countries operate the fully integrated SAS air line.

As we have seen, the Nordic countries constitute a passport union, with more intensive customs cooperation than any other group of countries. On the cultural dimension of integration, the Scandinavian states have also gone further than other groups, EEC included. This also applies to coordination of research and education and to cooperation in the areas of radio and television. As far as international groupings and organizations are concerned, Nordic cooperation is well advanced. This goes for representation in such bodies as the United Nations, the Council of Europe, the OECD, GATT, and EFTA. The Scandinavian states have also shown intensive collaboration in their relations with, and aid to, the developing countries. Finally, the impressive increase in trade inside the Nordic group within EFTA in recent years should be mentioned.

The Scandinavian countries constitute a partial economic union. As for integration of capital and services, regional policy making, and the coordination of rules of competition, the Nordic countries have achieved less than might have been expected. The same may also in part be said of the EEC.

In particular, the following features are conspicuously lacking in Nordic integration: a customs union or common external tariffs; a common trade policy regarding third countries; a common agricultural policy; and coordination of economic policies. These are considerable drawbacks to work with if the goal is, as it is claimed, the successful political integration of the countries. On the other hand, the important fact is that several impressive results have been achieved without the element of a supranational organization. It would seem that neither a customs union nor a common trade policy toward third countries would be possible without the introduction of supranationality in some form. A joint agricultural policy, or a fisheries policy, would hardly be possible without at least an element of supranationality.

The same may also apply to any efficient coordination of economic policies. This is where the main problem lies, which is that of bringing about integration of the main administrative offices. Alternatively the issue could be approached by sensible and realistic solutions of regional problems, either as they occur, or preferably in advance. There is a sufficiently advanced and useful machinery available in Scandinavia to make forecasting and planning possible.

However, two processes of roughly equal importance are required for the successful implementation of such policies. There is a need for people to stop thinking in national terms and to start thinking in regional terms instead, when looking for specific solutions to problems. By region I mean the subregional geographical areas of Scandinavia that in certain respects naturally belong to one entity, such as industrialization, energy, resources, and environmental control.

This change may come about by the pressures for a rational utilization of resources or by the industrial and economic demands of regionalism as they express themselves on different levels; but it will also have to be helped by processes of learning and adaptation. In this respect microintegration is, as I have shown, an important concept for the implementation of policy.

Finally, there may be an ultimate need to make inroads into the power and authority of the national administrators. There seem to be two ways in which this may be achieved. One would be through the institution of some sort of EEC Commission-type machinery or organization, as this was originally conceived to be, based upon the preexisting web of integration in Scandinavia. Alternatively, or concurrently, the result may be brought about through a mass movement or a broadly based political allegiance involving definite party programs that call for the required measures. Needless to say, the latter method seems somewhat idealistic and possibly even utopian; but the basis for successful political integration in practically all sectors exists in Scandinavia. More than that, integration has already been achieved in several important fields, and procedures have been adopted that may be considered superior to those used earlier. In a sense I think that much in Nordic integration is determined, as it will continue to be, from an evolutionary and gradualist point of view. Pragmatism has been useful in the steps taken so far. The problem is that the Scandinavian approach to integration may not in the short run be quite pragmatic enough. If this is so, the important fact is that this shortcoming is being realized when seen in the context of the evolving patterns of politics and economics, as we move into the last quarter of the twentieth century.

NOTES

1. Amitai Etzioni, Political Unification (New York: Holt, Rinehart, and Winston, 1965).

2. Karl W. Deutsch, Political Community and the North Atlantic Area (Princeton: Princeton University Press, 1957), and The Analysis of International Relations (Englewood Cliffs, N.J.: Prentice-Hall, 1968).

3. See Dagens Nyheter (Stockholm) 20, no. 7 (1970).

4. See Helsinging Sanomat (Helsinki) 7, no. 4 (1970).

5. See Etela-Suomen Sanomat (Helsinki) 7, no. 4 (1970).

6. Stanley Anderson, The Nordic Council: A Study of Scandinavian Regionalism (Seattle: University of Washington Press, 1967); Etzioni, op. cit.

7. Interview with N. G. Geelkerken, president of the Benelux Parliamentary Council, in Stockholm, March 1969.

8. See Dagens Nyheter, April 9, 1970.

9. See Dagens Nyheter, April 18, 1970.

10. For a good discussion, see Uwe Kitzinger, The Politics and Economics of European Integration: Britain, Europe, and the United States (New York: Praeger Publishers, 1965).

APPENDIX A

THE ORGANIZATION, METHODS, AND AIMS OF THE NORDIC COUNCIL:
REPLIES FROM PARLIAMENTARIAN MEMBERS

	Yes	No	Uncertain	No Response
Part 1				
1. Is the annual session of the Nordic Council long enough for its work load?	25	4	2	0
2. Is the best time of year chosen for the annual session?	20	7	4	0
3. If there sufficient contact between the minister and the parliamentarians?				
a. during the session	24	5	1	1
b. between the sessions	15	12	3	1
4. Should the government members have the right to vote in the Nordic Council?	1	30	0	0
5. Should the government members be more actively involved in its work?	13	12	3	3
6. Are all political parties in your parliament sufficiently represented in the council?	29	1	1	0
7. Are you satisfied with the size of the Nordic Council?	22	5	3	1
8. Is there enough interest in the council in your parliament?	10	19	1	1
9. Is the machinery of the council sufficiently utilized between the annual sessions?	19	7	5	0
10. Would you describe the organization of the Nordic Council as generally good?	19	6	4	2
Part 2				
1. Should the Nordic Council concentrate on fewer and more important matters?	18	6	4	3
2. Should the governments introduce more matters to the Nordic Council?	12	12	5	2
3. Is the Nordic Council too slow and cumbersome?	14	4	11	2
4. Might a central secretariat improve the work of the council?	15	10	5	1
5. Should the Nordic Council be given supra-national powers?	9	13	6	3
Part 3				
1. Should the aims of the Nordic Council be redefined and clarified?	9	14	3	5
2. Does the council create greater Nordic unity among the Nordic states in such organizations as EFTA, the Council of Europe, and the United Nations?	17	7	3	4
3. Is membership in the Nordic Council compatible with full (or associate) membership in the EEC?	24	0	2	5
4. Is the council at present capable of further Nordic integration?	6	12	7	6
5. Is there enough popular support for the Nordic Council in your country?	4	14	7	6

Source: Compiled by the author from a survey conducted in Oslo, Stockholm, and by mail of 83 officials connected with the Nordic Council in 1970.

APPENDIX B

THE ORGANIZATION, METHODS, AND AIMS OF THE NORDIC COUNCIL: REPLIES BY CIVIL SERVANTS

	Yes	No	Uncertain	No Response
Part 1				
1. Are the proposals from the Nordic Council on the whole useful?	31	0	4	1
2. Are they on the whole realistic?	23	1	11	1
3. Could the proposals have been planned better?	26	4	4	2
4. Should the Nordic Council concentrate on fewer and more important tasks?	15	9	9	3
Part 2				
1. Should the government members be more actively involved in the work of the council?	22	4	8	2
2. Should the governments introduce more matters, that is, make more proposals?	14	11	8	3
3. Should there be more cooperation and collaboration by the elected members of the Nordic Council with the ministers before proposals are put to the council?	14	5	12	5
4. Should ministers have the right to vote in the Nordic Council?	2	24	7	3
5. Is the Nordic Council big enough?	30	1	2	3

(continued)

(Appendix B continued)

	Yes	No	Uncertain	No Response
6. Is it too big?	1	28	5	2
7. Is the annual session of the council long enough for its work load?	25	2	5	4
8. Should the elected membership of the Nordic Council vary more?	3	18	12	3
9. Might a central secretariat improve the work of the council?	22	5	7	2
10. Is there enough interest in the Nordic Council among the parliamentarians in your country?	24	6	6	0
11. Is the Nordic Council's public relations machinery sufficiently developed?	8	19	8	1
12. Does it function well enough?	2	21	10	3
13. Is there enough popular support for the Nordic Council in your country?	5	22	8	1
Part 3				
1. Since a large number of important Nordic politicians participate regularly in the work of the council and since the council seems to play an important role in several ways, is it possible that the Nordic Council may become a future Nordic parliament?	14	16	5	1
2. Should the Nordic Council be furnished with supranational powers of decision making?	6	17	10	3
3. Are there any special problems in your country that could be more easily dealt with by a supranational Nordic Council?	6	14	14	2

	Yes	No	Uncertain	No Response
4. Do you think the Nordic Council is too slow and awkward for efficient solving of problems?	18	9	2	7

Source: Compiled by the author from a survey conducted in Oslo, Stockholm, and by mail of 83 officials connected with the Nordic Council in 1970.

APPENDIX C

THE ORGANIZATION, METHODS, AND AIMS OF THE NORDIC COUNCIL: REPLIES BY GOVERNMENT MEMBERS

	Yes	No	Uncertain	No Response
Part 1				
1. Is the annual session of the Nordic Council long enough for its work load?	14	2	0	0
2. Is the best time of year chosen for the annual session?	7	4	5	0
3. Is there sufficient contact between the ministers and the parliamentarians?				
a. during the session	12	1	2	1
b. between the sessions	10	3	2	1
4. Should the government members have the right to vote in the Nordic Council?	5	11	0	0
5. Should the government members be more actively involved in its work?	6	8	2	0
6. Are all political parties in your parliament sufficiently represented in the council?	14	0	2	0
7. Are you satisfied with the size of the Nordic Council?	10	2	4	0
8. Is there enough interest in the council in your parliament?	11	3	2	0
9. Is the machinery of the council sufficiently utilized between the annual sessions?	10	2	2	2
10. Would you describe the organization of the Nordic Council as generally good?	5	2	5	4
Part 2				
1. Should the Nordic Council concentrate on fewer and more important matters?	13	1	2	0
2. Should the governments introduce more matters to the Nordic Council?	4	8	2	2
3. Is the Nordic Council too slow and cumbersome?	8	3	5	0
4. Might a central secretariat improve the work of the council?	5	6	2	3
5. Should the Nordic Council be given supra-national powers?	2	10	3	1
Part 3				
1. Should the aims of the Nordic Council be redefined and clarified?	2	7	4	3
2. Does the council create greater Nordic unity among the Nordic states in such organizations as EFTA, the Council of Europe, and the United Nations?	5	6	4	1
3. Is membership in the Nordic Council compatible with full (or associate) membership in the EEC?	12	0	3	1
4. Is the council at present capable of further Nordic integration?	6	4	4	2
5. Is there enough popular support for the Nordic Council in your country?	2	5	5	4

Source: Compiled by the author from a survey conducted in Oslo, Stockholm, and by mail of 83 officials connected with the Nordic Council in 1970.

APPENDIX D

COOPERATION AGREEMENTS AMONG THE NORDIC COUNTRIES

General Agreements

Treaty of cooperation among Denmark, Finland, Iceland, Norway, and Sweden, signed in Helsinki on March 23, 1962, amended in 1971 and 1974 (Treaty of Helsinki)

Working procedure for the Nordic Council, 1971

Working procedure for the Nordic Council of Ministers, 1973

Treaty among Denmark, Finland, Iceland, Norway, and Sweden concerning cultural cooperation, 1971

Treaty among Denmark, Finland, Iceland, Norway, and Sweden concerning cooperation in the field of transport and communications, 1972

Convention on the protection of the environment among Denmark, Finland, Norway, and Sweden, 1974

Agreement among Denmark, Finland, Norway, and Sweden concerning a common labor market, 1954

Convention among Denmark, Finland, Iceland, Norway, and Sweden respecting social security, 1955

Passport Regulations

Protocol among the governments of Denmark, Finland, Norway, and Sweden concerning exemption of the nationals of these countries from the obligation to have a passport or residence permit while resident in a Scandinavian country other than their own, 1954

Convention among Denmark, Finland, Norway, and Sweden concerning the waiver of passport at the intra-Nordic frontiers, 1957

Development Assistance

Agreement among Denmark, Finland, Iceland, Norway, and Sweden concerning the administration of joint Nordic assistance projects in the developing countries, 1968

Technology and Industrial Development

Agreement among Denmark, Finland, Iceland, Norway, and Sweden on a Nordic fund for technology and industrial development, 1973

Statutes for a Nordic fund for technology and industrial development, 1973

Official Documents, Statements, Speeches, Pamphlets

Andersson, Arne F. "50 Ar i Arbeide For Norden." Pamphlet, Stockholm: Foreningen Norden, 1969.

____. "Vanorter i Norden." Pamphlet, Stockholm: Foreningen Norden, No Date.

Arnesen, Gerhard. "I Arbeid for Norden Foreningen Nordens Organisasjon og Virksomhet." Pamphlet, Oslo: Foreningen Norden, 1967.

Getz-Wold, Knut. Nordic Economic Cooperation. Hasselby, 1965.

Gislason, Gylfi. Free Cooperation of the Nordic Countries. Hasselby, 1965.

Hakkerup, Hans. "Nordic Cooperation in the Legal Field." Speech to The Consultative Assembly of the Council of Europe, Strasburg, September 20, 1963.

Häkkerup, Per. "Nordic Cooperation and the World around Us." Speech to the Norden Association annual meeting, Aalborg, Denmark, June 13, 1964.

"Helsingfors-Aftalen." Pamphlet, Kbhvn: Foreningen Nordin, No Date.

Industriella Utvecklingstendenser i Europa: En Studie Av Industrins Omstalling Till Stormarknader. Stockholm: Handelsdepartementet, 1967.

Kling, Herman. "Legislative Cooperation among the Nordic States." Speech to Nordic Council Conference for International Organizations in Europe, Hasselby, Sweden, June 2-4, 1965.

Nordic Committee on Social Policy. "Nordic Cooperation in the Social and Labor Field." Pamphlet, Oslo: Ministry of Social Affairs, 1965.

Nordic Council. Minutes of meetings. Stockholm: the Council, 1952-76.

____. Nordisk Kontakt. Stockholm: the Nordic Council, 1955-76.

____. Statutes of the Nordic Council. Stockholm, 1967.

Nordiska Radet. Nordisk Udredningsserie. Stockholm: the Nordic Council, 1960-76.

____. Nytt Fran Nordiska Radet. Oslo: the Nordic Council, 1960-74.

"Nordisk Framtid Ett Handlingsprogram Antaget af Foreningarna." Pamphlet, Stockholm: Foreningen Norden, 1967.

Ohlin, Bertil. "Nordic Cooperation and the Nordic Council." Speech to Hasselby Conference, Stockholm, 1965.

Petren, Gustaf. "The Nordic Council." Pamphlet, Stockholm: the Swedish Institute, 1962.

____. Nordisk Rattsgemenskap Och Nordisk Lagstiftningssamarbete. Pamphlet, Stockholm: Foreningen Norden, 1969.

Royal Ministry of Foreign Affairs (Sweden). Negotiations for a European Free Trade Area, 1956-58. Stockholm: the Ministry, 1959.

Sletten, Vegard. Five Northern Countries Pull Together. Nordic Council, Oslo.

Sverige Och EEC Romfordraget Ur Svensk Synvinkel. Stockholm: Handelsdepartementet, 1968.

Udvidet Nordisk Okonomisk Samarbejde. Kbhvn: Foreningen Norden, 1969.

Utvecklingen av Den Svenska Exporten Pa EEC—Marknaden. Stockholm: Handelsdepartementet, 1967.

Vignander, Haakon. "Vad Vi Skal Veta Om Varandra? Nordisk Laroboksgranskning." Pamphlet, Stockholm: Foreningen Norden, 1969.

Waris, Heikki. "Social Policy in the Nordic Countries." Paper read at the Hasselby Conference, Stockholm, 1965.

Wendt, Frantz. Nogle Resultater Af Nordisk Samarbejde Gennem 15 Ar: 1945-1960. Mimeographed, Copenhagen, 1960.

_____. The Nordic Council, Its Background, Structure, and First Sessions. Copenhagen: Danish Group of the Nordic Council, 1964.

____. "Nordiska Radet, Riksdagarnas Nordiska Samarbete." Pamphlet, Stockholm: Foreningen Norden, 1969.

Newspapers

Aftenposten, Oslo.

Berlingske Tidende, Copenhagen.

Dagbladet, Oslo.

Dagens Nyheter, Stockholm.

Etela-Suomon Sanomat, Helsinki.

Helsinging Sanomat, Helsinki.

Politiken, Copenhagen.

Scandinavian Integration, Cooperation, and Politics

Anderson, Stanley. The Nordic Council: A Study of Scandinavian Regionalism. Stockholm: Svenska Bokförlaget Norstedts, 1967.

Andren, Nils. "The Nordic Cultural Commission, 1947-57." The Norseman 15, no. 6 (December 1957).

____. "Nordiskt Samarbete Och Nordisk Integration." Utenrikspolitik, no. 1 (1961).

____. Government and Politics in the Nordic Countries. Stockholm: Wicksell, 1964.

Andren, Nils. "Nordisk Integration—Synspunkter Och Problem—Stallningar." Internasjonal Politikk (Oslo), no. 4 (1966).

____. "Nordic Integration." Cooperation and Conflict (Oslo), no. 1 (1967).

Apec. The Norwegian Approach to Regional Economic Development. Halifax, 1962.

Arneson, B. A. The Democratic Monarchies of Scandinavia. New York: Van Nostrand and Company, 1949.

Bonham, G. Matthew. "Scandinavian Parliamentarians: Attitudes towards Political Integration." Cooperation and Conflict (Oslo) no. 3 (1969).

Bonsdorff, G. Von. "Regional Cooperation of the Nordic Countries." Cooperation and Conflict (Oslo), no. 1 (1965).

Boyens, John. "Die Nordische Zusammenarbeit." Europa Archiv (Bonn), no. 22 (1963).

Brofoss, Erik. "Survey of Economic Developments and Economic Policies in Norway since World War II." Oslo, University of Oslo, International Summer School, 1963.

Burbank, L. B. "Scandinavian Integration and Western Defense." Foreign Affairs 35, no. 1 (October 1956).

Dolan, Paul. "The Nordic Council." Western Political Quarterly, no. 12 (1959).

Eckstein, H. Division and Cohesion in Democracy: A Study of Norway. Princeton, N.J.: Princeton University Press, 1966.

Elder, Neil C. M. "Parliament and Foreign Policy in Sweden." Political Studies, 1953, pp. 193-206.

____. Government in Sweden: The Executive at Work. Oxford: Pergamon Press, 1970.

Eriksen, Erik. "The Nordic Council's Fourth Session." Interparliamentary Bulletin 36, no. 2 (1956): 56-63.

Fagerholm, K. A. "Tionde Sessionen." Nordisk Kontakt, no. 6 (1962).

Friis, Henning, ed. *Scandinavia between East and West*. Ithaca, N.Y.: Cornell University Press, 1950.

Geisser, Max. *Das Beispiel des Nordischen Rates*. Hamburg: Europa Brucke.

Hedtoft, Hans. "The Nordic Council." *American-Scandinavian Review* 42, no. 1 (Spring 1954): 13-21.

Herlitz, Nils. "Der Nordische Rat: Voraussetzungen, Aufbau, Aufgaben." *Schriftenreihe des Deutschen Rates der Europaischen Bewegung*, Bonn, 1955.

____. "Nordiska Radets Tillkomst: Minnen Fran 1951-1953." Supplement to *Nordisk Kontakt*, 1962.

Hult, Marit. "Integrerende Og Disintegrerende Krefter i Norden Belyst Ved En Analyse Av Norske Stortingsmenns Holdning Til Planene Om En Nordisk Tollunion 1954-59." Ph.D. Diss., University of Oslo, 1968.

Jorgenson, Theodore. *Norway's Relation to Scandinavian Unionism, 1815-1871*. Northfield, Minn.: St. Olaf College Press, 1935.

Kleppe, Per. *Main Aspects of Economic Policy in Norway since the War*. Oslo: Oslo University Press, 1960.

Lange, Christian. "Nordisk Offentlig Samarbeid—En Regional Integrasjonsprocess?" *Internasjonal Politikk* (Oslo), no. 2 (1965).

Lange, Halvard. *Norsk Utenrikspolitikk Siden 1945*. Oslo: Johan Grundt Tanum Forlag, 1952.

____. "Scandinavian Cooperation in International Affairs." *International Affairs*, no. 3 (July 1954).

Lindgren, Raymond E. *Norway-Sweden: Union, Disunion, Integration*. Princeton: Princeton University Press, 1959.

____. "International Cooperation and Scandinavia." *Yearbook of World Affairs*, 1959.

Løchen, Einar. "A Comparative Study of Certain European Parliamentary Assemblies." *The European Yearbook* 4 (1958).

____. "Arbeidsformene i Nordisk Rad Og Europaradet." Nordisk Kontakt 8 (1963).

____. "Nordisk Samarbeid i Utenrikspolitikk Og Internasjonale Organisasjoner." Oslo: Foreningen Norden, 1966.

____. Norway in European and Atlantic Cooperation. Oslo: University Forlaget, 1964.

Lorendahl, Bengt. Regionpolitik i Norden. Stockholm: Foreningarna Nordens Forbund, 1969.

Olsson, Gunnar. The Common Nordic Labor Market. Stockholm: The Swedish Institute, 1968.

Petren, Gustaf. "Scandinavian Cooperation." The European Yearbook 2 (1956).

Seip, Helge. "The Pursuit of the Possible in Scandinavian Cooperation." The Norseman 14, no. 3 (May-June 1956).

Solem, Knut Erik. "Nordic Integration: Problems and Possibilities." European Studies, no. 9 (1969).

Störe, Thor. Nytten av Norden. Oslo: Foreningen Norden, 1969.

Storing, James A. Norwegian Democracy. Boston: Houghton-Mifflin, 1963.

Wallmen, Olof. Nordiska Radet och Nordisk Samarbete. Stockholm: P. A. Norstedts, 1966.

Wendt, Frantz. "The Norden Association." American-Scandinavian Review, Autumn 1956.

____. The Nordic Council and Cooperation in Scandinavia. Copenhagen: Munksgaard, 1959.

Orvik, Nils. "Integrasjon For Hvem, Mot Hvem?" Internasjonal Politikk (Oslo), no. 4 (1966).

____. Trends in Norwegian Foreign Policy. Oslo: Norwegian Universities Press, 1962.

EEC, EFTA

European Community Press and Information Office. European Community. London: the Office.

____. Community Topics. London: the Office.

____. Current Notes on the European Community. London: the Office.

European Economic Community. The Rome Treaty.

European Free Trade Association. Agricultural Agreements between the EFTA Countries. Geneva: EFTA, 1969.

____. EFTA Bulletin. Geneva: EFTA, 1959-70.

____. Building EFTA. Geneva: EFTA, 1968.

____. EFTA Trade, 1959-1967, with Some Analysis of Long Term Trends. Geneva: EFTA, 1969.

____. EFTA Trade 1959-1966. Geneva: EFTA, 1968.

____. EFTA Trade 1968. Geneva: EFTA, 1970.

____. EFTA Foreign Investment Changes in the Pattern of EFTA Foreign Direct Investment. Geneva: EFTA, 1969.

____. Using EFTA. Geneva: EFTA, 1968.

____. The Effects of EFTA on the Economics of the Member States. Geneva: EFTA, 1969.

____. Convention Establishing the European Free Trade Association and Agreement Creating an Association Between the Member States of the European Free Trade Association and the Republic of Finland. Geneva: EFTA, 1967.

____. The European Free Trade Association—A Single Market of 100,000,000 People. Geneva: EFTA, No Date.

____. European Free Trade Association, The Rules of Origin. Geneva: EFTA, 1967.

Regional Integration and Integration Theory

Alker, Hayward Jr. "Intergration Logics: A Review, Extension and Critique." International Organization 24, no. 4 (Autumn 1970): 869-914.

Avery, William P. "The Extra Regional Transfer of Integrative Behaviour." International Organization 27, no. 4 (Autumn 1973): 549-56.

Behrman, Jack N. "International Sectoral Integration: An Alternative Approach." Journal of World Trade Law 6 (May-June 1972): 269-83.

Brenner, Michael J. Technocratic Politics and The Functionalist Theory of European Integration. Ithaca, N.Y.: Cornell Univery Press, 1969.

Cantori, Louis J., and Spiegel, Steven L., "The Analysis of Regional International Politics: The Integration versus the Empirical Systems Approach." International Organization 27, no. 4 (Autumn 1973): 465-94.

Caporaso, James A. "Theory and Method in the Study of International Integration." International Organization 25, no. 2 (Spring 1971): 228-53.

Centre for Contemporary European Studies, University of Sussex. European Integration: Research in Progress. Centre for Contemporary European Studies. Brighton: University of Sussex, 1969.

Cobb, Roger W., and Elder, Charles. International Community: A Regional and Global Study. New York: Holt, Rinehart and Winston, 1970.

Cooper, R. N. "Economic Interdependence and Foreign Policy in the 1970's." World Politics 24 (January 1972): 159-81.

Dahlberg, Kenneth A. "Regional Integration: the Neo-Functional versus a Configurative Approach." International Organization 24 (Winter 1970): 122-28.

Deutsch, Karl W. Nationalism and Social Communication. Cambridge, Mass.: M.I.T. Press, 1953.

____. The Analysis of International Relations. Englewood Cliffs, N.J.: Prentice-Hall, 1968.

____. "Supranational Organizations in the 1960's." Journal of Common Market Studies 1, no. 3.

____ et al. "Integration and Arms Control in the European Political Environment: A Summary Report." American Political Science Review, June 1966.

____ et al. Political Community and the North Atlantic Area: International Organization in the Light of Historical Experience. Princeton, N.J.: Princeton University Press, 1957.

____ et al. France, Germany and the Western Alliance: A Study of Elite Attitudes on European Integration and World Politics. New York: Charles Scribner's Sons, 1967.

Etzioni, Amitai. "The Dialectics of Supra-National Unification." American Political Science Review 56 (1962).

____. "European Unification. A Strategy of Change." World Politics 16 (1963/64).

____. "A Paradigm for the Study of Political Unification." World Politics 15, no. 1 (1963/64).

____. Political Unification: A Comparative Study of Leaders and Forces. New York: Holt, Rinehart and Winston, 1965.

Galtung, Johan. "A Structural Theory of Integration." Journal of Peace Research 4 (1968).

Haas, Ernst B. "Regionalism, Functionalism, and Universal International Organization." World Politics 8 (1955/56).

____. The Uniting of Europe: Political, Economic and Social Forces. London: Stevens and Sons, 1958.

____. "The Challenge of Regionalism." International Organization 12, no. 4 (1958).

____. "International Integration: The European and the Universal Process." International Organization, Summer 1961.

____. Beyond the Nation-State: Functionalism and International Organization. Stanford, Calif.: Stanford University Press, 1964.

____. "Technocracy, Pluralism and the New Europe." In A New Europe?, edited by Stephen Graubard. Boston: Houghton-Mifflin Company, 1964.

____. "The Uniting of Europe and the Uniting of Latin America." Journal of Common Market Studies, June 1967.

____. Tangle of Hopes: American Commitments and World Order. Englewood Cliffs, N.J.: Prentice-Hall, 1969.

Haas, Michael. "A Functional Approach to International Organization." Journal of Politics 27, no. 3 (August 1965): 498-517.

Hansen, R. D. "European Integration: Forward March, Parade Rest, or Dismissed?" International Organization 27, no. 2 (Spring 1973): 225-54.

____. "Regional Integration: Reflections on a Decade of Theoretical Efforts." World Politics 21, no. 2 (January 1969): 242-71.

Hoffman, Stanley. "International Organization and the International System." International Organization 24, no. 3 (Summer 1970).

Jacob, Philip E., and Toscano, James V., eds. The Integration of Political Communities. Philadelphia: J. B. Lippincott Company, 1964.

Kaiser, Karl. "Transnationale Politik." Deutsche Vierteljahresschrift, Special Issue, 1969.

____. "The U.S. and EEC in the Atlantic System: The Problem of Theory." Journal of Common Market Studies 5, no. 4 (June 1967).

Lindberg, Leon N. The Political Dynamics of European Integration. Stanford, Calif.: Stanford University Press, 1964.

____. "Decision Making and Integration in the European Community." International Organization, Winter 1965-66.

____. "Integration as a Source of Stress on the European Community System." International Organization 20, no. 2 (Spring 1966).

____. "The European Community as a Political System." Journal of Common Market Studies 5, no. 4 (June 1967): 344-87.

____. Europe's Would-Be Polity. Englewood Cliffs, N.J.: Prentice-Hall, 1969.

Mitraney, David. "The Prospect of Integration: Federal or Functional." Journal of Common Market Studies 4, no. 2 (December 1965).

Nye, Joseph S. "Patterns and Catalysts in Regional Integration." International Organization 19, no. 4 (Autumn 1965): 870-84.

____. "Comparative Regional Integration: Concept and Measurement." International Organization 22, no. 4 (Autumn 1968).

____. "Comparing Common Markets: A Revised Neo-Functionalist Model." International Organization 24, no. 4 (Autumn 1970): 796-835.

Plischke, E. Systems of Integrating the International Community. New York: Van Nostrand, 1964.

Puchala, Donald J. "International Transactions and Regional Integration." International Organization 24, no. 4 (Autumn 1970): 732-63.

Rosenstiel, Francis. "Reflections on the Notion of Supranationality." Journal of Common Market Studies 2, no. 2 (November 1963).

Russell, R. W. "Transgovernmental Interaction in the International Monetary System, 1960-1972." International Organization 27, no. 4 (Autumn 1973): 431-64.

Russett, Bruce. "Transactions, Community, and International Political Integration." Mimeographed, 1970.

Saeter, Martin. "Hva er Integrasjon?" Internasjonal Politikk, no. 4 (1965).

____. "Integrasjon: Teori og Virkelighet." Internasjonal Politikk, no. 4 (1966).

Sanness, John. "Hegemony, Imperium and Integrasjon." Internasjonal Politikk, no. 4 (1966).

Schmitter, P. "Three Neo-Functional Hypotheses." Mimeographed, Chicago: University of Chicago, 1968.

Schmitter, Philippe C. "Further Notes on Operationalizing Some Variables Related to Regional Integration." International Organization 23, no. 2 (Spring 1969).

Taylor, Paul. "The Concept of Community and the European Integration Process." Journal of Common Market Studies 7, no. 2 (1968).

Western European Integration

Alting von Geusau, Frans A. M. European Organizations and Foreign Relations of States: A Comparative Analysis of Decision-Making. Leiden: A. W. Sythoff, 1964.

Armstrong, John A. The European Administrative Elite. Princeton, N.J.: Princeton University Press, 1973.

Baumann, C. E. Western Europe: What Path to Integration? Boston: D. C. Heath and Co., 1967.

Bell, Coral, ed. Europe without Britain: Six Studies of Britain's Application to Join the Common Market and Its Breakdown. Melbourne: Chesire (for Australian Institute of International Affairs), 1963.

Beloff, Max. Europe and the Europeans. London: Chattof Windus, 1957.

____. The United States and the Unity of Europe. New York: Vintage Books, 1963.

Beugel, E. H. van der. From Marshall Aid to Atlantic Partnership. Amsterdam: Elsevier Publishing Co., 1966.

Camps, Miriam. Britain and the European Community, 1955-1963. Princeton, N.J.: Princeton University Press, 1964.

____. European Unification in the 60's: From the Veto to the Crisis. New York: McGraw-Hill, 1966.

Cartou, Louis. Précis des organisations européennes. Paris: Dalloz, 1965.

Coombs, D. Politics and Bureaucracy in the European Community. London: Allen and Unwin, for Political and Economic Planning (PEP), 1970.

Coudenhove, Kalergi C. An Idea Conquers the World. London: Hutchinson, 1953.

Curtis, Michael. Western European Integration. New York: Harper and Row, 1965.

Deutsch, Karl W. "Integration and Arms Control in the European Political Environment: A Summary Report." American Political Science Review 60, no. 2 (June 1966): 354-65.

Direct Elections and the European Parliament. Occasional Paper No. 10, London: Political and Economic Planning (PEP), 1960.

European Coal and Steel Community, Common Assembly. Information Mensuelles (Luxembourg), Monthly.

Fawcett, J. "Britain and the EEC: The Issue of Parliamentary Sovereignty." World Today 27 (April 1971): 139-43.

Heathcote, Nina. "The Crisis of European Supranationality." Journal of Common Market Studies 5, no. 2 (1966).

Kitzinger, Uwe. The Challenge of the Common Market. Oxford: Blackwell's, 1962.

____. The Politics and Economics of European Integration. New York: Praeger Publishers, 1963.

Lambert, John. "The Constitutional Crisis 1965-1966." Journal of Common Market Studies 3, no. 3 (May 1966).

Lundgren, Nils. "Customs Unions of Industrialized Western European Countries." In Economic Integration in Europe, edited by G. R. Denton. London: Weidenfeld and Nicholson, 1969.

Meade, J.; Liesner, H. H.; and Wells, S. J. In Case Studies in European Economic Union. London: Oxford University Press, 1962.

Monnet, Jean. "Prospect for a New Europe." U.S. News and World Report, Supplement to Vol. 2, no. 2.

New York Herald Tribune, 10 March, 1953.

Pickles, William. "Political Power in the EEC." Journal of Common Market Studies 2.

"Political and Economic Planning: Direct Elections and the European Parliament." Pamphlet, London, 1965.

Pryce, Roy. The Political Future of the European Community. Marshbanks, 1963.

Puchala, Donald J. "Integration and Disintegration in Franco-German Relations, 1954-1965." International Organization 24, no. 2 (Spring 1970).

INDEX

ABOUT THE AUTHOR

ERIC SOLEM is currently with the Directorate of Strategic Analysis, Operational Research and Analysis Establishment, Department of National Headquarters, Ottawa, Canada, where he is engaged in work on specific defense questions as well as on problems of overall strategic planning in Canada.

Dr. Solem has been actively involved in cross-national research projects, and has written on the subjects of international nuclear materials control and regulation, arms control, political and economic integration and community building, energy and resource questions, and long-term planning and forecasting. He has contributed to several academic journals and other periodicals.

He is a graduate of the University of Manitoba, Canada, where he obtained his Bachelor of Arts in Political Science and Economics. He also holds a Master's degree in Advanced European Political Studies from Leicester University, England, and a Doctorate of Philosophy from Oxford University, England.